Stop Telling Us It's Fake:

A Wrestling Fan's Journey

1977–2012

Craig Higham

Thank you to my beautiful family Kristina, Zara, Connor, Ruby, Max and Abbey, who, whether this book gets published or not, are my greatest and proudest achievements in my life. And I apologise to my kids for taking up so much computer time!

This book is dedicated to my fellow wrestling fans, who enjoy the thrills, spills and excitement wrestling brings as much as me.

ISBN-13: 978-1489585509

ISBN-10: 1489585508

Foreword

I have just finished reading Mick Foley's 'Countdown to Lockdown' (Foley's fourth wrestling literacy masterpiece), and currently searching EBay for Chris Jericho's 'Undisputed' as his book is nowhere to be found in Dubbo, NSW where I currently live. I already have a nice collection of other wrestling autobiographies including those by Shawn Michaels, Hardy Boys, Edge, Hulk Hogan, Kurt Angle, Batista and Rick Flair, to mention a few. I have enjoyed reading these books as they are a great way for fans like myself to gain a great insight into how these great performers turned their love of wrestling into fantastic careers, their trials and successes, as well as how unglamorous the life of a wrestler can be (as Mickey Rourke's 'The Wrestler' also showed). I am not a huge reader of books, but these wrestling autobiographies have been an exemption to the rule, and in fact when asked what my favourite book of all time is I answer without hesitation Mick Foley's *Mankind, Have a Nice day*.

But after reading a few wrestling autobiographies I started to ask myself the question "what about all those people like me", who love wrestling just as much as these wrestlers, whom were just as passionate as these wrestlers about wrestling when we were kids, but for one reason or another did not choose the path of a wrestler (it has nothing to do with not having any talent, honest....). In my over inflated opinion, I believe we fans are just as important as those wrestling superstars we watch, because if it wasn't for us fans, then really, Stone Cold Steve Austin, The Rock, Hulk Hogan, CM Punk, Mankind, Sting, Ric Flair and The Undertaker would not be the household names they are now. There are only so many empty arena matches two wrestlers can perform before they'd get bored! So where is our story??? Where is the story/autobiography on 'The wrestling fan'...But I guess even more importantly, if there was a story on a wrestling fan, would anybody read it???

I have thought about that question for quite a while, as I feel I have had this book inside me waiting for the right time to be written for some time now. But there has never been the right time or I've simply been too scared to start. With work commitments, 5 kids and a generally busy life schedule, it was quite easy to keep putting off this dream I had of writing a book. So after completing reading *'Countdown to Lockdown'* I decided the time now was right, and with the support and encouragement of my, inspirational and very intelligent wife Kristina, I have decided to put pen to paper (or if you want to be more technical fingers to keyboard). Now whether this book gets finished, and/or published or not, *I am going to finally start to write it,* even if the only person who reads it is me, my wife (and Mick Foley as I intend to send it to him for a New York Times Best seller comment like, "fantastic book, couldn't put it down...").

Another reason I wanted to write this book, is to give all those non-wrestling fans out there an insight, into not only some of the history of wrestling, but also some insight into what makes a wrestling fan. We wrestling fans have been ridiculed all our life by you non-wrestling fans, and I feel this book may go some way in showing these people that we are not stupid, but just really love the world of sports entertainment. If you have ever been to a live wrestling event, you would know we wrestling fans are a weird but loveable bunch of people who come from all sorts of countries, cultures, sex and ages. We come together for the laughs, drama, and entertainment wrestling brings. Unlike sports such as soccer (or football if you are from Europe) or boxing there are very few fans turning on each other at wrestling events. So this book hopefully will give those non-wrestling fans an insight into what makes us tick.

I should also point out before you start reading the book that the majority of my wrestling enjoyment has been with the WWE Company (previously known as the WWF and the WWWF). While I have watched wrestling from numerous other wrestling companies, such as World Championship Wrestling (WCW), and TNA (Total Nonstop Action) and even IWA (International Wrestling Australia), the WWE has made up nearly 80% of my wrestling viewing and enjoyment. Here in Australia in the 1980's and 1990's, as you will read, we were very limited in our wrestling viewing options, which is one of the reasons the WWE became my main and sometimes only source of wrestling. So if this book seems a little WWE heavy, then now you know why.

Another major point that should be made before reading, is that I am no scholar, this will be my first book (and possibly last), I am no expert in ...well anything, I am not a wrestling *smark*, or a hidden WWE employee (although I am always open to running an Australia section of the WWE if you are reading Mr McMahon). I am literally a wrestling fan, and have been a wrestling fan for the past 30+ years, who has finally decided to complete one of his bucket list items of not only writing a book, but writing a book on being a wrestling fan. Even having a teaching background, I expect upon finishing an editor (or my beautiful wife) to spend hours fixing up my punctuation and grammar (spelling should be OK due to spell-check, what a wonderful invention). Like my wrestling and literacy idol Mick Foley, I was going to write this book by hand, but due to my spelling and handwriting, a computer is going to be a far better option (sorry Mick).

This book is not a complete history of wrestling over the past 30 years, however major incidents in that 30 years will be looked at but not in too much depth, nor is this a history of my life as I may not be as exciting to read about as I think I am, this book is a history of **wrestling in my life,** my life as a wrestling fan, and why and how wrestling has been a big part of my life. While some historical information is included, and you could even learn something about wrestling (which I hope any non-wrestling fans will do), the focus of this book was to explore an average wrestling fan, and what makes us leap out of our seats, scream at the TV, by the T-shirts, hats, games and other merchandise, order Pay Per Views, and hop on our computers to complain, whinge, praise, acknowledge and talk wrestling to other wrestling fans. It will also hopefully give an insight as to why people like me have been able to stay wrestling fans for over 30 years.

During this book I will mentioned a variety of wrestling terms. I have included at the back of this book, a glossary to help those non-wrestling fans understand any terms or phrases that do not make sense when they are reading this.

Finally, as the title states, we wrestling fans believe it or not are not stupid. We know that wrestling is entertainment and why many people perceive wrestling to be not entirely real, but to us fans we feel every hit, we feel every fall, we feel every chair shot, we feel every fall through a table, we feel every fall from 15 foot high steel cages and we feel every win by our favourites as well as the losses, which makes it real to us....

Chapter 1   My Wrestling Journey

"You know wrestling is not real! Don't you?"

"That blood is fake!"

"That is not even a real chair"

"That's a fake table"

"They are not even hitting each other"

"The results are rigged"

"The ring is really a trampoline"

"All wrestlers are friends out of the ring"

"All wrestlers take steroids"

If any of these sayings sound familiar, then like me you are a wrestling fan, who has had to put up with statements like those ever since we first watched our first wrestling match. To me there are two types of people in this world, those who enjoy wrestling, and the rest of the world, or simply non-wrestling fans (NWF)! The problem is that the typical NWF doesn't fully understand why we love wrestling so much, and therefore mock what they do not understand (and one of the reasons I wanted to write this book was to explain our love of wrestling to these NWF). Like many forms of entertainment you have those people who like it and those people who don't, entertainment forms such as the Theatre, Opera, Car Racing, or reality TV have their lovers and haters, and wrestling is no different, the unfortunate thing is those NWF people feel the constant need to try and stop or mock our enjoyment of professional wrestling. I do not like synchronised swimming but I don't go around saying, "synchronised swimming is not a sport, they are not even swimming, those nose plugs look ridiculous etc...", I just do not watch it, and let those that do enjoy it watch it in peace.

As we grow up, we do become more aware of exactly what professional wrestling is all about and usually have the debating skills to argue with those NWF, but as a kid hearing those comments is like someone telling you that Santa and the Easter Bunny are not real! I bet most people do not walk into a room while their kids are watching Spiderman, and say "you know Spiderman is only a comic book character". Yet the first thing a NWF will say when they see someone watching, or talking about wrestling even if it is kids watching, is "You know wrestling is fake don't you?" The question is usually said/asked like the NWF has some secret information that they are passing on to us, or that we are so stupid that we had no idea how the wrestling industry is run. What these NWF do not realise, is that most of us wrestling fans have been watching wrestling for most of our lives, and understand a lot more than the NWF does about our beloved sports entertainment.

Now before I go any further, just a little bit about myself and my background just to show that I am an average wrestling fan who has finally decided to tell his story about the role that wrestling has had in his life. I will not go into too much depth, because quite frankly I am a pretty average bloke, and I do not want to bore you readers before getting to the main purpose of my book.

I was born in Dubbo, NSW Australia, which is a town about 4 hours inland from Sydney. We moved when I was

1 to a small coastal community of Kiama (about 2 hours south of Sydney). I am blessed in that my parents are still together, and have been together for over 40 years. Both my parents would and have done everything for their kids, but go about it in different ways. Mum would be the emotional support, always there with an ear to listen, or just a great big hug if needed. While dad had the physical side covered, and would fix anything that needed fixing. Now throughout this book I mention wrestling heroes of mine, but my dad is and will always be my first real hero (and I will deny it if he asks). Over the last 3-4 years he has shown just what type of man he is by overcoming, prostate cancer, triple by-pass, a heart attack, and the return of a high PSA count. He has handled all these setbacks and still had the attitude during this time to make sure his wife and kids were always OK. (A quick side note for all wrestling male fans near or over 40 get your prostate checked regularly!!!)

I have an older brother Ron, who would grow up to be our "black sheep" of the family, he follows an alternative lifestyle to what I am used to, and he has 4 sons, 3 marriages and has given my mum and dad more greys hairs than the rest of us kids! I also have have a younger sister Sandii, who is more like me, with similar interests and attitude to life. She also has 2 boys, and at one stage poor mum had 8 grandsons and no granddaughters. But she is now lucky enough to have 3 beautiful granddaughters.

Like most kids in Australia at the time, I played cricket in the summer, and either soccer or league in the winter. While I was no Don Bradman on the cricket field (my top score would end up being 18 not out), I was a decent bowler, and pretty good fieldsman. On the soccer field I fared better, while my 2 years in rugby league netted me only 2 touches of the ball, however 1 try!

One of my fondest memories as a kid was visiting my grandparents, and helping my Grandfather who had his own dairy farm. I would help him out by rounding the cows into the dairy yard, putting on the suction caps on the cow's teats (except for those cows that would kick, which my grandfather knew by sight, even though I thought they all looked the same), hosing out the dairy when finished, and of course getting that fresh glass of milk at the end of the shift! My brother and I also had a great game we invented around the dairy which was kind of like hind-n-seek, except your goal wasn't just to find each other, but to throw a rock at the 'fresh' cow paddies in front of each other, splattering each other with the fresh cow poo!!

We moved to another coastal town of Taree when I was 10, as most of mum's family were (including my grandfather) in this area, and would stay there until finishing school in 1989. An average student at school, or to be more accurate I tended to coast along through school. Most of my teacher reports were "Craig would do better in class if he just applied himself more!" But in the end I did enough to get into a Bachelors of Teaching degree at the Wollongong University. One of my few life's regrets is that in all the time I have lived near beaches, I never learnt how to surf. Now while I have had one lesson, and did manage to last a whole 5 seconds on a surf board, I would like to at least double that before I die!

While at Wollongong University, I started what would become an 18 year association with The Department of Sport and

Recreation, beginning with being an vacation instructor on school holiday camps during my holidays at Uni. Teaching kids how to canoe, kayak, learn archery, rock climb, start and cook on fires etc. became a regular part time job. After University I would work at a variety of Sport and Recreation Centres around NSW before I obtained full time work at one of these camps. This camp was at Lake Burrendong which was very near to Dubbo, which is the town I was born in, so I managed to come full circle. It was during my work at Lake Burrendong where I would meet and work with another wrestling fan.

I went on to what I like to call a 'practice marriage', in which the only highlights were the birth of my two boys Connor and Max. After the ending of my practice marriage, I would move with the times and go on to try online dating. It was on the site RSVP that I would met my beautiful wife Kristina. After months of emails, texts and phone calls we finally went on our first date at The Cowra Japanese gardens. We chose this spot as being 4 hours away from each other; it was the ½ way mark. I still remember my first thoughts of WOW, as she stepped out of the car, as I had never been on a date with anyone as stunning as she was, and I would spend the next two hours thinking why on earth did she choose me? Kristina would then introduce me to Zara and Ruby, her two daughters, who I quickly opened my heart to, and have become my two daughters as well, (and yes we have been called many times the modern version of the "Brady bunch"). Connor and Zara are the same age, and we have nicknamed them the twins, due to how alike they are in personality, as well as Connor and Ruby sharing the same birth date of 12th December. We have been blessed that not only do all 4 kids get along really well, but without sounding too biased, they are the 4 best kids in the word! We had our little angel Abbey who was born on the 12 April 2011, before heading back to the Japanese Gardens to get married in March 2012. Without getting too emotional, Kristina has been a big motivation and support behind me starting to write this book, and even after 4 years I still have that question of "Why did she choose me?"

I now teach inmates at a correctional centre, which has its own challenges, but I enjoy the uniqueness of the teaching, we have just come back from our honeymoon through France, Switzerland and Italy, and have moved into our newly built house. We are planning our next family holiday to Vanuatu next year, and of course I would love to bring my family along for my book tour! (If that ever happens!!). The one constant which has been with me since I was young, until now is my enjoyment of professional wrestling, and it is something I look forward to keep enjoying until my last days on my death bed!

I was no different to many other wrestling fans out there with my love of wrestling starting when I was a young whipper snapper (kid for those non Australian readers). For me it all started by watching wrestling on Saturday mornings at my mates (John Pearson) house. We would wake up, have breakfast, then switch on the TV and wait for the wrestling to begin. What made this Saturday ritual of watching wrestling more fun at John's place was the moment the show finished the long cushions on his parents lounge become our opponents, and we became Hulk Hogan, Junk Yard Dog, Hill Billy Jim, George The Animal Steele, while the cushions became King Kong Bundy, Greg The

Hammer Valentine and Big John Studd. Thinking back, to this day I still believe we are undefeated and the current Pearson lounge room Tag team champions!

The wrestling company that started my wrestling addiction, and would be a very constant in what ever happened in my life was the World Wrestling Federation, or known to many as the WWF. Due to legal reasons it later changed its name to World Wrestling Entertainment or commonly known as WWE. Throughout this book I will refer to World Wrestling Federation/Entertainment as simply WWF/E.

Today's kids have far better options when it comes to acting out their favourite matches, or wrestler's moves with the large variety of action figures, computer games, wrestling rings (for their action figures) and costume/fancy dress gear available (yes I am jealous of what the kids of today get to play with). Here in Australia in the late 1970's and early 1980's we really only had the pre-mentioned cushions or our younger brother and sisters. My poor sister was put in the full nelson hold so many times; I think her neck became a little longer (just like one of those tribes people in Africa!). Another wrestling mate of mine Quin Penman, had an unfortunate brother who was constantly put in the figure-four-leg-lock, the sharp shooter, the camel clutch and other assortment of wrestling submission moves over the years, (sorry William). In the summer, it was our old lilo (blow up mattress) at home that I took into our pool that became my opponent, and this was where all of those high flying moves from the edge of the pool onto the floating lilo, such as Macho Man's flying elbow, the frog splash or my personal finishing manoeuvre of a 'pile driver from the top rope' were performed. As for action figures, well any wrestling had to be done between my Masters of The Universe action figures such as He-Man and Skeletor!!

As a parent myself now, I do in principal encourage wrestling companies' stand on not conducting some wrestling moves at home, however, I still enjoy hoping on our trampoline and taking on my kids in our wrestling matches. I should point out that all 'wrestling' done on our trampoline is very safe, and does not include any dangerous moves such as pile drivers,

DDT's or frog splashes from the roof although I see this happening once they move into the invulnerable teenage years! I hope I do not have to ever see a 'YouTube'/video of my kids jumping off the roof onto boxes like Mrs Foley had to endure!

As mentioned before, in Australia it was very hard to keep up with what was happening in the wrestling world. We had the choice of 2 TV channels only when I lived in Kiama. One of those channels was the ABC, which was very British dominated in its TV show programming in Australia, and also included news based shows, and younger kids television, no wrestling however. The other TV channel we had was either WIN or Prime depending where you lived and on those networks being able to watch any wrestling was always a lottery. When I was young however it was on Saturday mornings, it was those Saturday mornings that I became a wrestling fan for life.

We moved in 1981 when I was around 10, from Kiama to Taree (another coastal, farming town), and it would be a couple of years before I got a chance to see wrestling again. I now had 3 TV channels to choose from, but the new channel was SBS, which for those outside Australia showed foreign TV shows and movies, so again no wrestling on this channel. But I occasionally I did get to see *World Championship Wrestling* on our TV. It was in 1987 that my love affair with wrestling was totally re-ignited when Quin lent me his tape of Wrestlemania III. After watching and re-watching and re-watching the video tape of Wrestlemania III, I was back to being a full time wrestling fan. While wrestling was still not a regular on Australian TV, what was regular was the monthly WWF/E wrestling magazines I started to buy. These magazines were my internet of the 80's, and kept me up to date with my favourite wrestlers, feuds and upcoming PPV's. I first came across the WWF magazine while walking into a newsagency with my dad while he was buying his morning paper. While walking down the sports magazine section, the image of Macho Man Randy Savage stood out like The Big Show at a kindergarten! My first issue was the February/March issue in 1987 with The Macho Man Randy Savage on the cover. I then continued to religiously buy the magazines until my last issue being the August 1992 issue (with British Bulldog Davey Boy Smith on the cover). Sadly my extensive collection has passed away, and what makes it even sadder is that I found out doing some research on the internet that back issues are going for up to $30 a magazine!! I still get that little bit of nostalgia when I see the current issue at my local Newsagency, and do occasionally pick it up for a read.

The other way I kept my wrestling fandom addiction alive, pre internet days, was through hiring the WWF/E Pay Per Views (PPVs) when they came out on video. My friends and I became well known at The Wallace Corner store in Taree for our hiring out the wrestling videos, as it was the only video store in Taree smart enough at the time to have these videos in their store. It was here I first got to watch many of the great PPV's of the late 1980's such as the very first Survivor Series, the Very first Summer Slam, and Wrestlemania II. Though nowadays you can pick up wrestling PPV's from department store as well as hiring them from the video store and can usually get them just a couple of weeks or so after it happened, back in the late 80's and early 90's I would have to wait for up to 4 months before being able to hire and watch the latest PPV. But as a dedicated fan it always was worth it.

After finishing University and heading off into the real world (although becoming a teacher my dad considers I never made it to the real world), I struggled to keep up with what was happening in my wrestling world. I would flip through the WWF magazine at the newsagencies and still hire out the PPV videos, but like many fans in the early to mid-1990's wrestling just wasn't holding my attention (could it have also been the parties and drinking I was doing at Uni....). I started working with The NSW Department of Sport & Recreation at a Sport & Recreation camp at Lake Burrendong, just outside of Wellington, NSW. It was around this time that I just starting to learn about and use the internet, and as a wrestling fan, the first thing I did was look up the WWF (now WWE).

The end of 1997 was the beginning of what I am calling becoming a full time wrestling fan, as now I had an outlet where I could get weekly updates of shows such as Raw, that were still not yet available for me to watch in country NSW. This now gave me three ways to keep in touch with the WWF, through hiring PPV's when released on videos, the WWF.com website and my reading the WWF magazines at the newsagency (I do not encourage reading magazines at Newsagencies without paying, but as a poor University Student and young man new in the workforce money was tight, and usually beer was a priority over magazines). It was around this time that WCW had started catching WWF/WWE in the ratings and the Monday Night Wars were about to start, although since 95% of my wrestling world revolved around the WWF, I did not know of this.

I was living in a shared house with three mates in Dubbo around 1998/99 when we all decided to get pay TV (AUSTAR) on our home (I guess this would be cable in the US). For me it was a very quick yes decision as I knew that the pay TV supplier Austar was showing wrestling every week and not just any wrestling but WWE Raw! So now I had for the first time since I was 8 or 9 (nearly 20 years) access to a weekly professional wrestling TV show in WWF's RAW. It wasn't long after that that I ordered and saw my very first PPV event live, on

AUSTARs Main event, which was Wrestlemania XV, and I have not missed a Wrestlemania since. I have over the past 10 years ordered many PPV's, but Wrestlemania and the Royal Rumble are the two I will always order every year. Wrestlemania started becoming a yearly event at my house for a couple of years with friends, pizza and beers, while those PPV's I didn't order I still managed to hire at the Dubbo Blockbuster video store.

While the WWF/E was and has been my main source of wrestling through this time, I still managed to catch and watch the occasional WCW Nitro which I now also had access through my pay TV. While I didn't order any PPV's from WCW, and missed many shows as it was usually on Saturday nights, which was the night I usually went out after playing Rugby for the day, I was still fairly familiar with most of the wrestlers on the show. That's why in October 2000, along with a good friend from my work (Rhonda Pullbrook) and her son Zac, we drove over 4 hours to see our very first live wrestling event in Sydney, the WCW Thunder. While I will go on further in another chapter about attending live wrestling shows, this soon became a regular event for the three of us. I have also had the privilege in 2010 to take my own 2 boys Connor and Max, and my beautiful wife Kristina to their first wrestling event, the 2010 Smackdown Tour in Sydney , and then the following year I got to take my beautiful daughters Zara and Ruby to the WWE Raw tour 2011 also in Sydney. And just recently, I took all four of them to a live IWA wrestling show in Dubbo. I have promised my nephews Rhys and Jak and my brother-in-law that the next wrestling show I will invite them along, and in fact have just purchase tickets to the Raw tour in 2013 for them for Xmas. And once my beautiful daughter Abbey is old enough, I will take her along to a show as well.

I continue to enjoy watching wrestling and will switch it on when I get home after work, on Wednesday to watch WWE Raw, and Friday afternoon when I get to watch WWE Smackdown. I have continued ordering the PPV's of Wrestlemania and the Royal Rumble, while the Elimination Chamber PPV has now become a regular of mine as well. Those PPV I miss, I will still hire from our local Blockbuster, and I will religiously visit the internet for regular wrestling information on not just the WWE, but also occasionally TNA (total non-stop Action Wrestling). Even at 40+ years old I am still proud to admit I enjoy my wrestling, and as a dad being able to experience watching, going to live wrestling shows and enjoying wrestling with your kids is an awesome feeling, and an excellent family time activity.

But I guess for you NWF out there, I still hear you ask (and my dad says it best) "Why do you watch that shit"?

Chapter 2   Wrestling Fans

My first answer I always come up with is the action, whether it's Jeff Hardy diving off the top of a ladder, Mick Foley being thrown off a 15 foot cell, or Brett Hart and Shawn Michaels battling for over an hour for the WWF/E championship. What happens in or outside of a wrestling ring when wrestlers fight is very rarely dull unless you're watching a Great Khali match (I was going to re-use Mick Foley's Al Snow match comment again; however I actually enjoyed watching some of Al Snow's hardcore matches). You have athletes (and yes I regard them as athletes - but more about that shortly) that can perform some amazing stunts and moves, others that can show tremendous strength, tremendous endurance and then there are those wrestlers that are great to watch when working together with combination of move sets, reversals and generally great chemistry with their work during a match.

Whether it's a traditional 1 on 1 match, inside a cage, tag team, battle royals, us wrestling fans quite simply enjoy the battle between two (or more opponents). Such as the Romans did when watching the Gladiators battling in the Roman Colosseum, we humans beings have enjoyed watching people battle it out just for our entertainment. Whether it is wrestling, boxing, Mixed Martial Arts, Kick Boxing, Karate, football etc., the sight of two (or more) people or teams battling it out is a form of entertainment that is embedded into our DNA as much as eating and sleeping. We all have our favourite forms of gladiator battles, and like many mine is in the wrestling format.

While many see professional wrestlers as entertainers, as I briefly mentioned they should also be classed as athletes.

Athlete: a person trained or gifted in exercises or contests involving physical agility, coordination, stamina, or strength.
(www.definitions.net)

A professional wrestler, to be successful, must train every day, not just in their look and fitness, but also in performing moves correctly. It is no different than football players training for a special play, or divers and gymnast training for a special routine. I have already mentioned how professional wrestler needs strength to not only lift an opponent, but there is strength needed in making sure they are safe for the entire move they are performing. Agility, coordination and stamina are also standard qualities that are needed by professional wrestlers today.

Once I found out the results were planned out, that punches and kicks do not always "hit" their opponent, and that wrestling was not as real as I though it once was as a kid, it didn't stop my enjoyment, only changed my focus of what was happening in the match. My focus became the skills and athletic ability of the wrestlers. How they can go 10, 20 minutes or even up to 1 hour of fast paced running, lifting, falling and performing. It is no different to watching a great fight scene in a movie. You know when you're watching it that it is not real, but you enjoy it anyway. Growing up I loved the slap stick fighting in movies made famous by Terrance Hill and Bud Spencer, movies such as 'Trinity is my name', 'I'm for the Hippopotamus' and 'Go for it'. With the corny sound effects, and unrealistic situations, it only made the movies and fight scenes' more enjoyable to watch. Wrestling is no different, or as it is somewhat known as (especially in the WWF/E Company) 'Sports Entertainment'.

*"**Sports entertainment** is a type of spectacle which presents an ostensibly competitive event using a high level of theatrical flourish and extravagant presentation, with the purpose of entertaining an audience. Unlike typical athletics and games, which are conducted for competition, sportsmanship, exercise or personal recreation, the primary product of sports entertainment is performance for an audience's benefit, thus they are never practiced privately. Sports Entertainment is WWE's way of describing Professional Wrestling Commonly, but not in all cases, the outcomes are predetermined (such cases are*

not considered to be fixed, however, as it is an open secret)." Wikipedia.

And to show that wrestling companies such as the WWF/E have identified themselves as a sports entertainment genre:

Now It Can Be Told: Those Pro Wrestlers Are Just Having Fun

The promoters of professional wrestling have disclosed that their terrifying towers in spandex tights, massive creatures like Bam Bam Bigelow, Hulk Hogan and Andre the Giant, are really no more dangerous to one another than Santa Claus, the Easter Bunny and the Tooth Fairy.

But please don't repeat this. Millions of grown men and women just don't want to know.

In an attempt to free their exhibitions from regulations that apply to boxing and other sports that cause serious injury, spokesmen for the World Wrestling Federation testified recently before the New Jersey Senate that professional wrestling is just "entertainment" and that participants are trained to avoid serious injuries.

As a result, a bill deregulating professional wrestling passed the Senate today by a vote of 37 to 1.

Spokesmen for the federation said it had successfully pressed for deregulation in Connecticut and Delaware and was now trying to do the same in a number of other states. In New York, professional wrestling is regulated by the State Athletic Commission.

"If this thing were real, there would be broken bones all over the place," said Al Komjathy, an aide to the sponsor of the bill, Senator

Francis J. McManimon, Democrat of Hamilton. "Its entertainment. It's illusion." Such admissions, however, fly in the face of a longstanding fiction, a willing suspension of disbelief by millions of wrestling fans. The bizarrely clad giants who perform drop-kicks, flying body presses and a manoeuvre known as a "chicken wing" (sometimes called a "hospitalizer") in arenas and on television publicly maintain that they are engaged in real combat. Their groans, grunts and hollers, they say, are true expressions of rage.

Under the legislation, the state's Athletic Control Board would no longer license wrestlers, promoters, timekeepers and referees. The wrestlers would no longer be required to take physical examinations before an exhibition.

The bill, which still must pass the Assembly, would also remove the state tax on television rights.

The World Wrestling Federation asks in the legislation that professional wrestling be defined as "an activity in which participants struggle hand-in-hand primarily for the purpose of providing entertainment to spectators rather than conducting a bona fide athletic contest."

(By PETER KERR, Special to the New York Times Published: February 10, 1989)

So to those NWF, to very quickly sum up, yes we older wrestling fans know that the results of the matches in wrestling are worked out prior to the match. Yes we know that the punches and kicks do not always connect, and yes we know The Undertaker doesn't control the lights and lightning with mysterious powers. We know that wrestlers learn, and train for years to know how to fall, take a 'bump', and practise and train on how to wrestle. But as for wrestling being *fake*, well.....

> *Fake - to create or render so as to mislead, deceive, or defraud others* (www.definitions.net)

.......considering wrestling and especially the WWF/E have openly admitted of the type of entertainment they are, and shows such as 'WWE Tough Enough' and the many autobiographies written by ex-wrestlers show and discuss some of the training that goes into becoming a wrestler, hence the WWF/E is not misleading, deceiving or defrauding us, then I will have to disagree with my NWF friends and say, wrestling is NOT fake. In fact I couldn't say it any better than by Tom Clark (Featured Columnist):

> *"The automatic dismissal of the industry by people who really don't understand what it is and how it works, is, in a word, infuriating. At this point, the best thing to do when they start talking is to just tune*

them out, or change the subject. There is no

winning in that discussion. Not at all."

December 3, 2011

So what makes two wrestlers fight?, what makes The

Undertaker and Triple H put their careers on the line fighting in

Hell in a Cell, what makes Rey Mysterio fly over the top rope, or

The Dudley Boys put people through tables ? The main answer is

a shiny gold Championship belt. Whether it's The World

Heavyweight Championship, The WWE Championship, Tag

team championship, Intercontinental Title, NWA Championship,

or the IWA Trans-Tasman Championship, every wrestler that

pulls on a pair of tights wants at some time in their career to be a

champion.

Besides wrestling for a Championship, there are basically

3 typical wrestling matches.

First are the 'squash match', where one wrestler (or tag

team) is booked to look really strong and unbeatable, and they

will usually destroy the opponent/s very quickly. This will

usually involve an unknown wrestler as the opponent, or a

wrestler whose main role is to make these guys look strong (WWE 's Heath Slater did a fine job at this role with returning WWF/E legends and the way he performed his role is one of the reasons he has become fan favourite of mine).

The second typical wrestling match you will see is two well establish wrestlers (or tag teams) battle. The match will have little or no 'story' build up, and will usually occur as fillers for main TV shows (like WWE Raw), or be the main event on lower promoted shows such as WWE Superstars. Live house shows are another place that these types of matches are usually seen. The match might be of high quality and you may enjoy seeing one of your favourite's wrestler and win, or see a fantastic 'spot', but there is no real emotion invested prior to the match by the fans.

The third type of match involved two or more wrestlers (or tag teams) who are currently involved in a feud, and this feud, story or disagreement can only be settled in the ring. Whether it's for a championship, being the number one contender, respect, revenge, or just because they generally hate each other.

If wrestlers did not have a feud or story behind why they need to fight, then as good as the match can be there is no real emotion behind watching it felt by us fans, and that's the big draw of wrestling. The more emotion, time and reason a fan has invested into a match, then the more atmosphere they are likely to bring to the arena. If you think about Boxing and UFC/MMA it is why they have the press conferences prior, so that the fighters can build some emotion, hatred and publicity before their fights, so the fans become invested not just financially but emotionally into the fight between the athletes involved. A big part of why wrestling is so popular is not just the actual wrestling, but also the lead up to why these wrestling bouts are occurring.

Why do wrestlers feud???, Cowboys and Indians, Cops and Robbers, Jedi's vs. The dark side, we all love a good vs. bad, or hero vs. villain story, and at its core that's what wrestling is all about. And what makes those good vs. bad guy stories even better..... it is when our hero overcomes the odds, finally wins the championship or turns bad! Just as important to there being a feud, is how that feud came about. There have been many times when two wrestlers are feuding and we fans just do not care. This results in the match and possible show loosing atmosphere. I feel there would be nothing worse for two wrestlers to wrestle a match with the crowd being quiet. Feuds can be as simple as breaking up of a tag team, heel/face turns, stealing girlfriends, injury revenge, costing matches etc - there are many ways to get two (or more) wrestlers feuding. A common complaint amongst today's internet wrestling fans is that the 'story' is just a copy, rehashed story from years ago, or the same story between two other wrestlers. What these internet fans need to realise is that it is not just the wrestling genre that rehashes story lines, how many versions of 'Cinderella' or 'Romeo and Juliet' are turned into movies. Same thing for TV, how many sitcom shows run a similar story line to another, in fact a Season 6 episode 7 of *South Park* is titled "the Simpsons already did it" referring to the fact that there is no story a TV show can now come up with, that has not already been on done on The Simpsons. Here is some common feud/storylines that have been used regularly either by the same wrestling companies, or common feuds/storylines used by different wrestling companies:

- Employee vs. Their boss – done to near perfection by Stone cold Steve Austin and Vince McMahon.
- Jealous tag team partner
- Invading group of wrestlers
- Apprentice turning on their boss
- Stealing girlfriend/cheating girlfriend/kidnapped girlfriend
- Revenge from injury
- "I'm better than you" complex
- "I want my title shot" Hungry Challenger
- You cost me my title

To best demonstrate how the emotion invested by us fans can change the atmosphere and importance of a match then let us look at the three Wrestlemania matches between The Undertaker and Triple H. Individually three great matches, but the

Wrestlemania 28 match between the Undertaker and Triple H is the one I will look back on as the best, not just the match itself, but why I/we had to watch the match.

At Wrestlemania 17 the story behind why Triple H and The Undertaker were having their match at Wrestlemania was that Triple H felt that he deserved to be in the Wrestlemania main event having defeated everyone in the WWF, including The Rock and Austin. The Undertaker took exception to that and told him that "*Triple H had never defeated him*". While it was a good match, between two big stars, Wrestlemania 17 is not remembered for this match. This is mainly due to The Undertaker's streak not being acknowledged as a serious event yet, there was no real emotion behind the reason to fight ("you haven't beaten me") and like me, and the majority of the fans were more invested in the next match between The Rock and Stone Cold Steve Austin.

The Undertaker vs. Triple H II Wrestlemania bout was at Wrestlemania 27. The first thing many fans noticed was that during all the build-up, the WWE did not mention or focus on the

Wrestlemania 17 match which adds more to the fact that match did not have much importance. The story leading into this feud was that The Undertaker made his return after four months away from the WWE. However, The Undertaker's return was interrupted by an also returning Triple H. The two men stared each other down and with Triple H then looking at the Wrestlemania sign, suggesting a match and an attempt at ending The Undertaker's streak at Wrestlemania XXVII. With Triple H being good friends of Shawn Michaels (who the Undertaker retired at lasts years Wrestlemania in an absolutely fantastic match), this was booked as a bout Triple H was trying to break The Undertaker's Wrestlemania streak and get some revenge for Shawn. A no-holds-barred match was confirmed and many believe (including myself) that it was the match of the night at Wrestlemania 27 and the best match ever between these two. However, Triple H was just another superstar attempting to break the Undertaker's streak, so while the build up to this match was a big improvement on their first Wrestlemania match, again there was no real emotion behind the feud as many like myself believed Triple H had no chance in ending The Undertakers streak. However when you do get two fantastic performers in the ring then you can get a match that draws you in during the match, which is what this match did. Many people believed Triple H was never going to break the streak, but as the match went on this became a huge possibility. However great this match was though, it was very quickly replaced the following year at Wrestlemania as the best match between these two superstars.

The lead up to Undertaker vs. Triple H III at Wrestlemania 28, was billed as the "end of an era" and would be held in the Hell in a Cell. The previous year at Wrestlemania XXVII, in the post-match events, due to the physicality and punishment suffered by The Undertaker at the hands of Triple H, for the first time in his career, The Undertaker was carted away from the ring by the medical staff on a stretcher. After nearly ten months away from the WWE, The Undertaker returned on the January 30, 2012 edition of *Raw*, where he confronted and challenged Triple H to a rematch at Wrestlemania XXVIII. The Undertaker stated that he "did not want 'that scene' (of him being stretchered away) to be a lasting memory". Triple H refused the challenge, leaving the ring smiling and patting The Undertaker on the back. The next week on *Raw*, Shawn Michaels (Triple H's best friend and who had to retire due to losing to The Undertaker at Wrestlemania 26) asked Triple H why he didn't accept the Undertaker's challenge. Triple H stated he was willing to put his ego and personal agendas aside as he now had to focus on running the WWE, as well as he knew exactly what he would have to do to defeat The Undertaker - and that he would not be the one to end him. The Undertaker, still wanting his Wrestlemania rematch with Triple H, called Triple H a "coward", and comparing his abilities to be not as good as that of Shawn Michaels. Angered by these comments, Triple H accepted The Undertaker's challenge, saying that if *"he [Undertaker] wanted an end, they would go all the way"*, that they would compete in a Hell in a Cell match. On the March 5 episode of *Raw*, Michaels announced that he would be the special guest referee in their Hell in a Cell match at Wrestlemania.

Already the build up to the Undertaker vs. Triple H 3 had more raw emotion and feeling than the other 2, not just by the wrestlers but also the fans. Add in the emotion already invested by us fans through the Shawn Michaels vs. Undertaker rivalry, and his possible affecting the outcome, and already this match had people talking about it before it happened. As like the previous year, this was the match of the night (in my opinion), and the reaction and atmosphere of the crowd in attendance moments before the match, during the introductions, during the match and the afterwards showed just how much they were invested in this match. Like many I was exhausted after watching the match, and the first thing I really wanted to do was watch it straight away again, even though there was still matches to come.

We wrestling fans do not watch wrestling just because we like to see two people fight. If that was the case then I could just head down to the pub on Friday or Saturday night. We watch wrestling because they have given us a reason that they need to fight. Whether it's real or not (some feuds do have elements of real life, the Edge and Matt Hardy feud from 2005 being a prime example), it makes wrestling matches more part of a story than just a fight.

Movies such as Mickey Rourke's 'The Wrestler' and 'Beyond the Mat' a 1999 documentary directed by Barry W. Blaustein, and the autobiography books by wrestlers such as Mick Foley, Hulk Hogan and Chris Jericho have given the NWF, and us wrestling fans, a further insight into the world of wrestling. It has shown many of us the unglamorous side to the wrestling industries, tricks of the trade and how destructive it can be for the wrestler's lives. For me, it has given me more of an appreciation of what these wrestlers will do for us fans, what they put their bodies through and what they give up (family time with loved ones and kids) all for the love of the industry and performing for us fans.

With my beloved WWE, I see it going through a transition period with the retirements and limited matches from Triple H, The Undertaker and The Rock, However I am enjoying seeing the emergence of some future stars in the likes of Dolph

Ziggeler, Daniel Bryan, Damien Sandow, Ryback - just to name a few.

Due to a busy life with building a new house, raising 5 kids, 2 dogs and of course work, I find my viewing of wrestling on TV not as frequent as it once was. Thanks to the internet, I still keep up with the results and happenings in the world of wrestling, and out of my five kids I have my wrestling buddy in my daughter Ruby. While wrestling is not a major part of my life anymore, it is and always will be a regular and important pastime that I can enjoy and escape the grind of work and bills for a couple of hours a week when I can.

Now while I have grouped all of us wrestling fans into one group, I should point out just like any fan base, we all have our likes and dislikes about our favourite sports entertainment genre. We have our different favourite wrestlers (John Cena, CM Punk, The Rock, AJ Styles or Rey Mysterio for example), our different favourite wrestling companies (WWE, WCW or TNA), our different favourite wrestling match types (traditional, tag team, cage, ladder or submission), and we even prefer different wrestling from different countries (US, Japan or Mexico). It is like all of us that love the Rocky movies, while we all enjoy the series of movies and are all Rocky fans, we all have our favourite Rocky movie we class to be the best in the series. For me, you just can't beat Rocky IV.

John Cena is a prime example of a wrestler that splits us wrestling fans. If you listen carefully to the crowd at a wrestling show (whether on TV, or if you are at a house show) you will hear half the crowd cheer when Cena's music plays and he comes down to the ring, while the other half of the crowd will tend to boo the house down! It is not uncommon for these opposing fans to start a 'cheer off', with those pro Cena fans yelling "let's go Cena!, while those anti Cena fans will reply with "Cena Sucks!" And the good thing about this cheer off is that if you watch the faces of fans, there are smiles on both sides, with each side trying to be louder than the other. A great trait that, unlike other sports, wrestling has is that the fans can turn differences into a fun, enjoyable and friendly rivalry. As for which side I sit on regarding Cena, well that will depend on who he is facing.

As you will read later on in this book, while these differences can add to enjoyment of watching wrestling, there are those minorities of people out there that use these differences in a negative way. This is usually done by complaining and whinging online, abusing wrestlers, wrestling companies, writers or other fans, or just generally be negative to an industry that they are meant to enjoy. But more about them later.

Chapter 3   Seeing it Live

I enjoy sitting down Sunday nights with a beer in hand watching the football on TV. I <u>love</u> going to a match, sitting with thousands of other fans cheering my beloved West Tigers to victory. I enjoy putting on my favourite Def Leppard CD, and singing along to those well-known tunes such as *Pour Some Sugar on Me, Love Bites, Animal, Let's get rocked*, I <u>love</u> standing two rows back from the stage, singing those well-known tunes along with the thousands of other fans at the concert. Whether it's a sporting event, a concert or even the theatre (yes I have been cultured enough to see the likes of Phantom of the Opera), seeing something live with the added atmosphere just makes things better.

Saturday October 11th 2000 my good friend Rhonda, her young son Zac and I packed ourselves into her car, and drove the 4 hours from Wellington, NSW to Sydney. This was to be our very first live wrestling show. For a couple of years Rhonda (and Zac) and I had been swapping, ordering and taping PPV's for each other, and the three of us were very excited when we found out the wrestling company WCW was coming to Australia. Now all three of us preferred to watch WWF/E, however we were not going to miss an opportunity to see a live major company professional wrestling event!

We stayed at Rhonda's sister's house and after a quick coffee and refreshing shower we then drove to The Sydney Entertainment Centre for the WCW Thunder show. After arriving at the stadium, and finally finding a park after 10 minutes we walked to the front of the stadium where we had to line up outside, waiting for the doors to open at 6:30pm. Standing there amongst thousands of other wrestling fans, my first thought was finally I am amongst my fellow people. Standing there seeing everyone in the favourite wrestlers shirts, with their signs or dressed up, the buzz and excitement in what we are about to see, I had already thought the $65 dollar tickets were well worth the money. Front door would open, and after the bag checks, it was off to the squeeze of the merchandise stands where we bought a program, and a Sting mask for Zac. We then bought our expensive $20 stadium hamburger and chips, before finding our entrance door, and waiting until they opened at 7:30pm.

The first thing I noticed once the doors opened, was that the ring looked a lot smaller in real life than it did on TV, then again they say TV adds 10 pounds, so the same must occur on wrestling rings. Up in the nose bleed sections I was pleasantly surprised that the ring wasn't that far away, and the wrestlers didn't look like ants moving around a toy wrestling ring, although I did wish I was up the front with the rest of those lucky people. The roar of the crowd (or the jeers) when someone's music hit, reading everyone's signs and seeing everyone's smiling faces, showed me that there was 10,000+ other people who had been waiting for this day as much as I had.

Many times we hear commentators state that TV doesn't do justice to us fans in appreciating the size of some of these wrestlers (Big Show, Khali etc), but when Kevin Nash waked through those curtains, I finally understood what these commentators were talking about. I would later be just as in awe of the size of superstars such as Brock Lesner, The Undertaker, Kane, Mark Henry and of course the Big Show when seeing them live.

Now as mentioned, at this time I didn't watch a lot of WCW, so while there was a few wrestlers I did know such as Jeff Jarrett, Goldberg, Book T, Scott Steiner, Kevin Nash and of course Hacksaw Jim Duggan, there were quite a few I hadn't heard of yet I. That didn't affect my excitement of the night, my appreciation of what the wrestlers did in the ring, or my enjoyment of the sports entertainment that is known as wrestling. It did give me my first glimpse of future stars such as Billy Kidman and Chavo Guerrero, as well as future great Rey Mysterio. What this night also did, was give me (and Rhonda and Zac) a taste for live wrestling which we would continue to feast on over the next couple of years. Highlights for the night included seeing Zac wear his Sting mask for most of the night, watching Rey Mysterio fly around the ring, Goldberg's strength and power and absorbing the atmosphere that you never get to feel watching it at home on the TV.

I would like to pause just for a second and talk about Zac Pulbrook. Unfortunately, Zac has become one of many young men who have tragically lost their lives due to falling asleep at the wheel while driving. On Saturday the 4th of September 2010, after a 21st birthday party planning night, Zac left his mum's house to go home so he could get some sleep before work the next day. Living just over an hour away, Zac believed he was able to do this drive, even though it was very late at night. He had done this drive many times, so felt even though it was late, he could get home safely. However, he didn't make it, crashing only 10km's away from where I live. It was a tragedy that still saddens me today, as he was turning into a great young man who had his whole life ahead of him. As you will see in this chapter I have some great and fond memories of Zac on our wrestling excursions, and wish to thank him for those. One of my fond stories I have of Zac was due to our yearly wrestling excursions, a rumour began where Rhonda and I worked. The rumour was that Zac was actually my son, and that these yearly excursions were all part of my child support payments. Considering Zac was 8 when we first met it did give the three of us many hours of fun playing to those rumours. I was and still am very proud to be known in some circles as Zac's fake dad.

After the WCW show we were back down to Sydney in October 2001 for the "World Wrestling all-stars" tour. The World Wrestling all-stars was a short lived company that came about during the ending of WCW and ECW, and just before the start of TNA. We were sitting close to the entrance ramp, (the closest we would ever get in a major wrestling event), and even managed to catch Road Dogg's bottle of water...well wore some of Road Dogg's bottle of water. The night was a wrestling tournament to crown the very first World Wrestling Allstar (WWA) champion. The final match was held inside a steel cage, my first and only cage match I have seen live, and had Brett Hart at ringside as a guest announcer. Both Road Dogg and Jeff Jarrett used Bret's Sharpshooter during the match, before Jarrett finally coming out on top.

WWA Title Tournament 2001

October 26, 2001 in Sydney, Australia

```
Jeff Jarrett_____
                   |Jarrett_____
Nathan Jones_____|              |
                                  |Jarrett (winner)
Battle Royal_____         |           |
                   |Buff Bagwell_|      |
Battle Royal_____|                     |


|Jarrett__
Psicosis_____                  |
                   |Lenny & Lodi_    |
Juventud Guerrera_|          |       |
                                     |Road Dogg_|
Konnan_____           |
                   |Road Dogg____|
Road Dogg_____|
```

<u>Note</u>: Bagwell won a battle royal to advance to the second round. Guerrera beat Psicisos, but was injured so Lenny Lane and Lodi replaced him to create a triangle match.

Just like our first live wrestling experience, the wrestling stars involved on the night were a mixture of wrestlers I had watched during their run with the WWF/E, as well as those high profile names from the now ended WCW. On this night while he didn't actually wrestle a match, I got to witness Brett Hart apply his Sharpshooter on Jeff Jarrett to end the night, one of the many highlights of a great night out.

On the 10th of August 2002, as The Rock would say "Finally the WWE has come to Melbourne" for the WWF/E World Global Tour. For me this was a dream come true, as it was something that in all of my years of watching the WWF/E, they had never toured Australia before. To put it into perspective, my previous wrestling trips was like going to watch the "Australian Meatloaf" tribute show, while the artist would look like and sing all of Meatloaf's well known songs, perform and display many of Meatloaf's mannerisms, and it was a great show, it just wasn't really Meatloaf. Seeing Meatloaf live in Australia in 2011 was a fantastic show, and a bucket list item crossed off. The WWF/E to me was like seeing the real Meatloaf concert!

Now to get to this show and to be a part of the 56000+ record attendance at the Melbourne Colonial Stadium (now known as Etihad Stadium), Rhonda, Zac and I had to travel near 12 hours to get from Wellington, NSW to Melbourne, Victoria (as any true wrestling fan would). A mixture of cars, buses, trains and scary taxi drivers got us to Melbourne late on the Friday night. A restful day of shopping, and sightseeing in Melbourne, before off to the Stadium for the show. The only disappointing thing was that once we arrived at the show we found out that Hulk Hogan would not be performing. One of the few wrestlers I did not get to see live, which will always go down as a disappointment on my wrestling viewing career.

Prior to our trip to Melbourne, I did design and make three wrestling signs for our trip. A great part of the atmosphere of seeing a wrestling show live is reading all the signs made by us fans. Now without blowing my own trumpet too hard, my signs tend to be the best at each show. One sign for each of us, with Rhonda having The Undertaker's, Zac having The Rock's, and I had a sign for 'The Hurricane' Gregory Helms. I think that I still have these somewhere collecting dust and spider webs in my garage.

There were 9 matches on the card that night with the main event being a triple threat match between Triple H vs. Brock Lesner vs. The Rock. Seeing the Rock deliver the Rock Bottom and people's elbow live will always be a highlight , as was seeing Triple H perform a "people's elbow". Brock Lesner looked huge, especially when he stood next to Paul Heyman. As mentioned many times by commentators, TV just doesn't do any justice to appreciating the size of these athletes. The crowd nearly blew the roof off when The Rock grabbed the mic and started his "Finally, The Rock has come to....." A quick side note to all future wrestlers who attend Australia, Melbourne is pronounced *Mel burn* Not *Mel born*.

Other highlights of the night for me include hearing "Jericho's a wanker" chants, and then when Jericho said he "doesn't even know what a wanker is", Edge then went and gave him a visual explanation! Edge climbing up the scaffolds around the ring, while taking his own video of the night and Rikishi delivering his classic stink face (speaking before about things that are bigger in real life.....). Seeing some of my favourite wrestlers live for the first time including The Hurricane, Edge, Jericho, The Rock, Kurt Angle and Triple H was something up till that moment I didn't think was ever going to happen in Australia. This is still one of the best things I have seen, experienced and been a part of (obviously with the exception of marrying my beautiful wife Kristina, and my kids), and I was glad to experience it with Rhonda and Zac. The only downfall was the early start and 12 hour trip back home the next day!

Results

- Rikishi defeated Rico in a Kiss My Ass match
- Mark Henry & Randy Orton defeated D-Von & Batista
- Jamie Noble (c) (w/ Nida) defeated Hurricane Helms to retain the WWE Cruiserweight Championship
- Chavo Guerrero & Hardcore Holly (w/ Maven) defeated Billy & Chuck (w/ Rico)
- Kurt Angle defeated Test

- Lance Storm & Christian (c) defeated Billy Kidman & Rey Mysterio to retain the WWE Tag Team Championship
- Edge defeated Chris Jericho
- Torrie Wilson defeated Stacy Keibler in a Bra and Panties match
- The Rock (c) defeated Triple H and Brock Lesnar (w/ Paul Heyman) in a triple threat match to retain the World Heavyweight Championship

Our next live experience, had me just as excited, as I would finally get to see The Undertaker wrestle, in 2004's 'The Return of the Deadman tour'. After experiencing the WWF/E during the Global world tour, I was just thrilled that the WWF/E would be returning to Australia this year, and especially thrilled at the thought of experiencing The Undertaker live. The Undertaker has become to me (and many others) the last link, between the 'old school' of wrestling in the very late 80,s early 90's, and today. He has managed to stay as one of the top stars in the WWF/E for over 20 years, something many other WWF/E superstars have not managed to do.

I use the term 'experience' while watching The Undertaker, because that is exactly what happens – you experience The Undertaker. From the moment the lights go out, and the first 'bell' of his entrance music starts, goose bumps went down my spine, (this has only happened twice since, while my wife Kristina walked down the aisle at our wedding, and standing looking down upon the Great Wall of China, after my boys and I climbed it for over an hour). The goose bumps continued through The Undertaker turning the lights on by raising his arms, his lifting off of his hat, and seeing those famous Undertaker eyes, watching him perform his signature moves such as 'old school', 'chokeslam' and of course the 'tombstone piledriver'. While I have seen The Undertaker since at other shows, experiencing him here is one of my great wrestling memories.

Other than The Undertaker match, the other highlight of the night was the Eddie Guerrero vs. Kurt Angle match. Seeing both Eddie and Kurt in their prime was just amazing, and I feel blessed that I got too see Eddie wrestle before his untimely death. We also happened to see match 3 of the best of 5 series for the US title between John Cena and Booker T for the US championship. This was very unique for a 'house show', as usually you can count on no title changes or anything seriously affecting any current stories being currently run on TV. But here in Sydney, we got to see this match (won by Booker T to go to a 2-1 lead), which made the night and show and us in Sydney feel pretty important.

From 2004 to 2011, I only have missed one wrestling tour, (and unfortunately this year's 2012 WWE world tour will make it 2) and I have yet to be disappointed at any show I have been to. The 2010 WWE Smackdown tour and the 2011 WWE Raw tours I have very fond memories as these tours I got to take my kids along to. In 2010 I got to experience a wrestling show with my two boys Connor and Max, as well as my non wrestling fan wife Kristina who managed to have a great time with us which says a lot about how much fun a live wrestling show can be. To see my boys dressed in their Rey Mysterio masks and shirts, holding the signs we made the week before, and watching them experience the joy at seeing Rey live, is a priceless memory that all wrestling dads (and mums) should enjoy experiencing with their kids. Having my wife along joining in the fun only added to my enjoyment of the night and my appreciation of her, as she was a NWF, now she at least fake's interest for us (I am yet to return the favour as I refuse to sit down and watch Midsomer Murders with her!). In 2011 it was the turn of my beautiful daughters Zara and Ruby to come and enjoy the wrestling with me. Ruby who is my main wrestling 'buddy', and I was just as excited to see her reaction to the action and matches, than I was of my own viewing of the action and matches.

Besides the actual wrestling, the four hour drive to Sydney, staying in a hotel room, buying our WWE shirts, and other merchandise and of course drawing our wrestling signs all adds to the whole experience of going to a WWE show. To walk around the thousands of other fans with their signs, their $500 replica belts, dressed as Hogan, Undertaker or John Cena make the night a friendly and visual experience even before seeing the actual wrestling. It is an event that I have always felt safe in bringing the family as everyone is friendly, you can see by people taking photos of those with the replica belts, and those dressed up. I have always experienced a politeness and courteous between fans during the line up at the merchandise stands, as well as the food stands and toilets.

While I have witnessed many of the high end production of live wrestling shows, I have always shied away from independent, or the local wrestling product in Australia. This has to do with a late night viewing of International Wrestling Australia (IWA) on a local pay TV site. The show was filmed at Rooty Hill RSL Club, I think there would have been lucky to be 20-30 fans in attendance. Now while the action and wrestling was pretty good, I felt it lacked the atmosphere due to the low numbers. It is the lack of atmosphere that has kept me away from these shows. Now due to a busy schedule, I was unable to attend the WWE show touring Australia this year. Due to missing out on my yearly live wrestling fix, I decided to take my 4 kids, Rhonda and myself to the IWA show at our local Dubbo RSL club this year (23rd June 2012), and it is something I am glad I did.

My first thought as we found our seats was that there is way more than 20 people here, in fact the show ended up having about 200-300 people in attendance which meant that this show was not going to lack atmosphere. Add the tournament formula for the night, and that there was a wrestler by the name of Tyson Gibbs, who was actually from our town of Dubbo (after believing this to be a kayfabe, I later found out this was actually true!). While there were certain moves that would not be able to be performed due to the low roof, I was extremely impressed with the quality of wrestling especially some of the risks these Aussie wrestlers did for our entertainment. Moves that included diving through the ropes onto a wooden floor (no mats for protection here at the Dubbo RSL), as well as some great technical in ring action. As most of us fans did not know any of these wrestlers, they all performed their roles well, so that we cheered for the faces, and booed the heels.

The standard performer for the night for me, was a wrestler named Jack Bonza, the main heel of the night, who managed to have all the kids in attendance absolutely hating him, while wrestling fans like myself admiring his performance all night. I still have the image of my daughter Ruby shocked when Jack pulled his pants down to show us his bare bum! Jack managed to enrage the fans through his attacking our local boy, picking on the kids in the front row, and his 'Rick Rude' posing in the ring. The other image that I have of the night is my young son Max screaming for Tyson not to tap when held in Jack Bonza's submission STFU move. That image showed me that wrestling is still alive and well despite what many internet wrestling fans believe (but more about them later). The bonus of these small local or independent shows is at the end of the night my kids (and other fans) get a chance to talk to the wrestlers as well as get autographs and photos with their favourite wrestlers of the night. What impressed me was the willingness of these wrestlers (some who have had to wrestle 2 or 3 matches) to talk and mingle with us fans. I left the night with only one real thought, that I and my family will be back!

A quick side note - one of those occasions where information would have been better a week ago - on the Monday morning after the IWA show, at work I ran into the Correctional Centre Chaplin who I happen to quickly see on Saturday night, but did not get a chance to say hello. On discussing the night, it came out that he is the dad of Tyson Gibbs, the local boy from Dubbo and eventual winner of the IWA Trans-Tasman Champion! Information that would have benefitted my kids and me, had we known this a week ago. Tyson Dad has informed me he is now trying his luck overseas in America, having tryouts with the Ohio Valley Wrestling (OVW), I wish him good luck with this.

I expect many more wrestling nights and trips, and hope to one day take my little baby Abbey to her first wrestling show. Live wrestling shows have become a big part of my wrestling viewing, and this now will include WWE shows and the local product when it comes to Dubbo. If you have never experienced a live wrestling show I highly recommend it, as a family night out, however bring plenty of money as merchandise is not cheap, or either is the food at some of the stadiums. But you can pack your own food and buy your shirts on EBay before the show, if you want a cheaper option. Remember to make your signs to hold up, and as a parent make sure you take the time to watch your kid's faces during the night, the images on their faces you will keep forever.

Upon nearing completing this book, I have just bought tickets for my family and my sister's family to the WWE Raw Tour, in Sydney July 2013. My two nephews Rhys and Jak, are big wrestling fans, so I look forward to watching their little faces light up when they see their heroes for the first time. On top of my two nephews, my four older kids Zara, Connor, Ruby and Max, my sister and Brother -in- law will be also attending, it has the making of a fantastic night! I will be in contact with my sister and challenge her to outdo me in the sign department. I think the loser will be on lining up duties at the merchandise stand to buy

the 6 shirts!

Chapter 4   Wrestling Companies

When I walk into a supermarket to buy a packet of corn flakes, I will walk straight up and grab the 'Kellogg's Cornflakes packet. Why? Because that's what I grew up with, that is what I feel comfortable with, that is the corn flakes I enjoy. If they are out of 'Kellogg's' Cornflakes, then sure I will grab the "Skippy's" Cornflakes instead. I will still get my cornflakes fix, and it is a nice change, and even maybe a little cheaper, but I still would of preferred my Kellogg's cornflakes instead. Wrestling is no different, as a wrestling fan I enjoy watching wrestling when I can, whether it World Wrestling Entertainment (WWE), World Championship Wrestling (WCW), Extreme Championship Wrestling (ECW), Total Nonstop Action (TNA's), or International Wrestling Australia (IWA). As mentioned earlier in the book, the majority of my wrestling viewing has been the WWF/E product, this is the company that I grew up with, this is the wrestling product I feel most comfortable watching, and this is the wrestling I enjoy the most.

In Australia in the world football, you are either follow Rugby League or follow AFL (Australian Rules football). There are other football codes such as rugby union and soccer that have their dedicated fans, but the majority of the country is divided up into either League or AFL. You might have a favourite team from the other code, but if a choice came down to Friday on TV between an AFL game or watching a Rugby League game, then you will watch the code you prefer (I would be watching my West Tigers on Rugby League). However if you follow Rugby League, and someone offered you free tickets to the AFL Grand Final you would gladly take it. If you were a Rugby League supporter and there was no League on TV, then you possibly would watch AFL, Rugby Union or soccer to get your football or sports fix. If your favourite player switched codes, you wouldn't switch with him, however, you might watch the other code a little more just to see how he is going.

Other examples of this 'line drawn in the sand' that affects fans of the same genre of entertainment include in the world of sci-fi, where you are either a Star Wars or Star Trek fan

(I side with the Star Wars fans). There is no love lost between the Trekkies and Star Wars fans, which is well documented in the movie 'Fanboys'. In the world of comics and superheroes, you either prefer to read and follow the DC superheroes such as Superman, Batman, Wonder Woman and The Green Lantern or Marvel Heroes such as Spiderman, Captain America, Wolverine and Thor (I prefer my DC heroes), or in the fantasy world of Vampires and Werewolves you are either on Team Edward or Team Jacob (not that I have ever watched 'Twilight"...........).

Wrestling in the late 1990's during the Monday Night Wars was no different. Even though you were a fan of wrestling, you either supported WWE or WCW, and that is the company you would prefer to watch. When I finally got my pay TV, I would always try and tune in every week to WWE's Raw & Smackdown. If I missed it, then I would always go on WWE.com to find out what had happened. I would, if I could afford it, order the WWE's PPV's (or got a video copy of my friend Rhonda as we took turns ordering them), and if I missed one then you could guarantee that I would be one of the first to hire it on Video when it came out at Blockbuster or Video Ezy. WCW was always there and I would tune in if I needed a wrestling fix, or if there was nothing else on. I very rarely went onto the WCW website, or ordered their PPV's as when it came to which wrestling product I wanted to spend my money on, it was always the WWF/E. In Australia we were lucky during the 'Monday night Wars' that WWE Raw, and WCW Nitro were never on at the same time, so if like many fans you wanted to watch both to compare shows you could. But being a WWF/E fan I did really enjoy the Raw episode where DX (Degeneration X) arrived at a WCW show in an army jeep to stir up trouble, and of course the episode in March 2001, when the WWE finally won the wars and the Shane McMahon twist at the end.

Even though some of my favourite wrestlers 'switched' from WWE to WCW, such as Hulk Hogan, Randy Savage, Brett Hart and The Ultimate Warrior, I still preferred to watch the WWE. I would read via the internet how my favourites were doing over in WCW, however, my enjoyment and viewing loyalty stayed the same. Having these favourite wrestlers leave, opened the way for other stars in the WWE to gain my support, such as Stone Cold Steve Austin, The Undertaker, The Rock and of course Mick Foley (Mankind).

Now since the Monday night wars are over, I do find myself switching on the computer to 'you tube' hiring DVD's and finding and watching many matches, and moments that I missed due to my viewing loyalty to the WWF/E company. Matches that include the greats such as Flair and Sting who I have never really got to appreciate, as well as some of my all-time favourites such as Mick Foley (as Cactus Jack), Hulk Hogan, Brett Hart and Chris Beniot (more about the controversy about his legacy in a later chapter). I have enjoyed viewing the matches that were the focal point of why WCW was winning the war for so long such as:

- Rey Mysterio vs. Eddie Guerrero (Halloween Havoc 1997-Mask -vs.- Title)

- Chris Benoit vs. Bret Hart (WCW Monday Nitro 1999, Owen Hart Dedication Match)

- Nasty Boys vs. Cactus Jack/Kevin Sullivan - Slamboree '94 (5/23/94 - Tag Titles, Falls Count Anywhere match)

- Chris Benoit vs. Kevin Sullivan - GAB '96 (6/16/96 – Falls Count Anywhere Match)

- Ric Flair vs. Vader (Starrcade '93)

- Ric Flair vs. Ricky Steamboat (WrestleWar 1989)

- Sting vs. Ric Flair (Clash Of Champions I)

- Bill Goldberg, vs. Hollywood Hogan for the WCW Championship July 6, 1998 edition of *Nitro*.

- The Outsiders (Kevin Nash and Scott Hall) and Hulk Hogan vs. Randy Savage, Sting, and Lex Luger (the Hogan turning heel moment),

Now to my knowledge, Australia did not have Extreme Championship Wrestling (ECW) on our TV's so besides reading the book "The rise and Fall of ECW", watching the DVD (of the same name) and WWE's watered down version and reign of ECW my knowledge and experience of this company is limited. Besides my favourite wrestlers having a run on the show such as Cactus Jack (Mick Foley), and The Dudley Boys I did not know too much about the main wrestling stars of the company. After the WWF/E 2001 'invasion' story line I was introduced to many of the house hold names of ECW including Sabu, Sandman, Tommy Dreamer and Rob Van Dam.

My understanding of the true ECW brand, is that besides the WWE's one night stand PPV's, the weekly ECW shows that were produced by WWE were in nowhere near the type of shows run by Paul Heymen in its heyday. This I personally feel was due to the WWE moving into its 'PG era' and could not broadcast what was typically shown on ECW. While hardcore, extreme wrestling, Japanese and lucha libre styles of wrestling are not every fans cup of tea, I feel that I would have been one of those who, if I had regular access, would have become a big ECW fan. Due to my limited knowledge on what would be the best way for other non ECW fans to get a good taste of what ECW was all about (before its WWF/E days) here is a top 10 match list I found online by Julian Williams, posted on 411mania.com on the 6th June 2006. If you are a fan of ECW and do not agree with his top 10, then take it up with him, not me:

The Top Ten ECW Matches – Julian Williams 6ᵗʰ

June 2006 411mania.com

10) Cactus Jack vs. Sabu (Hostile City Showdown '94)

This was the first dream match in ECW's history. It pitted two hardcore legends, Sabu and Cactus Jack, against each other in a match that fans of hardcore wrestling were dying to see.

9) CW Anderson vs. Tommy Dreamer (Guilty As Charged '01)

This was the last great match in ECW on ECW's last show. It was an I Quit match that saw the Innovator of Violence, Tommy Dreamer, battle CW Anderson who had become an increasing pain in Tommy's ass. These two men put on an awesome match that saw a lot of brutal spots including Tommy being suplexed through two chairs, a Death Valley Driver from the top rope through a table performed on Anderson, and Tommy finally making CW quit by wrapping the metal band of the table around his eyes.

8) Sabu vs. 2 Cold Scorpio (Cyberslam '96)

If you like spotfests, you'll love this match. These two men just went back and forth for 30 minutes straight hitting big move after big move. Some of the many highlights in the match include a reverse 630 legdrop by Scorpio, an over the top rope senton by Sabu onto Scorpio(who was in the crowd), and Sabu crashing through a table set up in the crowd after Scorpio moved out of the way. This is one match you can watch numerous times and never be bored because the action is absolutely nonstop.

7) Rey Misterio Jr. vs. Psicosis (Hardcore TV, 10/17/95)

This match was EXTREME lucha libre at its finest. Rey and Psicosis went out there and had a terrific match that had the crowd hanging on the edge of their seat. The match saw Rey dive into the crowd not once, but twice, Psicosis dive into the crowd as well, Rey deliver a running hurricarana from the ring apron onto the concrete floor, Rey hit a one and a half springboard sitting senton onto the floor, and Psicosis deliver a top rope legdrop through a table on the floor.

6) Mike Awesome vs. Masato Tanaka

(November 2 Remember '99)

If you thought their match at One Night Stand was incredible, you ain't seen nothing until you check out this classic. This match saw a sitout powerbomb from the ring apron to the floor THROUGH A TABLE by Awesome, a top rope superplex through a table by Tanaka, and a top rope Awesomebomb which finally finished off Tanaka after a grueling match. This match was hard-hitting ECW action at its best and should be mandatory viewing for anyone trying to catch up on some ECW history.

5) The Pitbulls vs. Stevie Richards and Raven

(Gangsta's Paradise, 9/16/95)

This was a match with a lot on the line with the tag titles up for grabs as well as the stipulation that the Pitbulls would have to split up if they lost the match. It was a 2 out of 3 falls dog collar match and turned out to be a brutal affair. This match was classic ECW overbooking which somehow always seemed to work out. You had Stevie Richards not participating in the match at first only to be later dragged out, you had Tommy Dreamer replace a Pitbull temporarily after he was knocked out, you had Bill Alphonso reverse the decision after Tommy Dreamer pinned Raven, you had Todd Gordon come out to restart the match, you had 911 finally shut Fonzie up with a big ass chokeslam, and finally you had the Pitbulls win the tag titles after delivering a double powerbomb from the top rope on Raven and Richards. A great match that intertwined many different storylines and had the crowd loving every second of it.

4) Rob Van Dam vs. Jerry Lynn (Hardcore Heaven '99)

Whenever RVD and Jerry Lynn stepped in a ring together, it seemed like the results were always a classic match. This match was no exception and I dare say it was the best of their numerous matches against each other. This match included Lynn falling face first onto the concrete after getting kicked off the top rope, a Van Daminator in the crowd, a sunset flip powerbomb from Lynn to RVD from the ring apron through a table at ringside, and two of the prettiest 5 star frog splashes you'll ever see.

3) Great Sasuke/Gran Hamada/Masato Yakashiji vs. Taka Michinoku/Terry Boy/Dick Togo (Barely Legal '97)

This match stole the show on ECW's first ever Pay-Per-View. These six men introduced the Japanese style of wrestling to a nationwide North

American audience and the fans just ate it up. The pace in this match was just insanely fast and saw so many highspots and sick moves that it would take forever to mention all of them. If you have never seen this match do yourself a favor and find it as this match still holds up well over time and will leave you in amazement.

2) Chris Jericho vs. Pitbull #2 vs. Shane Douglas vs. 2 Cold Scorpio (Heatwave '96)

This was a four corners match for the TV title held by Jericho and it was 40 minutes of great, nonstop wrestling action.. Jericho and Scorpio had some terrific interaction in the match that included an insane spot where Scorpio dropkicked Jericho in his head while he was upside down in mid-air performing the lionsault. Eventually Jericho and Scorpio were eliminated which left it down to P#2 and Douglas. P#2 kept fighting back even after getting hit with brass knucks, a splintered piece of table, a chain, and the title belt. Eventually he would fall to Douglas'

belly to belly slam, but that couldn't tarnish what

was an absolutely unbelievable match.

1) Eddie Guerrero vs. Dean Malenko (Hardcore

TV, 8/26/1995)

This was Eddie and Dean's final match in ECW

before joining WCW. It's funny that one of the

greatest matches in ECW's history would be a

technical masterpiece rather than a hardcore

brawl, but that was one of the great things about

ECW. These two men went out and told a great

story in the ring in a 2 out of 3 falls match.

Usually in a wrestler's final match in ECW before

joining a rival promotion, they would be booed

out of the building with chants of "You Sold Out"

echoing throughout the arena. Not in this case,

though, as the fans were instead chanting "Please

Don't Go" and were even more vocal about it

after witnessing this phenomenal match.

For me the thing I did enjoy about WWF/E's ECW run, was Christian returning and becoming the ECW Champion, and his run as the ECW champion. Also the fact it gave other WWF/E stars a run at a major world title such as Matt Hardy, Mark Henry and Kane. I also enjoyed the Edge/Foley/Lita vs. Terry Funk, Tommy Dreamer and Beulah McGillicutty match at 'ECW One Night Stand' in 2006, Rob Van Dam winning the WWE title from John Cena and The Miz and John Morrisons "The Dirt Sheet" internet show, and of course ECW introducing us to CM Punk.

I have included below a very quick timeline of what I feel are the main events of each of WWF/E, WCW and ECW from the 80's Rock 'n' wrestling era up until the end of the Monday night wars. It is only a brief timeline and if you would like any more information then there is plenty of information to be found on the internet. If that sounds like too much work then there are some great DVDs (although possibly very WWF/E biased) such as The Rise and Fall of WCW, The Rise and Fall of ECW or The

Monday Night wars, or if this book has inspired you to read more, then you can try these:

- *The Rise & Fall of ECW: Extreme Championship Wrestling (by Thorn Loverro)*

  ECW burst onto the sports entertainment scene in the early 1990s, and redefined the industry with a reckless, brutal, death-defying, and often bloody style that became known as 'hardcore'. In the process, it attracted a rabid, cult-like following that is still going strong today. The ECW 'hardcore' style changed the wrestling business forever; and more than any other single factor, it was the adoption of this 'new breed of wrestling' from the young upstart company by the WWE that was largely responsible for the subsequent WWE domination of the industry. Through extensive interviews with former ECW talent and management, fans will have an inside look at what made the company great - and what led to its ultimate demise

- *The Death of WCW: WrestleCrap and Figure Four Weekly Present . . .* (by <u>R. D. Reynolds</u> <u>Bryan Alvarez</u>)

  This detailed tell-all of the demise of the former top pro wrestling company World Championship Wrestling explores the colourful personalities and flawed business decisions behind how WCW went from being the highest-rated show on cable television in 1997 to a laughable series that lost 95 percent of its paying audience by 2001. Behind-the-scenes exclusive interviews, rare photographs, and probing questions illustrate with humour and candour how greed, egotism, and bad business shattered the thriving enterprise. Wrestling fans will devour the true story of this fallen empire, which in its heyday spawned superstars such as Sting, Bill Goldberg, and the New World Order.

- *Eric Bischoff: Controversy Creates Cash (by Eric Bischoff)*

  Under Eric Bishoff's watch as president of WCW, the company went head to head with Vince McMahon's WWE and beat them at their own game before WCW itself spectacularly imploded. But by then, Bishoff had made an indelible mark on televised wrestling, producing shows that had appeared more dangerous, sexier, and more edgy than anything that had come before. He did this to such an extent that in 2002, McMahon seized the chance to bring in his former nemesis as General Manager of RAW; since then, true to form, Bishoff regularly surprises fans with matches that would once have been unthinkable for television. In this revelatory look at his life and career, Bishoff frankly discusses the things he did, both right and wrong, as he helped shape the sports entertainment industry into today's billion dollar business.

World Wrestling Federation/Entertainment

(Timeline for the WWF/E adapted from Legacyofwrestling.com)

1982-'83 - Vincent K. McMahon bought out his father

Late 1983 - Vince McMahon signed a chiasmic athlete away from the American Wrestling Association Terry Bollea who would become better known as Hulk Hogan.

23 January 1984 - Hulk Hogan defeated the Iron Sheik and captured the WWF World Heavyweight Title and "Hulkamania" was born

29 May 1984 -, Vincent J. McMahon died at the age of 69 in North Miami, Florida of cancer.

1984-'85 - Appearances for Cyndi Lauper, on WWF Television. A connection between wrestling and music began the "Rock and Wrestling" era of the '80s. Lauper began a feud with Captain Lou Albano, and included Lou in her music videos "Girls Just Want to Have Fun" and "She Bop."

September 1984 - Vince McMahon invaded Calgary and bought Stu Hart's Foothills Athletic Club Ltd… signing Brett "Hitman" Hart.

31 March 1985 Wrestlemania I was shown on a Pay TV format and was a huge success

07 April 1986 - Wrestlemania II was held in three separate locations and was the first broadcast on pay-per-view.

29 March 1987 - 93,173 fans packed the Pontiac Silverdome in Pontiac, Michigan, breaking an

American indoor attendance record.

Late 1987 - The World Wrestling Federation continued to not only go "national," but "international."

WWF Wrestlers ventured into Milan, Italy and an estimated 10,000 in attendance

05 February 1988 - Andre pinned Hogan and captured the WWF World Title only to try and sell the belt to the "Million Dollar Man" Ted DiBiase. This was classed as illegal and the belt declared vacant.

11 January 1993 - The first ever Monday Night Raw was broadcast live on the USA Network from the Manhattan Center in New York City, New York. 01 February 1993

04 September 1995 - The WWF and Monday Night Raw received a jolt when World Championship Wrestling's

18 December 1995 - WWF/E Women's World Champion Alundra Blayze appeared on WCW Monday Nitro with the WWF Belt. She shocked when she tossed the belt into the garbage bin.

08 January 1996 - The "Ring Master" Steve Austin made his

World Wrestling Federation debut he would later become better known as Stone Cold Steve Austin.

31 March 1996 - Wrestlemania XII, WWF World Champion Bret Hart and Shawn Michaels in Anaheim, California, went 61:52 in an Iron Man Match

23 June 1996 - Austin won the King of the Ring Tournament, and Austin 3:16 was born

22 September 1996 - A WWF-ECW relationship was formed.

09 November 1997 – The infamous" Montreal Screwjob", where WWF/E owner Vince McMahon 'screwed' Brett Hart out of the WWF title. Brett Hart then moved to WCW. This also was the elevation of Shawn Michaels and Tripe H's group known as degeneration X

11 August 1998 - Shane McMahon, the fourth generation McMahon in the business, became the President of New Media for Titan Sports Inc., and the World Wrestling Federation.

1999 - Titan Sports became "World Wrestling Federation Entertainment Inc, WWF "Smackdown" was broadcast on the

UPN Network. It quickly became an important factor in the World Wrestling Federation's continued success.

23 May 1999 – Owen Hart died tragically during an in ring entrance stunt at the WWF/E second annual "Over the Edge" pay-per-view 23 August 1999.

October 1999 - Two WWF creative directors left the organization for its rival, WCW. They were Vince Russo and Ed Ferrara.

31 January 2000 - Perry Saturn, Eddy Guerrero, Dean Malenko and former World Champion,

Chris Benoit moved from WCW to WWF/E

October 2000 - The WWF changed its symbol from WWEF to simply "WWF." Also, the group continued to beat WCW in the ratings.

March 2001 - Shane McMahon appeared in Panama City Beach, Florida and announced that he had purchased WCW ending the Monday night wars

25 March 2002 – the WWF/E brand expansion where superstars were assigned to either Raw or Smackdown

05 May 2002 - The World Wrestling Federation officially changed its name to "World Wrestling Entertainment, WWE

World Championship Wrestling (The Ted Turner years)

Pre 1988 – Various promotions affiliate with the NWA (National Wrestling Alliance) under the World Championship Wrestling (WCW) title.

Nov 21 1988 – Ted Turner's WCW begins

Dec 1988 – WCW first PPV under Ted Turner Starrcade is held

Jan 1991 – WCW splits from NWA, forming its own championships

Early 1993 – Eric Bischoff is appointed Executive Vice President of WCW

1993 – The 'Shockmaster' incident occurs on "A Flair for the Gold" TV spot.

Late 1993 – Rick Flair becomes WCW after his non competing clause with WWF/E expires

1994 – Eric Bischoff declares war on WWF/E. Recruits Hogan and Savage. This is the start of wrestling contracts that include large guarantee yearly money and wrestlers having creative control of their characters. This would later lead to the downfall of WCW.

1994 – WCW Bash at the Beach, Hogan vs. Flair finally happens

Sep 4 1995 – WCW Nitro begins

1996 – Scott Hall and Kevin Nash join WCW and begin the New World Order (nWo)

– Bash at the Beach, Hogan turns heel and joins Hall and Nash in the nWo

- WCW would go onto win 84 consecutive Monday night ratings against WWF/E
- Time Warner buys the Ted Turner Cable empire, Ted Turner is still biggest stock Holder.

1997 – WCW Starrcade PPV is the Biggest ever buy rate in WCW history

Jan 1998 – WCW Thunder show premiers

April 13 1988 – WWF/E wins its first head to head rating in nearly 2 years

1998 – Goldberg's undefeated streak ends at the hands of Kevin Nash

Jan 1999 – The Hogan vs. Nash 'finger poke' incident

Sep 1990 – Eric Bischoff removed from control of WCW, replaced by former WWF/E writer Vince Russo

Nov 1999 – Russo revises nWo story line

Jan 2000 – Chris Beniot wins the WCW world Championship, only to hand title back the following day and announced he has signed with WWF/E along with Eddie Guerrero, Dean Malenko and Perry Saturn.

April 2000 – Bischoff reinstated by WCW

March 23 2001 – WCW brought by WWF/E

Extreme Championship Wrestling

1989-1992 – Started out as Tri State Wrestling, then sold and called Eastern Championship Wrestling.

1993 – Paul Heyman becomes head booker of the company

1994 – After a NWA championship tournament victory, Shane Douglass throws the NWA Championship in the garbage bin and declares himself the first ever ECW world champion. ECW changes its name to EXTREEME CHAMPIONSHIP WRESTLING.

1995 – Paul Heyman becomes owner of ECW. At a WWF/E show fans start chanting 'ECW' alerting Vince McMahon to the company

1997 – ECW and the WWF/E work together

April 13 1997 – ECW's first ever Pat per view "Barely Legal' is held.

1999 – ECW sign TV deal with TV station TNN

2001 – WCW wrestler Mike Awesome loses ECW world title to WWF/E wrestler Taz at an ECW event

2001 – ECW fold due to Bankruptcy

Obviously with the closing of two wrestling companies, there were many wrestlers looking for work, especially those not wanted by the WWF/E or who themselves did not want to wrestle for Vince McMahon and the WWF/E. After the folding of WCW and ECW, there were few wrestling companies that came about one of the first was the World Wrestling All-stars (WWA) which I have mentioned in the previous chapter. WWA ran from October 2001 until May 2003.

Total Nonstop Action (TNA) was formed by Jeff and his father Jerry Jarret, and Bob Ryder and has become the main company to form as a main alternative to the WWF/E. Initially just focussing on PPV's and using the internet, TNA slowly built a small but strong fans base and in 2002 TNA explosion was launched on TV. This would be later relaunched to the TNA Impact we can see today. Like back in the Monday night Wars days, there seems to be a very strong fan base that is either TNA or WWE. However at this stage TNA as not yet the numbers to complete in ratings against the WWF/E.

I will also include a quick historical timeline of what I feel are the important dates and moments in TNA for those of you readers who are interested, and like I mentioned before, if you would like a more thorough history try Google and/or Wikipedia.

May 2002 – Jeff and Jerry Jarret with the backing from Health South Corp, start the wrestling company NWA: TNA

Jun 2002 – Ken Shamrock wins first NWA: TNA Championship

Oct 2002 – Panda energy buys Controlling Interest

- The company starts by showing weekly PPV, rather than a syndicated TV show.

2004 – Become first American wrestling company to use hexagon shaped ring

Jun 2004 – TNA: iMPACT starts on Fox Sports

Jun 2005 – TNA: iMPACT move from TV to now being broadcasted on the internet

Sep 2005 – Sign new TV deal with Spike TV

Mar 2006 – Start performing House shows

Apr 2006 – Impact moves to Thursday nights

May 2007 – TNA officially break away from the NWA

Oct 2007 – Impact moves to a 2 hour format

Mar 2008 – Impact is shown Live on Spike TV

Oct 2009 – Hulk Hogan & Eric Bischoff form a partnership with TNA

Jan 2010 – Hulk Hogan debuts on TNA Impact and TNA returns to using 4 sided ring

Mar 2010 – TNA tries to re-start Monday night wars by moving Impact back to Monday nights, with the last hour of Impact going up against the first hour of Raw. Results are disastrous, and war ends before it really begins. Impact moves back to Thursdays.

Jun 2010 – Sting becomes first inductee to YNA hall of fame

Jul 2010 – ECW invades TNA, again with poor results as friction occurs between ECW stars and TNA stars

May 2012 – TNA files a lawsuit against WWE. *TNA's lawsuit alleges that that Wittenstein, who worked for the company for three years before departing in 2011, provided WWE with inside information on TNA contracts and other matters from his time working in TNA's talent relations and live events departments*

Just like WCW, I have not watched a great deal of TNA programming due to it's on and off availability on TV in Australia and my TV. Although while Christian and Mick Foley had their runs with TNA, I did regularly hop onto the TNA website to see how they were both doing, and was thrilled that they both got a TNA World Heavyweight champion title run. I also, through websites like www.wrestleedge.com, keep a casual update to see what is happening in the world of TNA, as there are performers currently on the brand who I have enjoyed watching over the years through their WWF/E tenors, such as Kurt Angle, Mr Anderson, Bully Ray Dudley and of course Hulk Hogan. Through my reading and small knowledge of the TNA company I hear a lot of good things about wrestlers such as A.J. Styles, Samoan Joe and Abyss. Just like with the ECW brand, I wouldn't feel right trying to list matches that showcase the TNA brand as I have only seen a few, and the list would be dominated by Kurt Angle, Christian and Mick Foley matches! So I will find someone else to do that. Although I have watched both Mick Foley's and Christian's TNA World Heavyweight championship title victories and recommend these:

| Christian Cage vs. Jeff Jarrett | 2006 |
| Against All Odds | |

| Mick Foley vs. Sting | 2009 Lockdown |

As for the best matches TNA has to Offer, after doing a search on Google, these were the common matches that kept re-occurring on different fan base chat lines and wrestling sites.

While I am off to watch them all this weekend, if you want to find out what TNA is all about, and the best it has to offer then these are the matches recommended:

AJ Styles v. Christopher Daniels v. Samoa Joe – *[Unbreakable 2005]*

-recommended by many top lists as the number one match in TNA history.

Kurt Angle v. Samoa Joe – *[Turning Point 2006]*

- recommended by many as the best in the series of matches between these two wrestling superstars.

AJ Styles v. Chris Sabin v. Petey Williams for the TNA X Division Championship in an Ultimate X match – *[Final Resolution 2005]*

- a matched that many recommend that showcases TNA x-division

Kurt Angle vs. Mr. Anderson

- Lockdown 2010-many believe to be the match of 2010

Christian Cage .Vs Kaz-#1 Contender-Ladder Match-Genesis '07 (You know I had to find a match that involved Christian to be on this list!)

While in Australia there are quite a few small wrestling companies that are either state specific or even City specific, while some do travel country wide. In NSW there are two main companies that I know of. These companies provide live wrestling entertainment around the country touring not only the major cities but also (lucky for me) country towns as well. The first is the IWA (International Wrestling Australia) who I just happened to see a show on the weekend of 23rd June 2012 (see my previous chapter about seeing it live).

".........Mark Mercedes who is a 15 year pro wrestling veteran who has wrestled for WCW in the USA & major companies in Japan and Europe. Mercedes adds 'IWA Pro Wrestling has been Australia's #1 in sports - entertainment for the past 11 years and is often referred by many venue managers as "Australia's hottest live

touring act". IWA's success has surprised many and really revived pro wrestling in Australia'...."

The Australian Wrestling Federation (AWF) is the other wrestling company based in Sydney and has been around since 1999, and

......"consists of action packed, visually spectacular professional wrestling events that utilize wrestling talent from Australia and abroad. AWF events feature matches, interviews and storylines incorporating all the hype that is pro-wrestling today....." (http://www.awfwrestling.com.au/company/in dex.htm)

As mentioned in the last chapter I have enjoyed watching the IWA live when it came to Dubbo, and look forward to watching the AWF to compare the companies. Throughout Australia, and USA, Canada, Mexico, Japan etc.

there are many other small wrestling companies that have been just as important to wrestling's history, and current wrestling legacies. I would love to witness and see live wrestling in both Mexico and Japan where wrestling is huge in both countries....I will add that to my wrestling bucket list.

Chapter 5   Wrestling eras

Through my many years of supporting and watching wrestling I have witness the wrestling product transform, update, disappear from Australian TV, change, adapt and repackage its product to suit the fans, the decade and the generations (such as generation x and y). We have gone from the 1980's *Rock' n' Wrestling* era, moved into the 1990's with the *Monday night wars, the Attitude and ruthless aggression* eras, to now currently in what is known as *The pg* era. Each era has its supporters and detractors, and there is constant debates over which era is best, which era has the best wrestlers, matches, feuds etc. For many the Attitude, and Ruthless Aggression eras are separate, however for the purpose of this book I am combining them, as both were very similar in styles.

As a child of the 1980's I was introduced into wrestling through the *Rock 'n' Wrestling* era, this is the era that means the most to me as it involves a lot of my favourite wrestling memories, matches and wrestlers. I have, and still enjoy watching wrestling today in its *pg. era*, and enjoyed immensely the *attitude* era and the Monday Night Wars, (in which I was a WWF supporter in their battle with WCW). I feel when people start to compare era's (which I am about to attempt to do), depending which era you were introduced to in wrestling, that era is going to hold some sub conscious bias when you begin to compare it against the others. (I apologise in advance when my comparisons tend to favour the *Rock 'n' Wrestling* era). There are also those non wrestling fans, who will compare each era differently as well, with usually the *attitude* and Ruthless aggression eras coping most of the flack due to its apparent bad influence on the kids at the time. When comparing the three generations against each other, you are always going to have two-thirds of the readers disagreeing with you, and if that's the case then go and write your own book!

There are many ways we can compare each era, to try and work out which era was wrestling at its best. The criteria I have decided on for this book is a:

- Brief History of each era, of when they occurred and some of the main points leading to that era, that happened in that era, and that lead to the completion of that era.

- Who were the biggest stars of each era?

- The biggest and main feuds and stories that defined each era.

- Who was the biggest tag teams as well as how strong the tag team division was.

- What were the main titles and who was battling for them?

- Shows (TV and PPV), who had the best, the announcing team.

The **Rock 'n' Wrestling era** is said to have started in the early 1980's when there was a major change in the wrestling structure. This was the era that I was to start my journey into becoming a lifelong wrestling fan.

Disappearing were the regional territories in the USA and Canada, and the emergence of two wrestling companies that were going first national and then global. These companies were Vince McMahon's World Wrestling Federation (WWF/E) and

Ted Turner's World Championship Wrestling (WCW). Each company had a different focus, with WCW focussing on the more technical side of wrestling, letting the matches be the star of the show, while WWF/E went more into the entertainment side, joining forces with music industry stars such as Cyndi Lauper, and hence the Rock 'n' Wrestling name was born.

WWF/E started signing up the big names in wrestling across the USA and Canada including Hulk Hogan, Roddy Piper, Jesse 'The Body' Ventura, Junk yard Dog, Andre the Giant and Harley Race. Then with introduction of cable TV and Pay Per Views (PPV), Wrestlemania was born, and the Rock 'n' Wrestling era were in full swing. Very quickly the WWF became the number 1 wrestling show as its colourful over the top characters were a huge hit with kids (and those kids at heart), and its PPV events such as Wrestlemania, Summer Slam and the Royal Rumble soon becoming a yearly must see for wrestling fans. The peak of this era would be Wrestlemania III, as record attendances of over 93 000 people in the outdoor arena and PPV, helped cement wrestling into the 1980's culture.

The Rock 'n' Wrestling era is said to of finished in the1990's with the so called passing of the torch (championship) from Hulk Hogan to The Ultimate Warrior at Wrestlemania VI, in one of the very first major babyface vs. babyface matches that I had seen. While the torch (championship) was handed very quickly back to Hogan, the fun and comic book imagery of wrestling was about to end. With steroid accusations surfacing, and kids (including myself) from the 1980's now becoming teenagers and young adults in the 1990's, our interests and tastes not just for wrestling, but many things changed. With the majority of wrestling fans gained in the 1980's falling into the now teenage/young adult age bracket, wrestling companies had to change to keep these fans. A lull in wrestling occurred especially here in Australia, and the two main wrestling organisations would have to develop a completely different 'attitude' on how they run their shows to get fans to return, and bring new fans along with them.

The biggest star of the *Rock 'n' Wrestling* era at the WWF/E), was Hulk Hogan. He became the face of the 80's wrestling boom, and was well known even to those NWF. He was our ultimate hero, the ultimate good guy who 'took his vitamins and said his prayers'. Coming out to the ring in his customary red and yellow, with "Real American" blasting away, he was who most people went to a wrestling event for, or tuned into a wrestling show wanting to see and hear. From his customary comebacks (Hulking up) in his matches, his over the top promos or his poses at the end of the matches, he inspired a generation of wrestling fans. But for Hogan's light to shine so brightly he needed some competition/villains/heels to defeat. King Kong Bundy, Andre the Giant, Rowdy Roddy Piper were just some of the big name stars that I feel helped elevate Hogan to the heights he reached. His feuds and matches with the likes of Piper, Bundy and Andre, gave us as kids proof that good can triumph over evil.

Besides Hogan the other, wrestler that made the rock n wrestling essential viewing for many wrestling fans, which obviously includes myself was 'The Macho Man' Randy Savage. Throughout the 1980's (and early 1990's) Savage was a part of many great wrestling feuds, and you always knew his matches were going to steal the night. Savage could have a fantastic match against all types and styles of wrestlers, and his feuds with Jake 'The Snake' Roberts, The Ultimate Warrior, Rick Flair and Hogan were what made viewing wrestling in the late 80's such an essential part of my life.

Other performers who inspired my love of wrestling during this era include The Junkyard dog, The Ultimate Warrior, Brutus 'The Barber' Beefcake, Jake 'The Snake' Roberts, Ricky 'The Dragon' Steamboat and Hill Billy Jim. For all those wrestlers I cheered for there were those 'heel' wrestlers that were that good either on the mic, or in the ring at getting us fans to hate them. The best heels during the 80's include Ravishing Rick Rude, The Million Dollar Man Ted DiBiase, Greg 'the Hammer' Valentine and Harley Race. And of course those pesky annoying managers who always cost the good guys their matches by interfering, none were better than Bobby 'the Brain' Heenan and Jimmy 'The mouth of the south' Hart, Mr Fuji, Slick or The Sensation Sherrie.

As mentioned in the last chapter I didn't get to see much of his work prior and after his WWF/E runs, Rick Flair (Wooooo!!!), was the other biggest star for many, many wrestling fans during this Rock 'n' Wrestling period. His battles with Dusty Rhodes and Harley Race, the formation of 'The four Horseman' with, Tully Blanchard, Ole Anderson and Arn Anderson, and his famous quotes.....

"This ain't no garden party, brother, this is wrestling, where only the strongest survive."

"I'm a limousine ridin', jet flyin', kiss stealin', wheelin' dealin' son of a gun. WOOOO!!"

"To be the man, you've gotta beat the man!"

". Wooooo!"

"All the women want to be with me, and the men want to be like me."

.....helped cement Flair as 'the man' in WCW during the 1980's Rock 'n' Wrestling era.

You cannot talk about big stars of the rock n wrestling without mentioning Cyndi Lauper and Mr T. These big name music and acting stars helped the WWF/E move more into the mainstream media and TV. Cyndi Lauper's relationship with Lou Albano, having him appear in her music video, then the publicity surrounding her feud with Lou during a wrestling storyline, helped bring in new fans to wrestling. Cyndi Lauper continued her relationship with wrestling by constantly including wrestlers in her videos. Through his role in the TV show 'The A Team', Mr T was one of the biggest stars of the early 80's and his feud with Rowdy Roddy Piper was used to help establish Wrestlemania as they were in the main event as tag team opponents with Hulk Hogan on Mr T teams, and Paul Orndoff on Piper's. Twelve months later at Wrestlemania II, Piper and Mr T battled in a boxing match that saw eventually Piper being disqualified for slamming Mr T in the 4th round.

Not only were the superstars of the 80's fun to watch, but their feuds and intense rivalries that occurred during this time made tuning in or buying PPV's a must (or in my case hiring the PPV video when it came out at the local corner store). In the WWF/E there were many fantastic feuds that grabbed a hold of me, and made making their matches seem that more important, and the good thing about the rock 'n' wrestling era, there was always 'that' match, or 'that' moment that either defined the feud, or ended the feud. Some of those moments that I remember even 30 years on and have recently revisited thanks to you tube are:

- Randy Savage tied to the ropes, while Jake 'The Snake' Roberts held a large cobra and made it bite Savage's arm, during the Savage / Roberts's feud, which also included Roberts giving a snake as a gift to Savage and Elizabeth during their wedding.

- Hogan Slamming Andre at Wrestlemania III. While these two would go onto to wrestle more matches, it was that image to many that ended Andre's dominance over Hogan.

- Ravishing Rick Rude's tights with Jake Roberts's wife on them, and then he being stripped naked. Possibly would not be as affective in today's wrestling environment but worked well back in the 80's.

- Randy Savage embracing Elizabeth after losing his retirement match to The Ultimate Warrior. This signalled the end of their wonderful feud (1990/91) in a fantastic match, as well as Savage's in ring career (for a while anyway).

- Shawn Michaels throwing Marty Janette through a window on the barber shop, started 'The Rockers" splitting up and some great matches between the two.

- 1984 'Piper's Pit' segment where Piper smashed a coconut over Jimmy Snuka's head!

Other notable rivalries and feuds from those glorious 80's in WCW include: Rick Flair vs. Ricky The Dragon Steamboat; and Rick Flair and Dusty Rhodes While back in the WWF/E they had Hogan vs. Roddy Piper, Hogan vs. King Kong Bundy and one of his best feuds during 1989 Hogan against Savage, The mega powers exploding feud leading to their great match at Wrestlemania V.

While the big names starts such as Hogan, Savage and Andre 'The Giant' main evented wrestling shows, the rock n wrestling era also had a great variety and a strong tag team division. In my opinion many of the greatest tag teams were around and performed during this era and I have not seen the tag team division done as well or being as strong (especially in the WWF/E) since. The teams that dominated the WWF/E during this time, and the teams that I enjoyed watching include; The Hart Foundation (Brett Hart and Jim 'The anvil' Niedhart); The British Bulldogs (Davey Boy Smith and The Dynamite Kid); Demolition (Ax and Smash); The Powers of Pain; The Rockers (Marty Janette and Shawn Michaels); Iron Sheik & Nikolay Volkoff; The Brain Busters; Money Inc (Ted Debase and Irwin R. Shiester);The twin Towers (Akeem and the Big Boss man); The Colossal Connection (Andre the Giant and Hauk); Strike force (Rick Martel and Tito Santana); Legion of Doom (L.O.D); and my person favourites The Bushwhackers (Luke and Butch)!

In WCW the tag tam division was just as strong with teams such as; Ricky Steamboat and Jay Youngblood; The Rock 'n' Roll Express; Arn Anderson and Tully Blanchard; The Steiner

Brothers; Doom (Butch Reed and Ron Simmons); The Fabulous Free birds and of course The Midnight Express.

Like their single competitors counterparts in the 80's, it was the feuds between these teams that made the tag team matches enjoyable to watch. To fully appreciate how good traditional Tag team wrestling can be then I suggest the following matches to view:

Brain Busters vs. Hart Foundation (SummerSlam 1989)

Dream Team vs. British Bulldogs (Wrestlemania II)

Hart Foundation vs. Demolition -- Two out of Three Falls for the World Tag Team Championship – 1990

The titles that I saw many battles for during the rock n wrestling era included the WWF (later to be the WWE championship), the Intercontinental Title, and the WWF/E Tag Team Title. Due to only being 2 singles title, to me every title match was important and meant something, and if you won the title it represented to us fans that you were a major player at WWF/E. Unlike today there were some long reins with Hogan (the WWF title), Honky Tonk Man (Intercontinental title) and Demolition (WWF Tag team titles) all going on to have record reigns with their respective titles. This meant that when they finally lost their titles it was a big event, and the wrestler or team that beat them was/were something special.

The WWF title was the main title held as mentioned in the previous paragraph mainly by Hulk Hogan. He defended it regularly against as mentioned superstars such as Piper, Bundy, Savage and Andre 'The Giant'. The WWF title headlined most PPV's and when it didn't it was because the WWF Champion was involved in the main event tag team match. Other wrestlers to hold the title during this rock n wrestling period include Andre the Giant, Macho Man randy Savage, The Ultimate Warrior and Sergeant Slaughter. Huge battles main eventing Wrestlemania 2,3,4,5 and 6, helped cement this as the title everyone wanted, and those who won it were the top of Wrestling. A full list of the WWF/E champions from 1980 to 1991:

Bob Backlund   December 17, 1979

Held Up[†]	October 19, 1981
Bob Backlund	November 23, 1981
The Iron Sheik	December 26, 1983
Hulk Hogan	January 23, 1984
André the Giant	February 5, 1988
Vacated	February 5, 1988
Randy Savage	March 27, 1988
Hulk Hogan	April 2, 1989
The Ultimate Warrior	April 1, 1990
Sgt. Slaughter	January 19, 1991
Hulk Hogan	March 24, 1991

Often stealing the show at many PPV's was the battle for the WWF Intercontinental Title, none more famous than The Macho Man Randy Savage vs. Rickie 'The Dragon' Steamboat match at Wrestlemania III. My other fond memories of this title was during The Honky Tonk Man's reign where I hoped every opponent he faced would take the title off him and wipe that smug Honky Tonk smile off his face and take the intercontinental title from around his waist, but he always managed to avoid losing it! The Honky Tonk's claims to be "the best Intercontinental champion of all time" is one I still feel he has a strong claim to. The battle between Rick Rude and The Ultimate Warrior was a major highlight for this title for me, as I enjoyed this almost yearlong battle in 1988/1989. From Pat Patterson winning the very first WWF Intercontinental title, to legends such as Savage, The Ultimate Warrior and Brett Hart, this title was often the start of a WWF/E superstars rise to main event status. Winners or the Intercontinental title during the rock n wrestling era were:

1	Pat Patterson	September 1, 1979
2	Ken Patera	April 21, 1980
3	Pedro Morales	December 8, 1980

4	Don Muraco	June 20, 1981
5	Pedro Morales	November 23, 1981
6	Don Muraco	January 22, 1983
7	Tito Santana	February 11, 1984
8	Greg Valentine	September 24, 1984
9	Tito Santana	July 6, 1985
10	Randy Savage	February 8, 1986
11	Ricky Steamboat	March 29, 1987
12	The Honky Tonk Man	June 2, 1987
13	The Ultimate Warrior	August 29, 1988
14	Rick Rude	April 2, 1989
15	The Ultimate Warrior	August 28, 1989
—	Vacated	April 1, 1990

16	Mr. Perfect	April 23, 1990
17	The Texas Tornado	August 27, 1990
18	Mr. Perfect	November 19, 1990
19	Bret Hart	August 26, 1991

Not to forget the other major title during this era was the NWA World Heavy weight Championship, which has a long and complicated history due to merges with other companies, non-recognised titles changes and Champions being stripped of the title. During the 80's like Hogan in the WWF/E, the title belonged to one man, Rick Flair. While he did not have a three year run with the title, he did manage to capture/hold the title for a total of around nine times from 1980 to 1991. Other notable winners of this illustrious title during this time include; Harley Race, Dusty Rhodes and Ricky Steamboat.

The Rock 'n' Wrestling era also introduced us to the Pay Per View, none being more important to (what I feel) not just the WWF/E but to wrestling in general. A quick definition of what exactly is a Pay Per View (PPV):

....provides a service by which a television audience can purchase events to view via private telecast. The broadcaster shows the event at the same time to everyone ordering it (as opposed to video-on-demand systems, which allow viewers to see recorded broadcasts at any time). Events can be purchased using an on-screen guide, an automated telephone system, or through a live customer service representative. Events often include feature films, sporting events and entertainment.
(Wikipedia)

WWF/E then produced PPV's such as Summer Slam, Royal Rumble and Survivor Series. Unlike today there were only 4-5 PPV's a year, which I felt made them more important, and allowed for greater build-up of feuds before the matches. While in Australia, I usually had to wait three months to read what happened through the WWF/E magazine and four months to hire the PPV on video, it was usually worth the wait. What made these PPV's also extra special was that each was different, you had the big "super bowl' or 'grand final' of wrestling in Wrestlemania, and then in the summer another spectacular known as SummerSlam. The traditional Survivor Series of tag teams of 5 superstars vs. 5 superstars in an elimination style tag matches, and finally the Royal Rumble, an over the top battle where entrants come into the ring at 1 minute intervals.

While officially the **attitude/ruthless aggression** eras didn't officially start until September 1995, it was what occurred during the early 1990's that lead to this change in the 'attitude' of wrestling. In my opinion shared with many I found during my research there were 3 main decisions that were instrumental in starting the *Attitude* era and the *Monday Night Wars*:

1. WWF changed its main Monday night TV show *WWF Prime Time Wrestling* from a discussion based show, to a live show that had original matches between WWF stars and not Jobbing/squash matches. The show was also used to introduce and build stories up before upcoming PPV's

2. WCW had hired Eric Bischoff to the position of Executive Vice President, and after a difficult beginning, he started to find his feet, and decided to go to 'war' with the WWF. This including starting to hire and recruit some of the biggest names from the WWF including; Hulk Hogan, Randy Savage, Brett Hart, Scott Hall (aka Razor Ramon) and Kevin Nash.

3. We wrestling fans changed, from supporting the fan favourite babyfaces, too it becoming cooler to support the heels of the wrestling organisation, and enjoying more hard edge and risky story lines, (hence the attitude name), especially those that merged backstage politics associated with wrestling into mainstream stories. In my opinion this started during Hulk Hogan's heel turn and the emergence of the New World Order (now) he formed with Scott Hall and Kevin Nash.

All of a sudden with its ex WWF starts, risky hard edge

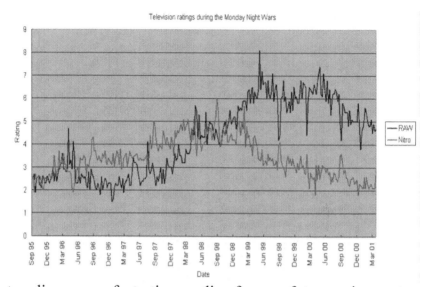

story lines, some fantastic wrestling from up future main event

wrestlers such as Chris Jericho, Eddie Guerrero, and Rey

Mysterio, WCW overtook the WWF in the TV ratings as the

main wrestling company. Vince McMahon and the WWF had to

very quickly adapt and change from its tired and out dated

formula to survive.

The emergence of stars such as Stone Cold Steve Austin,

a repackage Rocky Mavia to 'The Rock', Shawn Michaels,

Triple H, The Undertaker as well as the forming of factions such

as DX, The Nation of Domination and the Hart Family, the

WWF/E started to regain some ground. But it was I feel Vince McMahon himself who using a persona developed after the backlash and hatred over his dealing with in the infamous "Montreal Screwjob', and an ongoing feud he developed with Stone Cold Steve Austin, that really started to turn the ratings.

At WCW behind the scene dramas involving older vs. younger talent, overpaid wrestling stars with different and personal agendas, some inconstant story lines, matches and TV shows being changed on the spot, eventually WCW would fall below the WWF constantly in the ratings. Until on March 23, 2001, WCW was bought by the WWF, ending the Monday night War era. The *attitude* era however hung around little longer (and from the years 2001 to 2008 the Ruthless Aggression Era) to give us "The invasion" story line, WWF changing to World Wrestling Entertainment (WWE), the WWE brand split to Raw Show and Smackdown Show.

For me in the WWE/F there were many wrestlers that shone brightly during this era, these include Shawn Michaels, Triple H and the Undertaker. The attitude era also gave us the rise of Chris Jericho upon his arrival on Raw on the 9th August 1999. On a personal level some of my all-time favourites emerged during this time, including Mankind (Mick Foley), Edge, Kurt Angle, and of course Christian.

The 2 stars that took the *attitude* era by storm and eventually helped win the Monday Night wars were Stone Cold Steve Austin and The Rock. However, I feel the main star for the WWF/E during this time was the Mr. McMahon character. Without Mr. McMahon, Stone Cold Steve Austin does not become the massive star he did. Vince McMahon took an incident (The Montreal 'Screw job' of Brett Hart) that really should have been the end of the company, and used it to create one of the most hated heels in wrestling history. We fans loved every time he was given a stunner by Austin, the Rock Bottom or even a choke slam by the Undertaker. The Mr. McMahon character gave us all the fantasy image of an employee being able to 'lay the smack down' on their boss (who hasn't had a boss that they would love to do that to!!!). While other companies have tried to do the 'evil' boss story line before and since, I feel the Vince McMahon version has been, and will always be the best evil boss character in wrestling that we will see.

The Emergence of Degeneration X, originally with Shawn Michaels and Triple H (with Chyna), and later the degeneration X version of Triple H, Road Dogg, Billy Gunn and X-Pac, had many fans like myself in stitches with their humor, behavior and of course 'attitude' during this era. Feuds with other stables such as the Nation of Domination, The Corporation and the Ministry of darkness, showed that these guys were as good in the ring as they were outside it.

While Rick Flair and Hulk Hogan were still big names while in their WCW run, the other big names at WCW at this time were Scott Hall and Kevin Nash and their new World order (nWo) stable. However, during the Monday night wars at WCW it would be Sting and Goldberg that helped WCW win many Monday night ratings.

The feud between Stone cold Steve Austin and Vince McMahon is what many believed help the WWF/E win back the ratings from WCW. The feud, which has been voted by many as the best feud ever, started over Mr. McMahon not thinking Stone Cold Steve Austin, was a suitable Champion for his company. From this we witnessed many great moments and matches that helped set up the attitude era. These included:

- Stone Cold filling Mr. McMahon's car full of concrete
- Stone Cold attacking Mr. McMahon in the hospital (this segment also included the birth of Mankind's Mr. Socko)
- Stone cold giving Mr. McMahon and his cohorts a beer bath, form a beer truck
- Mr. McMahon Winning the Royal Rumble
- Stone Cold driving a Zamboni and crashing into the ring
- The many 'stunners' Stone Cold delivered to Mr. McMahon

Besides Mr. McMahon, Austin's feud with Brett 'The Hitman' Hart was the feud that many feel elevated Stone Cold to main event status, especially after their Submission match at

Wrestlemania 13, which in the course of the match, Austin went from Heel to face, due to his performance in the ring that night. Austin would go on to have a great rivalry with The Rock through the attitude era, as these two were destined to meet as they were the biggest stars of this era. The feud with The Rock led to some classic Wrestlemania matches, classic verbal confrontations and classic out of the ring moments. Mankind, The Undertaker, Triple H and Shawn Michaels were others to enjoy battles with Stone Cold.

One of the reasons that Mick Foley has become one of my al time favourite wrestlers was because of the many feuds and matches he had during this era. Foleys feuds with the likes of The Undertaker, The Rock, Stone Cold and Triple H showed many non-believers that he was a main event star. While he usually ended up losing many of the feuds and matches, what it did for me was show me for the first time, that your favourite winning a wrestling match was not as important as the quality of match they delivered. And there are many matches during Foleys feuds that he lost, however, I still enjoy watching over and over again. (The one I recommend is the Street fight vs. Triple H at the Royal Rumble, which many believe was the making of Triple H as a believable main event star thanks to the match with Foley).

Other feuds that defined this era in my opinion include:

- Kurt Angle vs. Chris Jericho vs. Chris Beniot – these three were possibly the best technical wrestlers of this era and were responsible for some great submission matches, ladder matches and just genera one on one matches. But to really appreciate all three then I recommend watching the triple threat match at Wrestlemania 2000.

- Brett Hart vs. Shawn Michaels – These 2 in my opinion saved the WWF/E, as when the likes of Hogan, Savage, Nash, and Hall left the WWF/E, these two lifted their games and become the re-building blocks of the WWF/E. The feud of course would end via the infamous Survivor Series match of 1997, now dubbed "The Montreal Screwjob".

- The moment Paul Bearer walked down the ring with Kane during the first ever Hell in the Cell match that was happening between The Undertaker and Shawn Michaels, we knew that The Undertaker had met his equal. The Undertaker and Kane, who we learnt was his younger brother, would finally meet at Wrestlemania 14 where it took 3 tombstones for the undertaker to win. Inferno matches followed, and these two would battle and feud many times over the next 10 years, with each match just as intone as the last.

- Edge and Christian, vs. The Hardy Boyz vs. The Dudley Boys, the rivalry between these three teams gave us some awesome matches. Battles of the Tag team Championship, or the services of valets, these three teams battles included tables, ladders, cages and of course it was these three teams that gave us the now awesome TLC – Table, ladders and chairs match.

Over at WCW during this time the main feuds that were occurring during this time and helping them lead the Monday night wars was the nWo vs. WCW. Included in this was the eagerly awaited feud between Hulk Hogan and Sting!

In the WWF/E the tag team division was headlined by three teams, Edge and Christian, The Hardy Boyz and The Dudley Boys. Their feuds and matches as mentioned above highlighted this division for a lot of the attitude era. While these three teams stole the limelight of the tag team division during this era, there were many more teams to shine during this period, many included some of the big name stars at the time, which goes to show the importance the tag team division still had in this era.

There was also a couple of 'dream' teams to develop during this time including The Rock and Mankind forming their Rock 'n' Sock tag team, as well as Kane and The Undertaker forming their "Brothers of Destruction' Tag team, while of course we had the dream pairing of Triple H and Shawn Michaels with Degeneration X. The re-vamp DX also gave us Road Dogg, and Billy Gunn, The New Age Outlaws. Other teams that were a major part of this era included:

- The APA (Farooque and Bradshaw)

- Mankind and chainsaw Charlie

- X-Pac and Kane

During this period in The WCW, The Steiner Brothers, and The Nasty Boys had their fair share of time in the spotlight. Harlem Heat (Booker T and Stevie Ray) would dominate the tag team titles with 10 reigns as WCW tag team champions. But it would be the team of Scott Hall and Kevin Nash, 'The Outsiders' who would be the real dominate tag team. Numerous tag team titles, forming the nWo, and dominating WCW TV, and PPV's were the reason these two were considered one of the reason WCW was winning the Monday night wars for a long period of time.

While there were two major wrestling companies, each company had their respective titles that could be won. In the WWF/E you had; WWE title which was the main title of the company, Intercontinental Title; European Title; Light Heavyweight title; Women's Title and WWE tag team titles. While over at WCW the titles that were sought after were the

World Heavyweight Championship, the main title of WCW;
World Television Champion; World tag Team Champions;
United States Champion and the Cruiserweight Champions.
Once WCW lost the Monday night wars, we had a situation
where as 'Commissioner Foley' said there were too many titles
in this company; there were more people with titles than without.
From this the WWF/E started having unification matches to
shrink the titles down. At the end of the unification process we
were left with the WWF/E Undisputed Championship,
Intercontinental Title, Cruiserweight and The WWF/E tag team
champions.) The unification matches included:

- Edge (United States) defeated Test (Intercontinental) at
  Survivor Series 2001 to be the unified Intercontinental
  Champion.

- The Dudley Boyz (WCW tag team) defeated The Hardy
  Boyz (WWF) at Survivor Series 2001 to be the unified
  WWF tag team Champions

- Rob Van Dam (Intercontinental) defeated Jeff Hardy
  (European) on Raw July 2002 to be the unified

Intercontinental Champion. Rob Van Dam would later help Unify the Hardcore Title into the Intercontinental title in a match against the Hardcore Champion Tommy Dreamer.

- At Vengeance 2001, Chris Jericho would beat The Rock, and the Stone Cold Steve Austin back to back to become the First ever WWF/E Undisputed Championship.

Once the Raw and Smackdown brand expansion happened and titles could only be fought and won on the respective shows, the US title was added to the Smackdown Brand, while The World Heavyweight Championship became the main title on the Raw Brand. Two Tag team titles would also occur so that each brand had one each.

One title that was added to the long list of titles that was actually I thought a good move, and was very sad to see it go, was the WWF/E Hardcore title. This Championship was first handed to Mick Foley/Mankind on the 2nd of November 1998, and was fought for with hardcore rules in mind. While watching hardcore matches is always enjoyable, it was when Crash Holly stated that he would defend the hardcore title 24/7 that this title took a life of its own. Title defenses in laundry mats, hotel rooms, Amusement parks, as well as the battle royals where the title change hands numerous times throughout the match made this title unique, and an exemption to the rule of too many titles during the invasion story line. The title ended with Rob Van Dam, although was quickly brought back to be co-held by Edge and Mick Foley; however Steve Blackman held the title the longest, at a total of 172 days, while Raven had the most title reigns at 26. The top 5 hardcore champions were (those with the longest reigns):

- Steve Blackman 172 days
- The Big Boss man 154 days
- Rob Van Dam 134 days
- Al Snow 129 days
- Crash Holly 108 days

In the battle for ratings and dominance, both major wrestling companies started giving us monthly Pay Per Views, instead of just the special events throughout the years. Now while personally I believe this to be a purely financial based decision, it obliviously worked as we still have monthly PPV's today. The WWE kept its big 4 (Wrestlemania, Summer Slam, Survivor Series and The Royal Rumble), and other events such as Backlash, Unforgiven and No Mercy.

One initiative I did enjoy for a while was that 8 PPV's a year were brand specific, which is for 4 PPV's only Raw superstars competed, while Smackdown had their own four PPV's. This made this gave a chance for more exposure for those mid cards from each brand to have a PPV match, while made the big 4 more important as it had all WWE superstars able to compete. When the WWE had ECW, they also got their own PPV (one night stand). I only guess this was stopped as not many people agreed with me on this concept, and buy rates were down.

Over at WCW Halloween Havoc, Bash at The Beach, Starrcade and The Great American Bash headlined their Pay Per View card.

Many believe that the *pg* era of wrestling which started in 2008 to be the start of the decline of the WWE and wrestling. Due to the change in the majority of fans bases with near 40% of wrestling fans being children and women, the WWE decided to tone down stories (sex and violence themes), stopping chair shots to the head, and the stopping of 'blading'(deliberate cutting yourself in the match to show a head wound). This toning down of the wrestling product has convinced many that this era is not as good as previous. But I agree with (and could not have said any better than) <u>Ryan Dilbert</u> (Featured Columnist on the Bleacher Report) who on February 28, 2012 stated:

....Is the PG Era as impotent and disappointing as fans want to believe?

WWE officially went PG in 2008, though there were signs before that pointed to them heading in that direction.

From that point to now we've seen an all-time classic in John Cena vs. CM Punk at Money in the Bank 2011, some phenomenal battles between

Chris Jericho and Rey Mysterio and perhaps the greatest match of all-time in Shawn Michaels vs. The Undertaker at WrestleMania 25.

To dismiss the PG Era is to dismiss the great work done by Randy Orton and Christian during their intense feud last year. Mark Henry's renaissance, Daniel Bryan's emergence as a heel and CM Punk's rocket to superstardom are all part of the much maligned period in wrestling.....

....The PG Era has taken away blading and chair shots to the head. It's been an unpopular decision among people not doing the bleeding.

But WWE should be applauded for its stance on avoiding concussions. Would we rather see the admittedly exciting impact of steel to skull or have our favourite superstars able to sustain longer careers devoid of dementia?

It's a trade I'm certainly willing to make.

As for the lack of blood, blading had gotten to a point where it was so overdone that it didn't have nearly the impact that it once did. If every time a wrestler hits a post or gets a stiff elbow across the brow, they start gushing blood, it becomes expected, not exciting.

Besides, years of blading leaves our heroes disfigured.

A good wrestling angle and a good wrestling match doesn't rely on blood anyway.

It's more than the lack of blood and chairs being bent on a man's skull that has fans bemoaning the current era. Visit any YouTube wrestling video, any online wrestling forum or the Bleacher Report comment section and you'll read countless tirades about the "good old days."

Our natural instinct is often to romanticize the past and undervalue the present.

There's no doubt that the Attitude Era was electrifying and that the Ruthless Aggression Era was marked with some of the best matches we've ever seen.

But we've chosen to remember Stone Cold and

forget Al Snow, pine for Eddie Guerrero and wipe

Nathan Jones from our memories.

As bad as we've made the PG Era out to be, it's full

of stars and future stars.

Cody Rhodes, Sheamus, Wade Barrett, Kofi

Kingston and Dolph Ziggler form a concrete

foundation for the WWE to build its future on.

Will its peak match what Rock and Austin did?

Maybe not, but it's too early to bury it.

The PG Era is just getting started.

History will decide if fans like me and Ryan are correct, or those who believe the pg. era is killing wrestling.

The pg. era has also seen the emergence of another wrestling company called TNA (total nonstop Action), which has given fans an alternative to the WWE 'pg.' product. Starting with a six sided ring, TNA focused on and had some great cruiser weight style wrestling (its X division which actually did not have a weight limit), as well as keeping those of us fans with the lust for blood, barb wire, and other hardcore action entertained. A good mix of ex WCW starts, ex WWE stars and new up and coming wrestling stars has made sure that this company has had a nice solid fan base. Sting, Kurt Angle, Hulk Hogan, The Dudley Boys and Jeff Hardy lead the list of big names to join the company, while AJ Styles, Samoan Joe, Abyss, Austin Aries, Bobby Rhodes and James Storm headline the list of stars that have made a name for themselves in TNA. While for a brief moment in 2010 the TNA Company tried to start a new Monday night wars with the WWE. While in the ratings it ended poorly, and they returned back to Thursdays to concentrate on their own product, they took with them a slightly larger fan base, and a higher profile of their existence in the Wrestling world.

Total Nonstop Action wrestling has been much maligned throughout its eight year history. Always fighting an uphill battle against cynicism and skeptics regarding viability, creative direction, and roster utilization (to name a few criticisms), TNA's very existence in today's landscape of professional wrestling is an accomplishment in and of itself.

TNA's brief history has seen the company experience a steady growth to the point where they are now the number two national wrestling company in the world, albeit a very distant number two to WWE. TNA's Thursday Night Impact program had seen a consistent string of satisfactory ratings upon landing a TV deal with Spike TV and subsequently earning a two hour time slot in prime time.

Although TNA was comfortable in its safe position as a distant second to WWE, TNA President Dixie Carter decided it was time to compete and push the small company to its limits in hopes of gaining mainstream exposure as well as a larger share of the pro wrestling audience.

In December of 2009, Spike TV used its synergy between two of its higher rated television partners (UFC, TNA) to make an announcement that was supposed to change pro wrestling forever. The shocking announcement would involve Hulk

Hogan, the most recognizable wrestling personality of all time who had recently signed with TNA, appearing on UFC's Ultimate Fighter finale and announcing that TNA would feature a Monday night telecast for its first show of the year.

The telecast was to air directly against WWE RAW, thus recreating the Monday Night Wars of the late nineties.

The inclusion of Eric Bischoff in yet another new regime in TNA did nothing but heighten prevailing skepticism about TNA and its creative direction. Bischoff and Hogan, while successful for a significant stretch of the Monday Night Wars, were also at the helm for WCW's eventual demise.

As was TNA's head booker Vince Russo.

The principles involved were cause for legitimate concern about the potential of TNA actually competing with WWE on Monday nights. Under Vince Russo, TNA had given pro wrestling some of the most creatively inept storylines, angles, and matches that the industry had seen since - well - WCW's dying days.

In any event, TNA debuted on Monday Night on January 4, 2010 in a Monday Night broadcast slotted for three hours and airing one hour before RAW.

A loaded show, packed with surprise (unadvertised) appearances by Jeff Hardy, Ric Flair, Scott Hall, and Sean Waltman would go on to draw the biggest rating in TNA history despite being crushed in the ratings war by a RAW show that countered with the return of Bret "the Hitman" Hart after a 13 year absence from the company.

TNA would return to Thursday nights, however the huge rating had given TNA the case of the itchy trigger finger, and it was only a matter of time before the trigger was pulled on a permanent Monday night timeslot.

TNA would return to Monday nights permanently on Monday, March 8 2010, with the show being highlighted by a surprise (unadvertised) appearance by popular wrestler Rob Van Dam. The show would also see Ric Flair's return to in ring wrestling after a much ballyhooed retirement following his standout match with Shawn Michaels at Wrestlemania 24.

With more bells and whistles being featured on the March 8th Monday night episode, and riding the momentum of the biggest rating in company history from its previous Monday night show in January, TNA's return to Monday night television would draw a disappointing 1.0 rating.

The ratings news would only continue to get worse with TNA dipping below a 1.0 rating for the first time in years, eventually bottoming out with a painfully minuscule .56 rating for its March 29th broadcast.

With ratings at historical lows for the small

wrestling company, the writing was on the wall for TNA's Monday night campaign. A strategic timeslot change, to avoid going head to head with WWE, was too little too late for TNA and the company would go on to announce that it would be moving back to its regular Thursday night timeslot just a few months into its foray into Monday nights.

The Monday Night Wars of 2010, if successful, could have been one of the biggest wrestling stories ever as competition between wrestling companies have proven to be good for business. However these Monday Night Wars served as a tale of TNA's failed experiment on a large platform as we learned (through comparatively low WWE ratings despite significantly outdrawing TNA) that the pro wrestling audience had eroded to some degree.

(By <u>Big Nasty</u> (Featured Columnist) on January 1, 2011)

The PG era at WWE has been dominated by one man, that of John Cena. With the likes of The Undertaker, Shawn Michaels and Triple H slowing down in their careers, John Cena was the one who stepped up to take their place, to become the 'face' of the WWE. I will talk briefly in a later chapter how this has divided the WWE fans, but the fact is John Cena has been a part of most of the main WWE story lines in the 'pg.' era.

However there have been other stars to come along and shine, Randy Orton, Rey Mysterio, The Miz, CM, Punk, Sheamus and Daniel Bryan are all new starts to come along. Some big names from the attitude era have managed to reinvent themselves to be a major part of WWE story lines including The Big Show, Mark Henry, (my favourite) Christian and Chris Jericho.

There has been less emphasis on blood, wrestling with objects, wrestling all over the arena, which means that this era has had to go back to wrestling roots, and rely on good promos, and good matches to entertain us fans.

The WWE champion and World Heavyweight Championships have been the dominate titles, and have had many great matches for them in the WWE, but this has led to other titles losing a little of their prestige and importance. Both the Intercontinental and Tag team titles have only just recently become something worth fighting for, while the US title is slowly reaching the importance it once had. The problem (and no offence to those wrestlers), has been WWE superstars holding these titles when not being believable champions. The likes of Santino, Jack Swagger and Zach Ryder are just three examples of wrestlers in my opinion who were not champion material at the time of holding the titles. While we all enjoy an underdog winning, it is how these3 characters defended and wore the titles which caused these titles to lose importance. On top of that there have been lots of incidents where either the intercontinental or US championship has gone months without being defended, or being involved in a well-developed feud. Thankfully the likes of

Christian, Cody Rhodes, Antonio Cesaro, The Miz and Wade Barrett have again lifted these titles to major importance.

A list of who has held each of the 4 major WWE titles in the PG Era are

WWE champion	World Heavyweight Champion	WWE Intercontinental Champion	WWE Us Champion
John Cena	Undertaker	Chris Jericho	Matt Hardy
CM Punk	Edge	Kofi Kingston	Shelton Benjamin
Rey Mysterio (and CM Punk)	CM Punk	Santino Marella	Montel Vontavious Porter
	Chris Jericho	William Regal	
		CM Punk	
	Batista	John "Bradshaw" Layfield	Kofi Kingston
Alberto Del Rio	John Cena		
	Jeff Hardy		The Miz

	Chris Jericho	Rey Mysterio	Bret Hart
	Jack Swagger	John Morrison (formerly Johnny Nitro)	R-Truth
			The Miz
	Rey Mysterio	Drew McIntyre	Daniel Bryan
	Kane	Dolph Ziggler	Sheamus
		Wade Barrett	Kofi Kingston
	Dolph Ziggler	Ezekiel Jackson	
	Christian	Cody Rhodes	Dolph Ziggler
	Randy Orton	Big Show	Zack Ryder
		Christian	Jack Swagger
	Mark Henry	The Miz	
	Big Show		Santino Marella

	Daniel Bryan Sheamus		Antonio Cesaro

The Tag team titles also suffered for many years in the background, and became second thought championships. After DX lost the titles at the end of 2009, these titles went on to be held by fraction such as Nexus and the Core, and mid card superstars thrown quickly together such as Santino Marella and Vladimir Kozlov, Air Boom (Kofi Kingston and Evan Bourne), Kofi Kingston and R-truth or David Otunga and Michael McGillicutty. With the emergency of some new tag teams and some unique but successful pairing of WWE superstars, such as Hell no (Kane and Daniel Brian) and Rhode Scholars (Cody Rhodes and Damien Sandow), The Usos, The Prime Time Players, Primo and Epico, and of course Rey Mysterio and Sin Cara, The WWE tag team titles have become something worth watching again.

TNA during this time also had a world Heavyweight championship, as well as a TV championship and its exciting x division. Its Tag team division was one area where TNA seemed for a while to put more effort into, and resulted in better tag team match ups, and some great tag teams. Teams such as The Dudley boys, Beer Money, The motor city machine guns, The British invasion and the main event mafia, made watching tag team matches in TNA a must.

There have been a few wrestlers who have managed to at one stage hold both a major title in the WWE (either the WWE championship or the World Heavyweight Championship) or WCW and then the TNA World Heavyweight Championship (or NWA World Heavyweight Championship as it was the TNA main title until 2007). These include:

- Christian
- Jeff Hardy
- Rob Van Dam
- Sting (held the WCW World Heavy Weight Championship)

- Kurt Angle

- Mick Foley

As mentioned before John Cena has dominated the PG era, and therefore has dominated some of the most important feuds of this era in the WWE. The feud which for me, turned my opinion of John Cena from one of I wish he would go away, to that of respect was his year long feud with The Rock. Their 'Once in a lifetime' yearlong Wrestlemania Match at Wrestlemania 28 including some of awesome in ring promos from both John and The Rock, some great one upmanship done on Raw and PPV's such as Survivor Series and then of course the final match itself. There have been rumours of a rematch, however, I hope this is not the case, as this rivalry is best left completed.

Now while John Cena has feuded with most of the current big names in the WWE, I feel the ones that I remember as some of his best work include:

- Batista 2008 and 2010

- JBL 2005

- Triple H 2006

- CM punk 2011 & 2012

- Edge 2005 and 2006

Other feuds during this so called poor 'pg' era have included some of the best and most anticipated feuds that I and many other fans have been waiting to see. These include:

- Brett Hart vs. Vince McMahon – Brett's return to the WWE after the infamous Montreal Screwjob. While the final match at Wrestlemania 26 was nothing flash, to see Brett back in the WWE was something us older fans had been waiting and hoping for.

- Matt and Jeff Hardy – we have seen numerous times, brothers or tag teams self-destructing. In what I believe was Matt Hardy at his ultimate best, the rivalry and matches these two produced was thrilling to watch

- Undertaker and Shawn Michaels – the feuds leading to their match at Wrestlemania 25 and their rematch at Wrestlemania 26, was nothing short of 'must see viewing' (sorry Miz). It showed why these two have been around for so long with their ability to tell a story leading up to a match, and a being able to tell a story during a match. The Undertaker would have a similar rivalry with Triple H, and would be just as intense, and just as enthralling viewing, however the one with Shawn I feel was done to perfection.

- Chris Jericho vs. Shawn Michaels – the intensity, the aggression, the promos and the quality of matches has made this feud in not just in my eyes, but fans many eyes the best of the pg era. Chris Jericho simply claiming to be better than Shawn Michaels gave us one of the most powerful feuds I have had a chance to witness. From Shawn's wife being punched, Shawn being thrown into a flat screen TV, and 2 matches where the ref had to stop the fights, had us wondering if this was actually real animosity between the two. We can only hope to see something half as good in the future.

While I have not watched that much TNA, I have done my research to come up with the best feuds in TNA history.

These are the most common feuds that came up in other people greatest TNA feuds:

- Awesome Kong vs. Gail Kim

- Kurt Angle vs. Samoan Joe

- Samoa Joe vs. Daniels vs. AJ Styles

- Bobby Rhodes vs. James Storm

- Kurt Angle vs. Aj Styles

The WWE has moved to many themed pay per views over the pg era, which events like Hell in a Cell, TLC (Tables, Ladders and Chairs) and The Elimination Chamber now major yearly events. It has kept its main 4 pay per views; however the survivor series has seen changes over the years with only 1 or 2 traditional survivor series matches taking place on the card. There is now 13 PPV's a year, and I personally feel 2 to 3 too many as some are only 3 weeks a part which sometimes does not allow for ample feud and hype build up.

TNA has their 'Bound For Glory' PPV in October, which is their main PPV of the year. Like The WWE they also have one PPV per month, and besides Bound for Glory there PPVs consist of: Genisis; Against All Odds; Victory Road; Lockdown; Sacrifice; Slammiversary; Destination X; Hardcore Justice; No Surrender; Turning Point and Final Resolution.

While I have enjoyed watching wrestling through the era's, my heart will always lie with the Rock 'n' Wrestle era, as this was the era that I identify with the most, and this was the era that started my love affair with wrestling and therefore I believe this to be the best era in professional wrestling. With the WWF/E product during this time, I enjoyed the colourful characters (compared to the WCW product at the time), I enjoyed the limited PPV, as it made the 4 or 5 a year worth the wait, gave enough time between the PPV to build up some great feuds (for all the matches on the card) and you appreciated them more when you watched them. I enjoyed the over the top managers, something which has gradually disappeared. The likes of Bobby 'The Brain' Heenan, 'The mouth of the South' Jimmy Hart, Mr Fuji, Slick and Harvey Wippleman made watching what was happening outside the ring just as fun as what was in the ring, and all of them had the ability to make you want to knock their teeth out! It had a good solid tag team division and holding a title meant something, very rarely was there such a thing as a transitional champ. I enjoyed the feuds, the interview shows such as 'The Pipers Pit', and the commentary of Gorilla Moonson and Jesse 'The Body' Ventura

But I guess if we really wanted to find out which era was the best then it could really only be settled in the ring. Now later in the book I will look at some of the fantasy match ups I would have loved to see, but here and now, to settle which era is best, I think we need a classic 21 man Battle Royal (I realise most battle royals are 20, but this gives each era 7 representatives). My selection criteria are basically the main players of each era, and will include what I believe the number 1 tag team from that era was. So here is my list of participants in the Battle of the Era's, Battle Royal. And I think it would be only fair that the three man commentary team to call this would be:

Jesse 'the Body' Ventura, Good old JR, Jim Ross and (and it pains me to say) Michael Cole, although on second thoughts replace Michael Cole with JBL......

21 Man - Battle (of the eras) Royal

Rock n Wrestle	Attitude / Ruthless Aggression	PG
Hulk Hogan	The Rock	John Cena
Rick Flair	The Undertaker	CM Punk
Macho Man Randy Savage	nWo - Kevin Nash	Beer Money – James Storm
Rickie 'The Dragon' Steamboat	-Scott Hall	- Robert Roode
Demolition - Ax	Stone Cold Steve Austin	The Big Show
-Smash	Sting	AJ Styles
Ultimate Warrior	Shawn Michaels	Randy Orton

The Future of wrestling over the last 12 months looks promising. With a transitional period occurring at the WWE with major stars retiring or working very limited shifts, I have seen the emergence of some great talent and performers who have me excited about continuing to watch the WWE and wrestling. The likes and rise of Daniel Brian, Damien Sandow, Cody Rhodes, Dolph Ziggler, Sheamus, Drew Macyntre, Ryback and even Heath Slater have shown that the WWE is in good hands, and doesn't have to rely on the likes of John Cena and Randy Orton anymore. We have some of the older generation delivering some of their best work such as The Big Show, Mark Henry and of course Christian. The tag team division is improving and there are some good teams that the division can be built around such as The Usos, Prime Time Players, 3MB and Epico & Primo. The importance of the non-main event titles is also improving thanks to more effort being put in on feuds over the titles, and wrestlers who carry themselves as champions holding the titles. There is still work needed to be done on the women's division, and maybe re-introduce some pesky managers (although I absolutely love what Vickie Guerrero brings to each show), but generally I see the WWE product re-establishing itself after a few years of resting on its laurels.

While I haven't followed much of TNA over the past 12 months, the feuds between Bobby Rhodes and James Storm I have read was amazing and along with Austin Aries have added variety to the World Heavyweight Championship scene. With Gail Kim, Tara and Mickie James they have a solid women's division they can build on, and they also have some experienced stars delivering some of their best work with the likes of Bubby Ray Dudley, Rob Van Dam and Jeff Hardy (if he has sorted out all his other dramas).

As we have seen the wrestling product has the ability to move and adjust with the times, and it is that flexibility that has allowed this product to consistently have a strong fan base which now included, of us old timer fans from the Rock 'n' Wrestle era, the young adults of the attitude era, and kids such as mine enjoying this pg. era.

Chapter 6   Wrestling & the Internet

In May 2012, at WWE's Over The Limit, The Big Show "shocked" everyone by turning heel, and attacking John Cena, and helping the General Manager John Lauranitus win his match.

Now depending which generation of wrestling fan you are, this incident either did shock you, OR you knew it was coming as on many different internet wrestling spoiler sites, wrestling blogs and wrestling internet chat sites prior to Over The Limit, there were people who 'new', or predicted that this was going to happen. Depending which generation of wrestling fan you are, you either looked forward to what was going to happen on RAW the following night, OR you took to your computer and complained about what just happened, how terrible John Cena or The Big Show were, or how the WWE, WWE writers or Vince McMahon have lost the plot.

The internet has changed dramatically how us dedicated fans view and interact with the world of professional wrestling.

We can hop onto our computers and find numerous professional wrestling sites to check results of TV shows, house shows or pay per views, we can read about of favourite wrestlers, tag teams or company, we can chat with other fans from across the world, and more commonly now we can voice our appreciating, or frustration to anyone who will listen (or read). It is this last point that I find as a generation X member hard to take.

Some modern generation Y internet wrestling fans apparently know more about wrestling than anyone. This includes us older wrestling fans, wrestlers, promoters, talent scouts, wrestling trainers, reporters and company owners. If you do not believe me, just ask them they will tell you! You have some wrestling fans who pull apart wrestling matches, shows, Pay Per Views (PPV) and wrestlers and try to tell the rest of the world how they would have done it, how to improve them, how to wrestle, how terrible a wrestler is, who should be hired or fired, what the story line should be and how those in charge should listen to wrestling fans more.

Many people believe it is the fact that the WWE has gone to a 'pg.' rating that is making wrestling (in the WWE) not as good as previous eras. I believe it has been the internet that has affected how people watch and enjoy wrestling. The internet has made it harder for us fans to be shocked and surprised anymore as there is always someone, somewhere posting something on the internet to spoil surprises. Whether it was a wrestler who was spotted in a particular town, or a wrestler who is thinking about or retiring, or a wrestler that is being suspended, it is on line way before it hits the TV, and therefore it loses its impact when it is finally shown on TV. <u>Mike Chiari</u> (Featured Columnist on The Bleacher Report) agrees as his article on June 19, 2012 states:

> ………*fans know when something is legitimate and when something is storyline related. Perhaps that isn't necessarily true for younger fans, but the vast majority of the audience isn't easily fooled. Since basically everything is out there on the Internet, WWE*

fans in general are very well informed with regards to the ins and outs of the business and feel patronized when something is being passed off as real rather than kayfabe.....

....Things such as John Cena being fired or Vince McMahon being removed from power might have been believable years ago, but fans understand the business side of things and realize that the WWE would never fire its top draw and that its owner couldn't really be ousted. .....

While I am guilty of reading these blogs, forums, and chats, I do enjoy reading the well thought out opinions and viewpoints such as those on The Bleacher Report for example. I do find it harder and harder to restrain myself to hop on these 'chats' and tell those internet wrestling fans, who just want to moan and complain about everything and everyone, to wake up to themselves! Wrestling is a form of entertainment, if you do not like watching, then don't watch, if you think you can do better, then go out and prove it, if you could run a better show, then start your own wrestling company. There are some internet wrestling fans that are very negative towards a product and industry they are meant to be supporting. The language used on these sites directed at wrestlers such as John Cena, Vince McMahon, Big Show, Hulk Hogan etc. is very degrading, abusive and insulting, language that would make sailors or bikies blush. I remember when wrestling was about cheering for the face, booing the heel, but admiring what they did in the ring, looking forward to what was going to happen next week and being shocked when someone turned heel or turned their back on their team mate. Nowadays watching wrestling seems to be about picking up all the mistakes that announcers make, story lines that don't match from two years ago, a wrestler botching a move, a wrestler that should be or shouldn't be pushed, who should or shouldn't have a title and bagging a company for releasing a wrestler or not hiring another, and then hoping onto the computer and telling everyone about it!

It's funny reading and listening to these fans telling people like Vince McMahon, Eric Bischoff, Hulk Hogan, Paul Heyman, Dixie Carter etc. how to run a wrestling company or show, what they are doing wrong, the flaws from each show and PPV, who should get more air time, who shouldn't and who should have the title. I wonder if they realise exactly how long Mr McMahon and co have been around wrestling and what they have done for the business world-wide. What is even funnier about these internet fan blogs, forums and comments is that you have different people having different opinions, and each person feeling their opinion is the only correct one, and that people like Vince McMahon should listen to them. I wonder how the WWE would look today if Vince did business just by listening to people from off the street???

The problem for wrestling companies is that no matter what they do someone will not be happy with the decision made, and they will complain about it. Currently CM Punk is in his 400+ day as WWE champion, the longest reigning WWE champion in 25 years. People complained online about there not being long major title reigns, and here they finally get one. But guess what, there are now those complaining that CM Punk should not have the title this long, or the title reign has run its course. Another recent complaint was that the same people were battling over the major titles all the time. All of a sudden we get the likes of Ryback in the WWE and Austin Aries on TNA battling for the major titles (and in Austin's case winning the TNA World Heavyweight Championship), and now we get people complaining that these guys are not ready to hold the major titles! So explain to me how a wrestling company can please everyone, all the time?

The internet has given people an avenue now to voice their disapproval for the whole world to read. Whether it's about wrestling, or politicians, or TV, these people believe it is their right to complain and express their opinions, yet usually have no experience, credentials or qualifications to back up their point of view. While back in the pre-internet days if you didn't like a decision, match or wrestler all you did was discuss the issue with your friends. Now we have many different forums for people to vent their frustrations, and opinions whether you want them or not. While we fans do not have to read them, and can just ignore them, there are those people who write on these chats, forums and blogs that do have some great view points and opinions. You unfortunately just have to read and scroll through the immature and offensive comments to get to them. What is worse now is they already have a term for those people whose only goal is to get a reaction out of a wrestler, a wrestling company or other fans, and that is of an internet 'Troll'. An internet troll is:

> *An Internet troll, or simply troll in Internet slang,*
>
> *is someone who posts controversial,*
>
> *inflammatory, irrelevant or off-topic messages in*
>
> *an online community, such as an online*
>
> *discussion forum or chat room, with the primary*
>
> *intent of provoking other users into an emotional*
>
> *response or to generally disrupt normal on-topic*
>
> *discussion*
>
> *(http://www.urbandictionary.com)*

Just recently in Australian a well know TV personality Charlotte Dawson tried to name and shame one of these Trolls for telling her and a fan of hers to "go hang yourself". The result of Charlotte doing this was to receive more abuse from other people, which resulted in her ending up in hospital.

It is this abuse toward an individual/s and towards wrestling and wrestlers that I find very hard to take, and as a teacher I look at it as a form of bullying. The internet has given people a false sense of "it's my right to say what I want", which many people believe means that they can abuse wrestlers (other celebrities, and other people), yet most will hide behind false names and accounts. I doubt anyone would walk up to The Big Show, and say "you're a waste of space and can't wrestle", yet in the safety of their rooms, they will type this onto a chat site!

As just mentioned when we talk about internet wrestling fans, I should point out that there are those internet fans, which watch the shows, PPV's and attend House shows and have general view points about the product, I like to class these internet fans into the general wrestling fan category. Then there are those internet fans that just read recaps and then rant and rave because their favourite wrestle didn't get enough TV time, or there is too much John Cena or Kurt Angle on TV, I like to call these fans disgruntle internet fans. Erik Beaston Senior analyst agrees by stating in Jan 9th 2012 on the Bleacher report:

Internet wrestling fans, it appears, often enjoy arguing over the current state of professional wrestling rather than actually watching the show. Somewhere along the line, a small portion of Internet fans became so enamoured with their own opinions that they stopped caring about the shows and, rather, voiced their opinion because they liked the attention it brought. Complaining about Daniel Bryan, CM Punk, Zack Ryder, Cody Rhodes, or anyone else not getting the push they deserve only works if you, in return, watch the show when those in charge give you what you want.

Chris Benoit and Eddie Guerrero saw shortened title reigns because the same bloggers and message board users that wanted them to be pushed to the top of the card never actually supported them by watching Raw and Smackdown.

Is this an indictment on all Internet fans? No. Hell, I am an Internet fan. I write for Bleacher Report, and most of what I write is opinionated work. But I watch the show. And a very large portion of Internet fans do actually watch the show. But there is that small contingent that would rather everyone read their written word, listen to their opinions, and stroke their ego than actually watch the show for which they have such strong words.

So to those of you across the Internet wrestling community that talk a big game but do not back it up by supporting their favourites when they are finally put in a featured position by WWE, do yourself a favor and give your fingers a rest for two hours on Monday nights and two hours on

Friday nights and actually watch the show.

Without you and without your IWC peers, the men

and women we voice our support for will see any

time the creative team has invested in them

dwindle and, eventually, disappear.

Another major issue for me about the disgruntled internet wrestling fans, is not so much the constant complaining, but is the language and attitude directed at the people involved in the industry. Now I may be showing my age and generation here, but when I was a young 'whipper snapper' saying the word 'bum' was considered a swear word. Nowadays you have kids younger than 10 dropping 'F' bombs and even the big 'C' bomb as swearing is becoming more commonly accepted in today's language. I remember when a swear word resulted in my mouth being washed out with soap, nowadays if us parents get the soap out we will possibly be charged with abusing our kids!

Here are two examples of writing about the same issue, the first is by a typical internet fan that watches and enjoys wrestling, while the second is a typical response by that 10% or so of disgruntled internet fans who believe they have a higher level of importance than the rest of the world.

*   Why do the WWE keep putting the WWE title back on John Cena. There are other wrestlers out there that I feel deserve a chance to shine. Wrestlers like Christian, or Kofi Kingston, or maybe give William Regal one good run before he retires fully from competing. I realise the kid's love John Cena, and that he sells the most merchandise, but us older fans are getting a little tired of him holding the title all the time....

*   F#$K the WWE, that useless, no talented piece of crap John Cena gets the title again, that's bullshit. What about other wrestlers who shits all over John in wrestling skills. If the WWE keeps shoving this shit down our throats, then I am going to switch to TNA!!

As you can see, while the issue is a common issue that a lot of wrestling fans debate about, example 2 to me shows that the person is not an actual wrestling fan, but someone who has a large inflated ego of themselves and who believes that everything that comes out of their mouth is the ONLY way things should be done. Instead of showing their intelligence by giving some points to back up their feelings they resort to abusing people that they have never met! They do not fully understand everything that John Cena goes through in the ring, and away from the ring, and all he does for organisations like "the make-a-wish foundation". I wonder if these abusive/disgruntle internet wrestling fans have ever tried out to become a wrestler and failed, or just can't get their arses away from the computer to join the real world. I wonder how these fans would go if someone came in off the street and critiqued their work in that way. Without being to stereotypical it is commonly thought that the abusive/disgruntled internet fan would fall into the teenager or young adult age group, and there really is a whole other book that can be (or already has been) written on the attitude of today's generation.

As the typical example above shows, John Cena is possibly the most abused, talked about, complained about and blogged about wrestler on these chat, forum or blogs sites. He cops abuse when he wins titles or matches, when he is placed in the main event or after one of his promos. His matches are pulled apart and dissected more than any other current wrestler, and when he does try something new or different he is criticized for it. You only have to look at the negative comments on web and chat sites after his 2012 'Money in the Bank' (MITB) win. He has never won the MITB, however, so many people were upset and whinged about him winning. Would I have preferred someone like Chris Jericho, The Miz or even Kane win...sure, but I'm not crying over the computer because Cena won! If I was Vince McMahon, would I listen to the small percentage of complainers on the internet, or the thousands of kids spending thousands of dollars on John Cena merchandise hmmmmmm.

What also annoys me about these people that complain about John Cena, is that they also attack those fans that enjoy watching him. As a parent and teacher it is this use of chat sites that concerns me the most. These 'Bullies'/trolls feel it is ok not only for them to abuse the WWE and John Cena, but also abuse those fans who like John Cena. I have seen and read many comments where a fan has posted something positive about John, only to receive multiple negative comments by these Bullies/trolls criticising their choice of favourite wrestler. The thing that is really good about wrestling is that there is a large list of wrestlers who you can choose to be your favourite, you shouldn't be abused for that.

Paul Wright, better known as The Big Show, is another easy target for people on the internet to whinge and complain about. Here we have a near 7 foot, "giant" wrestling, and people say he is not a believable champion?? If I was to pick either Big Show or someone like Zack Ryder to fight along with, I know who I would choose in a heartbeat! Over the past 12 months I feel that The Big Show has been at his best, he has had some great feuds and matches with Mark Henry, Daniel Bryan, and John Cena and now with Sheamus. As someone else in their low 40's, I do not think I am over the hill, and have a lot to offer my workplace, as does the Big Show. The thing I love about the wrestling entertainment is that you have such a variety of wrestling styles such as brawling, high flying, technical wrestling, hardcore etc., and Big Show is part of that variety. He is not going to fly around the ring, he is not going to produce high technical wrestling, but what he is going to produce is a dominate wrestler that his opponent has to find a way to overcome. I have also found The Big Show as one of those wrestlers who over the years has helped put over many superstars such as Cena, Brock Lesner, Daniel Bryan and now Sheamus.

Now just because I enjoy watching home renovation shows doesn't make me an automatic expert when it comes to building or renovating houses. I do not sit there watching 'Holmes on Homes' and say, "no Mike you should have used a flat head screw driver instead", or "Mike should have used 4 inch nails instead of those 6 inch ones". I don't do it because firstly I do not have any skills in the building department (which my dad will happily confirm), and second, Mike Holmes does. Quite a few of our internet wrestling fans however, seem to think that just by watching wrestling over the years they have developed skills and experience in the business of wrestling, without any form of training, work or work experience in the industry. Go onto to any chat forum and you will read many fans opinions on what should happen to certain wrestlers, how they would have them win titles, have face/heel turns or be promoted from mid-card status to Championship contender,

I always get a chuckle reading these internet fans wrestling story ideas, some I have had similar thoughts on, some I thinks that's a great idea, others I think that's a terrible idea which goes to show that you can't please everyone. I will tend to read chats/blogs that will start with "This is my idea.....", or "This is what I would do..." as is it just fans giving their opinions which is what chat forums are all about. What annoys me is when I see so called wrestling fans who believe they are better than those currently employed as wrestling writers by starting off their comments with "The WWE/TNA writers are a bunch of D*%#$...", or "The WWE/TNA writers should be fired.....". When a fan is bagging the writers for a current story line, champion, or face/heel change it shows me yet again that their focus is not on enjoying wrestling, but to try to make themselves feel much more important in the world than they really are. Have your wrestling story lines, ideas and suggestions of what you would do (I have in a later chapter), and ask fellow fans if they agree or not, don't however insult people for doing a job that you don't really know anything about, what constraints, or time restrictions, or pressures from above they are under. Think about a wrestling writer, they have to come up with a story that has to please their boss, the wrestlers involved, and of course us fans. Good luck trying to please everyone. To all those fans thinking they are better than current wrestling writers, get off your computers and arses and go prove it! It's always way easier to criticise someone, than it is to replace and do their jobs. Go and convince Mr McMahon or Ms Carter that you are the talent they need for their companies, rather than live out fantasies in your heads.

Back in my day, if we didn't like a wrestler (whether he was a heel or baby face), then we just supported his opponent they were versing. I was never a fan of Psycho Sid, however never felt the need to write him a letter and call him names, abuse him, or let the whole world know what I felt about his wrestling skills. I simply supported the guy he was wrestling, or had my toilet break when his matches were on. I do not know John Cena as a person, however (as mentioned) I know he does a lot of work for 'make a wish' foundation, supports the US troops (whether you agree with this or not), signs autographs for fans and generally seems like he enjoys his job…how many of us can say that? He is this generations Hulk Hogan, I grew up with Hulk Hogan holding the WWE title for nearly three years, imagine the complaining if John Cena did something like that today! The Honky Tonk man held the intercontinental title for one year, two months and 27 days, yet I wouldn't call him the best wrestler of his generation, funny, entertaining though, but not the best. But having the title for so long is what made his matches and title run more enjoyable as each match you hoped and prayed he loose, and when he didn't, you get frustrated, annoyed but just had watch and hope his next opponent could beat him. You didn't race around the neighbourhood and complain to everyone about it. It is from his long title run, however that he gradually became someone I enjoyed watching perform in the ring.

Another example of where internet fans taking offence and voicing their disapproval over a wrestling incident occurred last year (2011). When EDGE retired WWE superstar Christian won his first WWE World Heavyweight Title. As you will read later on, Christian is one of my favourite wrestlers of all time, so I, like a lot of fans were ecstatic about this happening. And then like many fans I was broken hearted when 2 days later he lost it on Smackdown to Randy Orton (it was actually 5 days later in TV time that is spoilers on the internet for you, but more about them later). Now here is the difference between general wrestling fans and today's disgruntled and abusive internet fans. The disgruntled internet wrestling fans bombarded wrestling sites voicing their disapproval to the WWE about what happened, the WWE's treatment of Christian, and their disdain for Randy Orton winning yet another major title. This distain and disapproval of what they claimed to be an injustice included threats of refusing to watch the WWE, hating and abuse on Vince McMahon, Randy Orton and the writers in the WWE. Had they, like me, been patient and just tuned in and watch over the next couple of months of Smackdown and PPV's that followed, they would have seen Christian and Randy Orton giving us some fantastic matches, and a fantastic storyline and feud in a typically slow period of wrestling between Wrestlemania and SummerSlam. I was happy to witness these matches and to see one of my favourites in Christian headline the company for a while.

Wrestlemania 3, Hogan vs. Andre the Giant there is a 'spot' in the match where Andre is meant to of head butted the ring post. By the camera angle it is quite clear that this didn't happen. Did that one moment spoil the match...NO, did that one moment change my opinion of Andre...NO, did that one moment spoil my opinion of the WWF/E...NO, did I feel the need to go out and let the whole world know that it happened...NO (I do realise that the last answer now should be a yes, however I am trying to prove a point here!!) Now if that same thing happened in the main event at Wrestlemania 28 between the Rock and Cena, I can guarantee both wrestlers, and the WWE would be pulled over the coals by these disgruntled internet fans, (who have never messed up anything or made any mistakes in their life) who would of focused on that incident and not the match as

a whole. By pulling apart a match, you lose focus on the whole,

the story that is told through a match, the athletic ability shown

by the wrestlers and therefore not enjoy the product. I mean do

we pull apart a hot dog before we eat it??? No we just eat it and

enjoy it, I bet if most people pulled apart what is in a hot dog

your enjoyment of that food would decrease!

So does all this complaining and moaning and bitching on

the internet work? According to Drake Oz (Featured Columnist)

on The Bleacher report on October 4, 2011, it unfortunately

does:

You can do many things through the World Wide

Web. You can make up rumours without having any

factual basis whatsoever to back them up, you can

watch a number of clips illegally through YouTube

and you can stalk your friends on Facebook.

If you're a wrestling fan, though, you can do

something else, too: You can complain about what

you don't like about the WWE, TNA or any other promotion out there.

In fact, wrestling fans across the world have gotten pretty good at this. Hey, I'll admit that I'm one of them, so no hard feelings, fellas.

Anyway, we often complain about the WWE on the Internet and then complain about the WWE not listening to our complaints about the WWE if you catch my drift.

Well, guess what? The WWE appears to be addressing this.

From PWInsider.com (via WrestleNewz.com) <http://www.wrestlenewz.com/wrestling/wwe-news/wwe-angles-to-please-internet-fans-piper-health-update-maryse-shoot/> :

'There has been talk within WWE of doing more angles that address some of the things that fans complain about on the internet.'

Well, if this is true, then you may no longer be complaining about the WWE not listening to your complaints about the WWE.

Are you confused? So am I.

Seriously, though, I think this is a good thing for the WWE and for us because we on the Internet do often make valid points that could help the company.

We wanted a better tag team division, and we (slowly) seem to be getting that. We wanted an Intercontinental Championship that matters, and it appears we are getting that as well.

So, now all we have to do is find a way to have title reigns that last longer than a month, and I'll believe that the WWE really cares what we think.

I think any company listens to its clients, especially when there is a common pattern in the complaints or suggestions department, and wrestling companies are no different. However,

I will still put faith in a man and company that has been around for over 30 years that they know what they are doing.

What is also becoming more and more frequent through avenues such as Twitter and Facebook is the amount of disgruntled wrestlers voicing their opinion over a former wrestling company, former co-workers, fans or the industry of wrestling. Just recently we have seen and read former WWF/E star Kenny (Kenneth Doane), comments on John Cena's divorce, relating back to issues that these two had when Kenny was working in the WWE, airing his dirty laundry about the relationship between him, John and former WWE diva Mickie James. Scott Steiner has been ranting and raving his personal feelings about Hulk Hogan and Eric Bischoff and their running of TNA, while Matt Hardy had what could only be described as a meltdown on the internet through some bazaar videos posted on line (more about his behaviour later). Is this a good thing?? Personally I don't think so. Thousands of people worldwide get fired, or have to leave their workplace due to work relationship disasters, differences with their bosses or other employees, failing workplace drug policies or inappropriate behaviour at the workplace. I left my workplace of over 14 years largely due to a new manager's attitude and dictatorship of our workplace. I didn't dwell on it, moved on and am very happy and content in my current job of teaching inmates at a Correctional Centre. Maybe people such as Kenny, and Scott Steiner should do the same, or as I tell my kids "toughen up Princess!"

The internet has also brought another common issue, that wasn't around years ago, that is of reporting and writing of results (spoilers) about wrestling TV shows, PPV or House shows before they are televised. Now there are people out there who are against this, saying you should be watching these shows, buying the PPV etc., which I agree in principal. However not all of us can afford PPV's all the time, so we need the internet to update us on the results. For many years wrestling was not on TV in Australia, so the internet was my only source to find out what was happening on Raw, Smackdown, Nitro etc. As for people writing spoilers (such as Big Show turning heel) well I feel a lot of the time it's a well educated guess due to knowing how wrestling shows work, rather than a spoiler, and like any sport or results if you do not want to know then don't read. I remember as a young boy, being banned from my next door neighbour's house every Sunday afternoon. My dad and I listened to the footy on the radio, my neighbour waited for the replay at night. I had the nasty habit of telling him the score or at least who won before he got a chance to watch the replay on TV. Both of us enjoyed our option of choice, so let those who want to spoil the show spoil it, if you do not want the show/results spoiled, then do not read, it's that simple.

There are other times when reading a spoiler/results has made me want to go out and buy the DVD of the PPV, or watch the replay of the show, just to see the match, or incident! A prime example of this was the 1998 WWE king of the Ring, Undertaker v Mankind hell in a cell match! At the time in Australia this was not shown on TV/pay TV however after reading the results I did everything I could to see the match, and have watched it over and over again, and use the match as a debate clincher when my non wrestling fans friends tell me that wrestling is not real! I didn't order the Extreme Rules PPV in 2011, but upon reading that Christian won the World Heavyweight title that night, I was first in line to hire it when it came out at the local video store!

WWE Smackdown and TNA impact results are two very common spoilers you can access prior to the shows being on TV. Now currently I do not get access to TNA wrestling on my TV at home, so reading the internet spoilers it is my only source of keeping up with what is going on over at TNA. Smackdown is currently shown on Fridays here in Australia, and with a busy life and 5 kids, I have trouble getting time to watch it every week. However as mentioned before, hearing that Christian loses his first WWE world heavy weight title via a spoiler, I made sure that I made time to watch that episode. So while spoilers may stop a majority of people tuning in, other times it may increase the TV audience, especially if something important happens. Look what happen to the TV ratings when on WCW they mentioned that Mick Foley (Mankind) was to win the WWE title on Raw. WCW lost over 100 000 viewers who switched over to watch the match!

My advice to those disgruntled internet wrestling fans (and those disgruntled wrestlers),…enjoy the show, appreciate the skills involved, the training, the travelling and the all year round performing required by these athletes. Understand that your favourite wrestler cannot always win or may not get to be 'the face of the company', understand that there are wrestlers who main role is to 'put over' other wrestlers. Understand just like any business, people have roles and particular job descriptions and restrictions. This is sports entertainment, not politics, not religion, not health, or education, Wrestling is all about fun and enjoyment, and if you cannot enjoy this without feeling the need to complain or whinge then maybe you should choose another form of entertainment to watch. If you have a comment to make, by all means make it, however there is no need to personally attack someone you do not know, or use abusive language, just because you disagree with something. There are a lot of well written and valid points of view that I enjoy reading, and I will continue to read these, as they do enhance MY enjoyment of the product.

While I seem to be saying that the internet has been a negative influence on wrestling, there have been a lot of positives to come from the internet. The internet has given us the ability to watch or re-watch our favourite matches and moments from previous wrestling eras. The use of 'you tube' has given me personally the opportunity to watch and experience matches from WCW, ECW and TNA that I have not had the previously opportunity to see. As mentioned in a previous chapter I have through the internet get to finally see the Flair vs. Steamboat match from 1989, as well as ECW classic Eddie Guerrero vs. Dean Malenko. Hopefully for those non wrestling people who read this book, or people like me who have favoured only one wrestling promotion, this book will give you a good start of what matches to watch. Besides matches, you can use the internet to look up, and learn more about your favourite wrestlers (from past era's or current), and find out about their careers prior to making it on a major wrestling company. You can also find out about all their titles they have won over their careers or even what they have been up to since retiring, what movies they are now staring in, or when they are bringing their comedy Tour to Australia (already have my tickets Mick!)

The other good thing about the internet and a lot of these wrestling blogs is that it does give wrestling fans from all over the world a chance to connect, discuss matches, PPV's and wrestlers. Questions posed on sites like www.wrestlezone.com <http://www.wrestlezone.com>, www.thebleacherreport/wwe.com , get a lot of interesting feedback and while I have yet to sign up and join in, it is something I do plan to do when I get the time. I enjoy reading the well thought out questions and replies to topics from 'How to fix The Tag team division',,' best matches of the year', 'who should be the next superstar given a push' or 'why isn't Christian WWE champion'.

Buying Wrestling show tickets online, finding out when wrestling is coming to your town (or in Australia's case country), are other ways the internet helps us wrestling fans.

While some people believe the internet is killing wrestling, I believe it is just changing how we view and enjoy it. Twitter, Facebook, and Tout are just new ways fans can interact with wrestling and their favourite wrestling stars. Like me and millions of others out in the world, we are going to continue to watch wrestling because we like the wrestling product. We have learnt to block out people telling us wrestling is fake all our lives, I am sure now we can block out those disgruntled wrestling fans who constantly feel the need to put down our wrestlers and the wrestling industries.

Chapter 7   Wrestling in Other Medias

The good old TV has been my main media source of my wrestling information and enjoyment for all of my life as a wrestling fan. From the weekly shows such as Superstars of Wrestling, Raw, Smackdown, and occasionally viewing of TNA Impact, WCW Monday Nitro and IWA, to the purchasing Pay Per Views (PPV's) such as Wrestlemania, Royal Rumble, SummerSlam and Survivor Series. However there have been other media outlets that have helped fan my love of wrestling, from the old VHS videos in the 80's to Blue Rays and DVDs today. Monthly magazines through to autobiographies and now varied internet sites, you tube and apps. Today my house is full of a variety of medias relating to wrestling, specific wrestlers and wrestling companies that include such media items as DVD, Blue rays, cd's, books, computer games and of course my mobile phone ring tones are currently wrestlers themes (my text message is Christian's theme, while my call ringtone is CM Punk's theme). I hope to add my own personal book to that collection.

Back in the late 1970's and early 1980's as I discussed in chapter 1, for me and every other wrestling fan that didn't live in a main city in Australia all we had was occasional TV viewing to keep up to date what was happening in the wrestling world. In 1987 I increased my wrestling media options by the purchasing of my first WWF/E monthly magazine which had now doubled my forms of wrestling information.

The WWF/E magazine started out as a bi-monthly publication. However by the late 1980's it became a monthly publication. In Australia the magazine was usually 3 to 4 months behind (I believe nowadays we are spot on or at least a lot closer with the release in the U.S), however, as there was no real other source of information I didn't mind being behind. The magazine, in its form of the late 80's to early 90's featured regular segments, as well as upcoming PPV reviews and then results from the PPV, or other big matches, profiles on wrestlers and current feuds as well as regular monthly segments. Using the online website www.wwebackissues.com/wwfmagazine.html I got a chance to look back at all the old covers of the magazines I used to own (and work out how much they would be worth now had I kept them!). Starting from 1987 Feb/March issue (With Macho Man Randy Savage on the cover), I would buy, read and collect the WWF/E magazine up until November 1990 (with The Ultimate Warrior on the cover). I still remember the joy and anticipation I had when I knew the latest magazine would hit my newsagency, and also my disappointment and frustration I had when they were late. My collection had pride of place in my room, all stacked neatly, in order, to read when I needed a wrestling fix.

I will occasionally now pass a newsagency and head to the sport section, to see the latest issue of the WWE magazine and get a feeling of nostalgia, and (without the newsagent looking), have a quick flip through for curiosity sake.

Below is the contents from the February 1990 issue to which shows what was in a typical WWF/E magazine when I was reading them.

Features

Departments

Also (briefly mentioned in chapter 1) I used to be able to catch up on the PPV's in the late 80's early 90's through hiring the video copies at my local video rental store. Just like the WWF/E magazine the release of the PPV's to video stores in Australia were also 3 to 4 months behind. While my first PPV I viewed was a recorded copy of Wrestlemania III, I would see most of the PPV's during the late 80's and early 90's through video hire.

Just like my anticipation in the arrival of the latest WWF/E magazine, I also remember the highs and lows of waiting for the video release of the PPV's. The obvious high of hiring out and watching, to the lows of the VHS tape already hired out, or worse the store not getting it in. I also remember that many of these hired PPV's would end up copied onto blank videos after I hired them; however I have completely forgotten how that happened.....

From the first ever Survivor Series, Wrestlemania 2 and the first ever SummerSlam, to the 2012 Money in The Bank, hiring or buying on DVD or Blue Ray WWF/E PPV's that I did not order or afford via purchasing the PPV have been a regular past time I have enjoyed over the past 30 years. And will continue to do this as long as the WWE keep making them.

Today besides hiring the PPV's, you can go to any department store and buy on DVD or Blue ray, the latest PPV, and only couple of weeks after it has been shown as well as many of the previous year's PPV's. We as fans can also buy (or hire) specific DVD's on specific wrestlers such as The Rock, Stone Cold Steve Austin or Hulk Hogan which tells their wrestling story as well as shows many of their greatest matches and moments. I personally have a nice collection of these at home including Mick Foley's Greatest hits and Misses; Edge: a decade of decadence; Shawn Michaels: Heartbreak and Triumph, Brett Hart: The best there is; TNA Kurt Angle Champion and Tombstone: The history of the Undertaker to name a few.

We as fans can buy (or hire) specific types of matches on DVD or Blue ray, I have just finished watching WWE's "Falls Count Anywhere" which has many of the best, hardcore, no disqualification matches shown on it, I also own the WWE bloodbath: The most incredible cage matches, WWE OMG the top 50 incidents in WWE history and WWE The Ladder match. We fans can even now own the entire library of Wrestlemania (1-29), as well as the entire libraries of the Royal Rumbles or SummerSlam.

Starting with WWF films in 2002 and now called WWE studios, we have been able to witness many current wrestlers move temporarily from inside the ring, to be in front of a movie camera. These wrestlers have been in some good films (notice I didn't say great films, but some have been pretty good), from Kane in 'See no Evil', John Cena in 'The Marine' Stone Cold Steve Austin in 'The Condemned', Edge in 'Bending The Rules', Triple H in 'The Chaperone' and of course The Rock started his movie career in a WWE co-produced film 'The Scorpion King'. This however is not a new concept, as wrestlers have appeared in many movies over the years. Wrestlers such as Hulk Hogan and Rowdy Roddy Piper, starring in films back in the Late 1980's. Classics from Piper include "Hell Comes To Frogtown, and 'They Live" while Hogan had No Holds Barred,

Rocky III and 'Suburban Commando'. While Piper and Hogan

will never win an academy award, I have always watched their

movies without any great expectations, and most of the time has

been reasonably entertained. While other notable wrestlers that

have turned up in some classic movies include Andre The Giant

in 'The Princess Bride'; King Kong Bundy in Richard Prior's

'Moving" Jesse The Body Venture in 'Predator' and Randy

Savage in 'Spiderman'. Then there is movies such the classic

'MacGruber', and Adam Sadler's 'The Longest yard', which has

a variety of our favourite wrestlers staring or cameo roles in the

movies. Kurt Angle also recently co-starred in the movie

'Warrior' which I class as one of my favourite movies of all

time.

While there have been many wrestlers staring in films,

there have been a few films based on the worlds of wrestling,

none better than Mickey Rourke's 2008 movie "The Wrestler".

If you ever wanted an understanding the world of wrestling that

does not involve wrestling for a large company, or a 'what ever

happen to' story, then this is it. It is a movie that has high place in my extensive movie collection. The other wrestling movie that is also high in my movie collection is the Barry W. Blaustein wrestling documentary 'beyond The Mat'. This Documentary focuses on three well known wrestlers, each at different stages of their careers. First, we see Terry Funk, who due to many injuries is contemplating retirement, yet still about to wrestle in ECW's Barely legal PPV. Second we see Mick Foley at the height of his career in 1999 and the risks he is currently taking in the ring, including seeing his family's reaction to the chair shots he takes during the 1999 Royal Rumble 'I quit" match verses The Rock. Finally we have Jake The Snake Roberts, a huge star and one of my favourite wrestlers in the 1980's now, a drug addict, wrestling in small independent shows. As a fan of Jake, it was very hard to witness him like this, after growing up with him battling the likes of Rick Rude, The Undertaker and Randy Savage. Seeing the families of these three wrestlers, and what their put through by their husbands and fathers, shows the real down side of the wrestling industry.

I will only quickly mention David Arquette's 'Ready to Rumble', as while I enjoyed the movie, the fact that David ended up WCW world Champion as a promotional stunt, was what I feel was a great blemish in the wrestling world and the less said about that the better. Back in the 1985, a 'mockumentry called 'Grunt – The wrestling movie' was released and one of my favourite movies at the time. If you have never seen (or heard of it) I recommend it to my entire fellow wrestling fans. Basically it is a story about a new 'masked' wrestler who may or may not be the same wrestler who accidently killed a man in the ring many years ago. I was very excited to actually find this movie on DVD for $5 the other day at an OP-Shop. Don't let the value fool you it is worth at least double that!

I mentioned above that my mobile phone does have a mixture of different wrestler's theme song that I can use as my ring tones, and as a family we have quite a few wrestling themes on our 'iTunes' on the computer including John Cena, Rey Mystrerio and Edge. Prior to mobile phones, MP3players and I pods, if we wanted to hear our favourite wrestling themes we brought the CD's. While the very first CD released by the WWF/E was "The Wrestling Album", which included great entrance themes from The Junk Yard Dog(JYD), Hill Billy Jim and of course Hulk Hogan's real America (for those WWE trivia buffs, The Real America was originally recorded for? ….........The Tag team US Express). My first Wrestling CD was *WWE the Music 4*, which had the track list of:

Track Title	Wrestler
1. Break down the Wall	Chris Jericho
2. Big	The Big Show
3. No Chance in Hell	The Corporation
4. Sexual Chocolate	Mark Henry
5. This is a Test	Test
6. Wreck	Mankind
7. Oh Hell Yeah (Performed by H-Blockx)	Stone Cold Steve Austin
8. Danger at the Door	D'Lo Brown
9. Blood Brother	Christian
10. AssMan	Billy Gunn

11. Ministry	The Undertaker
12. My Time	Triple H and Chyna
13. On the Edge	Edge
14. Know Your Role	The Rock

I would later add many more to my CD collection, including 'WWE music 5', 'WWE Forceable Entry' and 'WWE Wreckless intent'. The WWE has just released on ITunes the first 5 volumes of their "WWE: The Music" album series. They are available as an 80-song bundle.

Other music I have purchased based on being a wrestling fan, is that of the Chris Jericho's Band Fozzy. I have always enjoyed the heavy metal and hard rock genres, and finding out that Chris Jericho was leaving the WWF/E to work on his music spiked my interest on what the band would be like. I have thoroughly enjoyed Fozzy's albums *Happenstance*, *All That Remains*, and the 2010 album *Chasing the Grail* (which is currently in the CD player of my car). I look forward to their new album *Sins and Bones* to be released late 2012. Due to enjoying Edge's theme song "Metalingus", I have now become a big fan of the band Alter Bridge, and have added to my cd collection at home their albums 'One day remains' and Blackbird'.

I have managed to avoid the following albums released by other wrestlers including John Cena's "you can't see me', 'Be a Man' By Randy Savage and Hulk Rules by Hulk Hogan and the Wrestling Boot Band, and by all accounts so did a lot of other people. Albums by Lillian Garcia, Mickie James and Maria Kanellis were not my type of music so cannot comment on whether they were any good.

I am not a big reader of books, (and many after reading this might say I am not a big writer of books either!), however, I have become a regular reader of the biographies and autobiographies that are brought out by my wrestling heroes. Starting with Mick Foley's "Have a Nice Day: A tale of Blood and Sweat socks", which to this day is still one of my all-time favourite books, and the book that planted the seed in my head for the writing of this book. This book not only reinforced my interest in the wrestling business even more, but I found it very educational in regards to the world of the wrestling industry outside of a big company. It also brought to my attention the many of the backdoor politics that goes along with the wrestling industry. I would later go on to read Mick's other autobiographies "Foley if Good" and "The Hardcore Diaries" and after finally reading Mick Foley's "Countdown to Lockdown" book (which I did happen to read on the plane and trains while on my honeymoon!), being my final inspiration to starting this book.

I have enjoyed reading about how these wrestlers that I look up to started out just like myself as a wrestling fan. I have been interested in the many different paths taken by these wrestlers before they reached the heights of their WWF/E, WCW, ECW or TNA careers. The highs, the lows and the many injuries and hardships that have followed their wrestling careers have made for some great reading.

My current collection of wrestling autobiographies which I recommend to both wrestling and non-wrestling fans includes the following:

Book Title	Author / Wrestler
Adam Copeland on Edge	Edge
Batista Unleashed	Batista
The Rock Says	The Rock
The Hardcore Diaries	Mick Foley
Foley is Good	Mick Foley
Have A Nice Day: A Tale of Blood and Sweatsocks	Mick Foley
Countdown to Lockdown	Mick Foley
The Hardy Boyz: Exist 2 Inspire	Matt & Jeff Hardy
Heartbreak & Triumph: The Shawn Michaels Story	Shawn Michaels
Hollywood Hulk Hogan	Hulk Hogan
It's Good to Be the King…Sometimes	Jerry Lawler
The Stone Cold Truth	Stone Cold Steve Austin
To Be the Man	Ric Flair
Rey Mysterio: Behind the Mask	Rey Mysterio

A Lion's Tale: Around the World in

Chris Jericho

Spandex,

The rise and Fall of ECW

I would like to include Chris Jericho's second book (Undisputed), as well as books by William Regal, Dustin Rhodes and DX to my list.

The computer games industry has been an excellent source of wrestling entertainment for us fans, from humble beginnings on the Commodore 64, to the latest WWE'13 game on consoles such as PlayStation 3, WII and Xbox. These games have given us a chance to re-enact our favourite matches, moves, stories as well as give our favourites a chance at winning the WWE Title (Christian and Mick Foley are a multiply WWE champions on many of my wrestling games!!). While there have been numerous wrestling games throughout the past 30 odd years, I am only going to talk about the games that made it to my consoles, or caused me to use up all my spare change at the arcade.

We start with the commodore 64, and for those who weren't alive back in the 80's was a computer in which games had to be loaded via a tape cassette. This could have taken up to ½ hour, so you would start to load the game, go off and play outside for 30 minutes then come back and play the game. There were many times you would return to find an error, and you had to rewind and start the loading process all over again. But the good thing with this concept was if you had a double cassette player these tapes were easy to copy onto blank cassettes......or so I hear. My first wrestling game was 'Rock 'n' Wrestle' also known as "Bop'n'Wrestle" in other countries. As it was the only wrestling game I had seen and therefore I played it religiously, and it was always a good favourite to return to if bored on a rainy day. As Gorgeous Greg, you had to defeat ten unique wrestlers to become the champion, with each wrestler getting harder as you went through:

Hillbilly: Stereotype redneck. Easy fight; slow and easy to pin. Whiffs (misses) moves often. Practice against him!

Molotov Mike: *Bald guy with an eye patch. Tough, somewhat slow, hard to pin. Likes to head butt.*

Arab: *Stereotype Arab. Somewhat fast, but weak stamina and strength. Tends to do weaker moves; easy to pin. You can often break free of his holds. Molotov Mike is stronger.*

Biker: *Wears a biker cap. Tough, hard to pin. Messes around sometimes, giving you a second chance if you are low on stamina.*

Cowboy: *Wears a cowboy hat. Very tough, hard to pin. Likes to do body slams. Tends to finish you off as soon as possible.*

Vicious Vivian: *Punk rocker psychopath. Tough, hard to pin. Likes to head butt, and likes to finish you quickly.*

Indian Chief: *Wears an Indian head-dress. Very fast and manoeuvres well. Can finish you quickly if you are not alert and skilled. Likes to finish by flying off the corner post.*

Masked Mauler: Wears a green mask. Very tough, uses a variety of moves, moves in for the kill quickly.

Lord Toff: Wears a gentlemen's top hat. The strongest, and cunning. Does everything well. No time limit when fighting him.

Care of shawnZshihan on

http://www.lemon64.com/

My next venture into the world or computer game wrestling was one that took a fair amount of my 20 cent pieces and pocket money. "WWF Superstars by Technos 1989", I saw one day walking past a video arcade, and every spare chance and money I got went into this machine. It was one of those double look moments where you walk past, have a quick look, and it's not until you walk a few more steps forward that your brain processes what you saw, and you have to go back to confirm. In this case we were walking up a street in China town Sydney when we did our double take back into the arcade.

For the first time I was able to play as my favourite WWF/E superstars, which included: Hulk Hogan, "Macho Man" Randy Savage, The Ultimate Warrior, "Hacksaw" Jim Duggan, the Honkey Tonk Man, and the Big Boss man. The game play required you to choose two wrestlers to form a tag team, and fight three teams made up of the remaining wrestlers. Once you had defeated the three teams you faced Andre the Giant and 'The Million Dollar Man' Ted Dibiase for the title. If I remember correctly Andre was nearly impossible to do any damage on, so to win you had to stop Ted Dibiase from making a tag! My favourite combination of a tag team that I would always go to was The Ultimate Warrior and Big Boss man.

The next game to take all my spare change and pocket money was WWF Wrestlefest. Now you had two options of game play for this game. Just like the WWE Superstars, you could select two wrestlers to try and win the tag team titles, this time from The Legion of Doom. The second option for this game (the option I chose more often) was to try to win the Royal Rumble. Unlike the normal Rumble, besides eliminating people over the top rope you could also eliminate them via pin fall or submission. WWE Wrestlefest had an increase roster selection: Hulk Hogan, The Ultimate Warrior, "Million Dollar Man" Ted DiBiase and The Big Boss Man as from *WWF Superstars as well as now* Jake "The Snake" Roberts, Sgt. Slaughter, Mr. Perfect, Earthquake, Demolition Smash and Demolition Crush. My go to man in the rumble was The Big Boss man, while the demolition team of Smash and Crush for the tag team titles.

Both Superstars and Wrestlefest, being an arcade game, you could team up with your friends and try to win the titles together. However this became very frustrating if your mate didn't know how to play and got smashed by the computer, or even worse he didn't know how to tag you in, and lost the match before you had a chance to play, wasting your 40 cents!!!

WWF Royal Rumble 1994, once this game once it came out on SNES, it became part of my game collection. What I loved about this game was the fact you could not only play as your favourite WWF stars in one on one, tag teams, but also compete in the royal rumble! I could choose from: Bret Hart,

Crush, Razor Ramon, Shawn Michaels, The Undertaker, The Narcissist and Randy Savage,, Ric Flair, Tatanka, Ted DiBiase and Yokozuna.

Once I moved onto the Nintendo 64, WWF Wrestlemania 2000 was the game I would stay up all night playing, as well as ending up with many blisters on my thumbs because of the game. For the first time, I could create my own wrestler, and battle the likes of Stone cold and The Rock. This game let you play first blood matches, hardcore and last man standing matches. It had a huge roster of WWF superstars, and the ability to unlock more. This game also had Pay Per View mode, where you could create your own PPV, or recreate one from that year, and have your favourite win!! The big thing about this game I enjoyed was 'The road to Wrestlemania' story mode. Selecting one wrestle (and a tag team partner), fight through a whole year, to get to main event Wrestlemania. This story mode will become a regular in games that I buy from here on.

WWF here comes the pain is game I hired religiously from my local video store, as I couldn't afford to but it outright (all my money went on purchasing the PlayStation 2 system!!). While it was the last in the line of 'Smackdown' series of games, it was the first wrestling game since Wrestlemania 2000 that I had played, and from what I read the best in the 'Smackdown' series of games. While similar aspects remained the same, create your own wrestle, unlock bonus superstars, and match types like tag team, hardcore, royal rumble and cage matches, this game improved on the story, career or season mode feature. You chose a wrestler (could even be your created one), and your goal was to work your way up to having a Championship match a Wrestlemania. You had to make decisions, by talking to people back stage, picking rosters, and deciding who were heels and faces. Also add in the fact that you could play a WWF/E Diva Bra and Panty match, and then this game was well worth the wait!!

The Raw vs. Smackdown series from 2005 to 2011 became a regular yearly Christmas present to myself. Each year I would look forward to purchasing the game and try to conquer the career modes, road to Wrestlemania's, and have all my favourites with the titles. Each year they would improve the create-a-wrestler mode, and then introduce other create modes such as, stables, entrances and even finishers! You could wrestle in many common style wrestling matches including normal single and tag team, through to Royal Rumbles, cage, hell in cells (which included the ability to throw wrestlers off the top!!), elimination chambers, hardcore, car park, first blood, I quit and many more.

From 2006 through to 2008, the Raw vs. Smackdown games also gave us a General Managers mode. Here you had to put on a show, organise wrestlers, matches, feuds, and Pay Per Views to have the top / number one show by Wrestlemania. You had to watch out for wrestlers injuries, happiness (if they lost too many matches they would swap to another brand) and build up their crowd appeal. You had drafts to select your roster and could include legend and created wrestlers. This mode became my favourite thing from the game, as you could affect outcomes by participating in the matches, and of course affect who held the titles. I have been disappointed since this particular mode has disappeared and hope the powers at be bring it back for WWE'14.

Now due to a busy schedule, I have not yet had the opportunity to play WWE'12 or the just released WWE'13. However I did manage to borrow my nephews WWE'12 game, and look forward to playing that. And so far reviews for WWE'13 have been good, so that may also find its way into my PS3 collection.

Now being from the Commodore 64 generation, I would like to add that for someone like me who started with a joystick and 1 or 2 buttons, it does take me a long time to master the controllers that have up to 8 or 9 buttons, plus the button combinations! The wrestling games I always find are easy to get the handle of (even with combinations), and only have a few days of swearing when instead of punching my opponent, I end up performing a signature taunt and get smashed!!

Back in chapter 1 I spoke about my introduction to the internet, and then my introduction to www.wwe.com . It was for many years my source of information for what was happening in

the world of WWF/E, as well as a chance for me to catch up on

results of shows and PPV's I missed out on viewing. I now have

increased my internet library to include many other web sites

that are dedicated to wrestling. Starting with

www.impactwrestling.com for all my TNA information, through

to websites such as *www.**wrestling-edge**.com/*,

*www.**wrestlezone**.com/*, www.**bleacherreport/wwe**.com/,

www.**411mania**.com/ for my wrestling articles, news, reviews,

chats, spoilers and results. While *www.**iwawrestling**.com.au/* and

*www.**awf**wrestling.com.au/* I use for all my information on

wrestling in NSW, Australia. During the writing of this book,

Wikipedia has become a great source of information and just one

of the places I go to check dates and facts.

I have ventured into Facebook, and have 'liked' many

pages associated with wrestling, however, have not yet ventured

into the world of twitter, as I don't fully understand the

enjoyment factor of reading about how someone fed their cat last night. It may be something I look into (especially if this book gets off the ground).

I have previously mentioned that I have found 'YouTube' a great source to find and view all those classic matches, moments and promos that I remember and want to watch again, or want to see for the first time as didn't have the opportunity when they happened originally. 'YouTube' has given me the opportunity to experience, and enjoy wrestlers such as Sting and Rick Flair as due to them wrestling on other companies that I did not follow, I have missed many of their great matches. The same goes with stars on TNA such as Kurt Angle, AJ styles and Samoan Joe who have had great matches that I now get a chance to watch.

With new items happening on the internet and with new apps every day, who knows what will be next in the world of wrestling. In fact as I am writing this book, something new did occur, with the WWE forming a partnership with TOUT. On the 999th episode of Raw WWE fans got to send via a video message on line their responses to the question "What was your favourite

RAW moment. Very soon, fans will be able to have Q and A with some WWE superstars as well as participate in WWE 'TOUT Tuesday', a program on www.wwe.com, that will discuss the happenings on RAW the previous night. So what is TOUT? And how successful was it? Well according to an article by Nick Paglino after the 999th episode:

> *WWE today announced that immediately after WWE featured fan Touts - 15-second self-recorded videos - during Monday Night Raw, the social media platform's app skyrocketed from No. 37 to No. 6 in the Free Photo & Video category on the iTunes App Store. The Tout app was downloaded more than 30,000 times within hours of the broadcast.*
>
> *During last night's episode of Monday Night RAW, fans submitted Touts that were later aired during the live broadcast on the USA Network; Touts are also distributed across WWE's vast array of assets, including*

television, live events, WWE.com and to more than 100 million of its social media followers. Now, Tout is No. 116 on the overall Free Apps list (out of 900,000+ apps), speaking volumes to the power of the WWE Universe and the WWE brand.

This news comes a week after WWE's announcement that the global entertainment company became an investor and strategic marketing partner of Tout Industries, Inc.

Tout is a social media platform whose smartphone and Web applications enable real-time video status updates that can be shared instantly to Tout.com, Twitter, Facebook, Pinterest, SMS and email contacts. Through Tout's reply feature, WWE fans now have the chance to be seen and heard via Tout real-time video updates, encouraging a new dynamic social experience for WWE fans to interact with the brand.

"The partnership with WWE has proven that when you give enthusiastic fans the ability to easily share and interact with real-time video status updates, they will jump at the chance," said Michael Downing, CEO, Tout.com. "WWE's passionate fan base and tremendous reach across a variety of media assets create an extraordinary opportunity to engage fans and followers. We are uniquely positioned to provide this technology, and look forward to rolling it out across a diverse range of media and brand properties. "By Nick Paglino July 18, 2012

STAMFORD, Conn., Jul 17, 2012 (BUSINESS WIRE

We are blessed today with the amount of media options we can use to keep up with our wrestling addictions, and my enjoyment of the wrestling product has only increased with every new media option that has come along. And I will enjoy hearing my book on audio CD, or itunes as long as it is read by Mick Foley of course.

Chapter 8   Women in wrestling

From first seeing Cyndi Lauper in the ring with Lou Albano, Miss Elizabeth escorting Macho Man Randy Savage to the ring, and watching The Fabulous Moolah (c) defeat Velvet McIntyre at Wrestlemania 2, women have been a part of the wrestling product I have watched for the past 30 years. Women in wrestling can spark great discussions amongst wrestling fans, there are many who believe women should be limited to just valet's (and managers), while others believe that there is a place for women's wrestling in major companies. Personally, I enjoy watching female wrestling when the standard is high, and the competitors are professional wrestlers, and not models turned to wrestling, and believe it or not, I would prefer a traditional match done correctly rather than when it is a gimmick such as a bra and panties type match.

Wrestling Valet - *A female performer or wrestler acting as a wrestler's personal chaperone or manager; often used to distract other competitors, and attract and titillate male members of the audience.*

www.allword.com

Would anyone have watched or cared about a Test and Albert (T & A) tag team match had they not had Trish Stratus accompanying them to the ring? Or did anyone really care about 'Wildman' Marc Mero when Sable was at ringside? Or who had the better wrestling career Lita or Essa Rios? There have been many Valet's to shine over my wrestling viewing, and some even ending up being more successful than their wrestling counterpart. For me, it started with Miss Elizabeth escorting 'Macho Man' Randy Savage to the ring, and has continued through the years to currently Vickie Guerrero managing Dolph Ziggler, valets have been a major role in the history of wrestling. Whether it has been as a girlfriend, business partnership, relative or another arrangement, valets accompanying have added to the drama (and pleasant viewing) that can occur at ringside during a match.

Now there were many times a valet would distract the referee or opponent so their man or team could win. Whether it was the terrible screams at ringside from Melina, Debra showing off her puppies or blatant interference by valets such as

Sensational Sherrie, Chyna and Lita, these valets needed to be

watched at ringside. Some of the best known Valets that have

accompanied my favourite wrestling superstars (and did not go

on to have major wrestling careers) include:

Miss Elizabeth	Macho Man Randy Savage
Sapphire	The American Dream
	Dusty Rhodes
Peggy sue	Honky Tonk Man
Sensation Sherrie	Macho Man Randy Savage
	Shawn Michaels
Debra (Marshell)	Jeff Jarret
	Stone Cold Steve Austin
Marlene	Goldust
Sunny	The Bodydonnas
	The legion of Doom
Sable	Wildman Marc Mero
Stacey Keibler	The Dudley Boys
Stephanie McMahon	Triple H

While each of the above valets have all been somewhat memorable, the one valet that I have enjoyed watching the most is that of Vickie Guerrero. If the two words "Excuse Me" send shivers down your spine, then that is just an example of why in my eyes she will be known as the best Valet in WWF/E history. While Vickie had started appearing in regular WWE programming around 2006 (mainly on Smackdown with her nephew Chavo), it was her 'romantic' role with Edge, that took her from being Eddie's wife, to being the Vickie Guerrero character you see today. Since then she has been a regular part of the WWE Universe and I feel constantly been one of the best Heels of the last couple of years. You just have to watch the crowd reaction to her every time she speaks (especially those two words), when she comes down to the ring, interferes in matches, or is shown in a backstage segment. Vickie has taken many 'shots' from other wrestlers including being knocked off the ring aprons, speared and even suffered an Undertaker Tombstone! Vickie has the ability to quickly move from a formidable opponent and nemesis, to finding herself in comedy situations, usually at her own expense. Whether it has been managing WWE superstars such as Edge, Dolph Ziggler or Chavo Guerrero, portraying her 'cougar' persona with LayCool, as GM or as a women scorned, Vickie has been the shining light in a company that has lost its way with the way it has managed and treated its female superstar employees.

While a valet usually just accompanies a wrestler (or team) to the ring, and 'occasionally' gets involved or distracts the referee or opponent, there have been a couple of moments where the valet has stolen the whole show. There are two examples that quickly come to mind where the valet's actions outshone the match or event that was happening.

In 1988 at the first ever Summer Slam, The main event match was between Hulk Hogan and Macho Man Randy Savage vs. The Million Dollar Man Ted Dibiase and Andre The Giant . After her team of Hogan and Savage were being dominated during the match, Miss Elizabeth hopped up onto the ring apron, and removed her skirt, revealing a very unique one piece outfit, distracting Dibiase and the Giant, allowing Hogan and Savage to take advantage and win. Now while the incident and outfit would be classed as very tame compared to the standards set in the attitude/ruthless aggression era of bra and panty matches, this incident shocked (not only the competitors) us fans at the time, and is one of those moments that was done so well, it has stuck in my wrestling memory banks for over 20 years.

To further prove the different (moral) boundaries that occurred in the 'Rock n Wrestling era' compared to the attitude era, and one of the few times a valet is remembered more at a Pay Per View (PPV), than any of the matches, was at the 1998 Fully Loaded PPV. In a bikini contest between Sable and her former Wrestler Mark Mero new Valet Jacqueline, Sable would reveal her bikini top to be a pair of body painted hands! Jerry Lawler's reaction was priceless, as was the reaction of all of us fans! Nobody cared that Sable was disqualified, and for those who remember this moment I bet you cannot remember at least 1 other match from that PPV……..

Many Valets moved from outside of the ring, to inside and ended up having very successful careers as wrestlers. Trish Stratus, Lita and Chyna are just three examples of women who started out as valets, but ended up better known for their in-ring abilities. These former valets moved from outside the ring to each being at one stage WWF/E Women's Champions.

There are also others who just stared their careers as wrestlers (Beth Pheniox, Tamina and Mickie James to name a few). Women's wrestling has been a very hit and miss product, depending on who is in the ring. What company they wrestle in and what era they are wrestling in. Would you prefer to watch a Kelly Kelly vs. Torrie Wilson match or a Lita vs. Trish Stratus match??? For me the Lita/Trish match would win every time as the wrestling ability of both ladies, and the ability of both ladies to put on a decent wrestling match, for me is far better viewing than watching two barbie dolls "attempt" or try to wrestle. You only have to watch Trish stratus retirement match vs. Lita at Unforgiven 2006 to prove how good a women's match can be.

One of the common positives that keep coming from TNA that I hear, read and have seen briefly (prior to a channel move on Australian TV, in which I cannot watch TNA anymore) was that TNA has a very high quality women's wrestling (knockout) division. Not only have matches been done well, but there is an effort placed into story lines and feuds that at this stage of writing (this book), is leaving the WWF/E diva's division in their dust. You only have to look at the roster of women wrestlers that have worked there to understand why this division has shone so brightly. Knockouts which have included:

Awesome Kong

Ayako Hamada

Gail Kim

Madison Rayne,

Mickie James

Miss Tessmacher,

ODB

Tara

Velvet Sky

I did try and find lists on the best knockout matches in the history of TNA, but alas my research could not locate such a list. However the TNA Knockouts Championship/No DQ: Gail Kim vs. Awesome Kong (1/6/08, Final Resolution) was often mentioned as the best match in one of the best female feuds of all time.

There have many WWF/E divas who have entered the ring, and held the WWF/E Women's Championship or the now WWE Diva championship, however, when it comes to female wrestlers who can produce a great match, then the list of female wrestlers shrinks dramatically. From The Fabulus Moolah, through to Beth Pheniox, the WWF/E has had some great female wrestlers that have the ability to produce some terrific matches. As mentioned, Lita and Trish Stratus head the list, however, others who I feel were also able to produce great wrestling matches were:

Michelle McCool

Layla

Beth Phoenix

Molly Holly

Victoria

Mickie James

Melina

There is no surprise that Trish and Lita head my top 5 list of the best Women's matches I have seen as they are still to this day the best female wrestlers I have had the privilege in watching, in fact they hold the top 2 of the top 5 matches and at least one of them is involved in four of my top 5 matches! You will also notice that none of my top matches include those terrible gimmick matches of the attitude era, such as bra and panty, pillow fight, or those jelly and mud matches. My top 5 women's matches are:

Trish Vs Lita for the Womens Championship Dec 2004 Raw

Trish vs. Lita for the Womens Championship 2006 Unforgiven

Trish vs. Mickie James Wrestlemania 22

Victoria vs. Lita steel cage Nov 2003 Raw

Melina vs. Mickie James, Backlash 2007

Special mention Beth Phoenix vs. Melina, I Quit, not so much for the match, but for the ending, Beth contorting Melina's body in a position that you have to see to appreciate!!

Sadly the current women's division is lacking some major talent, and is in a lull, and needs some changes very soon, and it is not just me who thinks this. There are many blogs, articles, chat sites currently online explaining why the WWE diva's division is so bad or how they would fix the current Diva division. Articles such as Bill Atkinson on The Bleacher Report 26 September 2012, 6 ways the WWE division could be relevant again:

> *Quick! When was the last time you saw a truly meaningful, enjoyable WWE Divas match? Exactly. It's been a while. A lo-o-o-ong while. While the WWE Superstars continue to enjoy monster success in and out of the ring, the WWE Divas flounder in something that is less than mediocrity.*
>
> *The WWE slots their matches during times in the shows when both the attendees and the TV audience are heading to the bathrooms. You hear that Divas Champion Layla is going to*

wrestle on TV, but if you get up to go grab that soda or beer from the fridge, chances are the match has taken place, and Layla has changed back into her street clothes and gone home.

Face it. The WWE Divas matches are the show's equivalent of the seventh-inning stretch. Unless you're into "God Bless America" or "Take Me Out to the Ball Game," there's not much to see or do.

The Fabulous Moolah is spinning in her grave....

1. Dump the Diva Name......

2. Tone Down the T&A......

3. Allow for More Character Development......

4. Give Their Matches More Air Time......

5. Add More Titles— Perhaps a Tag Team Title.....

6. Create a General Manager for the

Women's Division... ....

Many valets and female wrestlers who have interfered during matches, or have been in the wrong place at the wrong time, and have ended up being on the wrong end of some frustrated wrestlers move such as spear, power bomb, stunner, rock bottom etc, or while involved in some mixed tag team matches, again have being on the end of some frustrated wrestlers move. The most memorable image of this was 77 year old Mea Young being power bombed through a table by Bubba Ray Dudley on RAW in consecutive weeks in 2000. The second power bomb being done from the entrance way on top of the ramp! However there have been those women wrestlers who have had the ability to mix it up with the men in the ring! This has happened 3 times at the WWF/E Royal Rumble with Chyna, Beth Pheniox and Karma not only entering the rumble but also eliminating people!

Royal rumble 1999 Chyna - she eliminated Mark Henry

Royal rumble 2010 Beth Phoenix – she eliminated The Great Khali

Royal rumble 2012 Kharma – she eliminated Hunico

Besides the Royal Rumble there have been also some women who have won male WWF/E titles. The most memorable one would be Chyna winning the Intercontinental Championship from Jeff Jarret at No Mercy 1999, in a memorable 'good housekeeping' match (kitchen items could be used as weapons). Chyna would have quite a few matches against Jarrett, and Chris Jericho over the Intercontinental title.

Trish Stratus and Molly Holly both held (briefly) the WWE Hardcore Title, during its 24/7 defending rule. While Lita got heavily involved in helping The Hardy Boys in the classic TLC II, with the likes of Edge and Christian and The Dudley Boys.

My Family getting ready for our zip line adventure in Vanuatu. Kristina, Abbey and Ruby (back),

Zara (Middle), Max and Connor at the front.

My wife and I on our Honeymoon in Paris 2012

Zara, Ruby, Connor and Max at the IWA show in our Home town of Dubbo 2012.

My "other son" and friend Zac Pullbrook

The fun of making your own signs at live show – WWE Sydney 2010

Max (above) Connor (Below) bet you can't guess their favourite wrestler....

A future WWE Diva Champion Ruby

Zara and Me at the WWE show in Sydney 2011

I have even managed to convince my wife Kristina to come to a live show. Here with Connor at the WWE show in Sydney 2010

I have even had a chance (even only for 1 minute) to meet my wrestling and writing idol Mick Foley!!

Chapter 9   Gone but not forgotten

Whether it has been due to injuries, drugs or even death there are many instances where we have lost one of our favourite wrestlers from either the wrestling ring, or even worse - permanently. While age will eventually force many to retire and pass on (unless you are Rick Flair or Hulk Hogan), too often we have seen and read about wrestlers such as Edge having to retire due to injuries, or Eddie Guerrero dying in a Hotel room, some (like these two) in the prime of their wrestling careers, main eventing Pay Per Views and battling for major titles. When you are watching someone every week on the TV, and when you have been supporting someone for many years, for us fans it is like losing a friend when they are no longer on the show, which is why many wrestling fans are so upset when a wrestler has to retire, gets released from a company or due to a death of a popular wrestler. For those female NWF, I would imagine that it would be the same feeling you had when Ridge (Ron Moss) left 'the Bold and The Beautiful'.

There are times where in a current story line that a wrestler gets injured, or fired or they quit their respective company. These are done as a way of giving the wrestler a rest (to heal minor injuries), participate in another endeavour (act in a movie), or have time off for family reasons. They will usually quickly return when the injury is healed or the movie is finished. There are usually many spoilers, on many wrestling websites that will quickly let you know which firing, injury or retirement are real and which are works.

There have been many instances where our favourite wrestlers have been lost to wrestling for very long lengths of time due to serious injuries, with Shawn Michaels missing from the ring for over four years being the one that stick outs the most. Who knows how many more titles he would have won or how many more great matches we would have seen had he not been forced away for so long? Stone Cold Steve Austin, Triple H and The Undertaker are just three other big names who have missed long periods of their careers due to injuries suffered in the ring. Even in the last year, my favourite Christian missed a lot of the year due to injuries, as did Wade Barret, Mark Henry and Evan Bourne (although he also had a suspension). We have even just seen Jerry 'The King" Lawler return from suffering a heart attack while commentating on a raw episode after competing in a match against CM Punk. From TNA, Chris Sabin tore his ACL and was out for a year, D'Angelo Dinero, Jesse Sorensen and Sting are currently on the injured list.

While many NWF call wrestling fake, the toll wrestling takes on a wrestlers body, mind and soul is huge and shows that while wrestling results may be scripted, and moves practiced and rehearsed, wrestling is definitely not fake! There are even some reports that show the average age a wrestler dies is between 40 and 50 years old. And that scared the sh*t out of me when considering I have just hit that age now (well low 40's). Whether its injuries from performing in the ring, the constant toll on a wrestlers body from travelling around not only the US, but nowadays even around the world all year or even just walking down to the ring (it is how Vince McMahon tore a quadriceps - watch the you tube video not only to see it happen, but how well he continued his role), or injuries and problems associated from drug abuse, the life of a wrestler is not always as glamorous as it seems. Like most sports there are common injuries suffered by wrestlers, and these can include:

- Broken bones – this has included necks, as well as ribs, legs and arms
- Concussions
- Torn muscles, included pectoral, groin, Quad and calves
- Joints injuries mainly knees, shoulders and ankles
- Sprains and strains
- Back injuries
- Cuts and wounds (not all are bladding/self-inflicted)
- Loss of body parts (Mick Foley's ear)

Wrestling moves that have gone wrong have caused many wrestlers to miss months and years off their careers, ended their careers, or worse still have left them in wheel chairs. We have all seen successful returns from injuries caused by these botched moves from many popular wrestlers such as Triple H, Stone Cold Steve Austin, Hardcore Holly and The Undertaker. Some however have not been so lucky. Brett Hart and Sid Vicious's careers were basically ended by moves that went wrong while Darren "Droz' Drozdov lost more than his career. A power bomb that went wrong has left Droz paralysed for life, and is now a quadriplegic due to the failed move.

> *Darren "Droz" Drozdov vs. D'Lo Brown (WWF "Smackdown" Oct. 5, 1999): This was a very tragic incident. The budding career of Darren Drozdov or Droz as he was known came to a screeching halt on an episode of Smackdown when D'Lo Brown botched a running powerbomb on Droz. The problem was that Droz was wearing a loose fitting t-shirt, and when D'Lo went to pick Droz up he could not get a firm grip on Droz, and Droz did not jump high enough to make up for the fact D'Lo didn't pick him up far enough.*

Basically D'Lo hands slipped, and he was trying his hardest to correct the mistake but did not have any leverage and could not get Droz up in the 90-degree angle needed to absorb the impact, instead dropping Droz directly on the back of his neck.

The Droz although alive, was paralyzed for life, and is now a quadriplegic due to the failed move.

Droz remains on the WWE's payroll as a journalist on the website most notably WWE Byte This, mostly doing pre-PPV predictions. It was truly neither man's fault that this happened, but it stands as a grim reminder that things can go wrong in the blink of the eye

<u>Alberto Cortez</u> on March 14 2009, The Bleacher Report

If you have a strong stomach, then there are many YouTube videos out there showing some horrific injuries such as broken legs, dislocated arms and fingers or wrestlers landing poorly on their necks, I stopped after watching just one YouTube video, which just happened to be the match between Sid Vicious vs. Scott Steiner at WCW "Sin" on January 14th, 2001, where Sid would break his leg.....(even writing this I feel queasy). Some of the most well-known 'incidents', accidents or injuries I have seen happen in the ring besides Mr McMahon's torn quads include:

- Jerry The King Lawler having a heart attack while on commentary 2012
- Bob "Hardcore" Holly Breaking neck after botched Power bomb 2002
- Brock Lesner's failed shooting star press at Wrestlemania 19
- John Cena tearing his pectoral performing a hip toss 2007
- Triple H Tearing His Quad breaking up a 'walls of Jericho' 2001
- Stone Cold breaking his neck, with botched pile driver 1997

- Wade Barret Dislocating his elbow in battle royal 2011

Wrestling, unlike many sports, does not have an off season, so a wrestler can or has to wrestle all year round. Those not fortunate to be signed by a major wrestling company, and are wrestling for smaller or independent companies will lose money when injured and not wrestling, which is why addiction to drugs such as pain killers, can be a common occurrence.

My teaching career has including many classes teaching about drug education. There is so much information available showing what can happen when people take drugs, whether they are prescription, performing enhancing or recreational. These classes also explain however, why so many people feel the need to take these drugs, even knowing the possible consequences. There are many jobs that have been associated with the need for taking drugs, or drug use and the world of professional wrestling is no exception to the rule, as there are many reasons wrestlers have turned to drugs. Depression associated with being away from loved ones, pressure to perform all year long, feelings of failure when not achieving success, or not being as successful as you once were, pressure to perform even with injuries are just some of the mental and emotional instability wrestler's face. Many of the deaths of wrestlers can be accredited to drug related issues, whether it is from heart related problems associated with drug use, blood pressure issues or overdoses. Drugs use can also lead to severe mental illnesses, such schizophrenia, deep depression, and possible suicide tendencies. Addiction to pain killers, alcoholism or high recreational drug use has been linked to many well-known wrestlers such as Jake 'the snake' Roberts, Scott Hall, Eddie Guerrero and Curt Henning (Mr Perfect). While it seems I might be justifying why wrestlers take drugs, due to drugs and drug addiction being an issue close to my family, and many of people I teach at a Correctional Centre affected by drugs and drug use, I feel that while I do not condone drug use, I understand how easy it is to fall into the drug lifestyle.

Some wrestling companies have moved with the times, such as the WWE introducing a 'Talent Wellness Policy'. In 2012 WWE main event stars Rey Mysterio and Randy Orton failed the test on this policy resulting in suspensions from the company. To explain the policy better, here is an article on 'The Bleacher Report" by Drake Oz (Featured Columnist) on June 1, 2012 called *The WWE Talent Wellness Program: A Casual Fan's Guide.*

A Brief Summary

The WWE Talent Wellness Program started in February 2006, and it is believed by many that the WWE's institution of the program was a direct result of the tragic death of Eddie Guerrero in 2005.

According to WWE's corporate Web site, the following is covered under the program:

- *Comprehensive Medical and Wellness Staffing*
- *Cardiovascular Testing and Monitoring*
- *ImPACT™ Testing (Concussion tests)*
- *Substance Abuse and Drug Testing*
- *Annual Physicals*
- *Health Care Referrals*

The WWE works with 10 physicians to help maintain the program, each of which specialises in a particular field, such as Cardiology or Orthopedics.

Banned Substances

The following substances are banned under the Talent Wellness Program, and more details on these substances can be found here:

- *Performance-enhancing drugs*
- *Stimulants*
- *Pseudoephedrine*
- *Narcotic Analgesics*
- *Benzodiazepines*
- *Barbiturates*
- *Diuretics*
- *Muscle Relaxers*
- *Sleep Aids*
- *Anti-Strogens*
- *Prescription Medications (See details on specifics for this one)*
- *Illegal Drugs*

- *Herbal and Dietary Supplements*

- *Synthetic Drugs*

The Three-Strike Policy

The Talent Wellness Program operates on a three-strike policy, in which three strikes results in termination from the company.

Here is the exact policy, courtesy of WWE's corporate website:

- *First Violation: In the event of an initial positive test for substances prohibited by this Policy other than marijuana and alcohol, the WWE Talent shall be suspended for thirty (30) days, fined an amount equal to thirty (30) days' pay deducted from the WWE Talent's downside guarantee on a weekly basis and WWE will publicly disclose the WWE Talent's name and duration of the suspension and indicating a first violation the Policy.*

- *Second Violation: In the event of a second positive test for substances prohibited by this Policy other than marijuana and alcohol, the WWE Talent shall be suspended for sixty (60) days, fined an amount equal to sixty (60) days' pay deducted from the WWE Talent's downside guarantee on a weekly basis and WWE will publicly disclose the WWE Talent's name and duration of the suspension and indicating a second violation the Policy.*

- *Third Violation: In the event of a third positive test for substances prohibited by this Policy other than marijuana and alcohol, the WWE Talent's contract with WWE will be terminated and WWE will publicly disclose the WWE Talent's name and that WWE Talent's contract was terminated for a third violation of the Policy.*

In Layman's Terms: One failed test equals a 30-day suspension, a second failed test equals a 60-day suspension and a third failed test results in termination.

Should anyone under contract with the WWE fail a third Wellness test, he or she can return after a one-year absence, but will have to abide by an even stricter policy.

Stance on Marijuana and Alcohol

WWE Talent do not receive a strike for testing positive for alcohol or marijuana, but they are subject to the following punishments for a positive test for either substance:

B. FOR POSITIVE MARIJUANA DRUG TESTS

In the event of any positive test for marijuana, the WWE Talent shall be fined Two Thousand Five Hundred US Dollars ($2,500.00) per positive test, which shall be deducted from the WWE Talent's downside guarantee.

The same $2,500 fine is in effect for positive

alcoholic substance tests.

Excuses such as "it is tradition" or "this is the typical culture" are no longer acceptable, as they were back in the 60's, 70, 80's and even early 90's. What happened out of the ring, when shows were finished, stayed in house (whether it be wrestling, football or rock bands). In fact the most common saying that is heard before any rugby trip that I went on was the classic "What happens on tour, stays on tour". But today with cameras and mobile phones everywhere, what 'happens on tour" ends up on the internet for everybody to view, comment on and criticize. In the wrestling world we fans now do not accept behaviour of wrestlers cheating on partners, taking drugs or drink driving. In a world where everyone that is classed as a celebrity is also looked upon as a role model, behind the scenes behaviour has to also change and adapt with the times. It is one of the many draw backs these days of being a professional sportsman, or entertainer, that there are always cameras on you waiting for you to make a mistake, in the world of wrestling there are no exceptions to this.

As you will see in a later chapter Edge (Adam Copeland) is one of my top 10 wrestlers who I have enjoyed watching over the past 30 years. So it was with mixed feelings to hear on the 12 April 2011 episode of Raw that he announced his retirement from wrestling due to injuries. Firstly, I was very disappointed to hear that we will not see Edge in a wrestling ring ever again. The intensity, skill, athleticism, humour and risks he brought to his matches throughout his career were why I enjoyed watching him in the ring. It would be those risks that would eventually shorten his career. I was however glad that he was given the chance by doctors to stop wrestling, and be able to continue to be able to live life to the fullest, and not risk one more match and end up in a wheel chair or worse. I will admit that during Edges farewell speech my eyes did swell up, but it must have been the onions I was cutting at the time....

Part of his speech made on the night of the 12th April

"......I started in the WWE when I was 23. I've been doing this for 19 years. 14 of them with the WWE. My first match was May 10th, 1996 at Hamilton's

Copps Coliseum. I was 23 years old, and I feel like I've grown up in front of all of you. I feel like I've made a whole lot of mistakes in front of you. I've learned from them, and I've become a man in front of you. I've come from being the silent guy running around the streets of New York with a trenchcoat that was way too small for him, to a pseudo vampire in The Brood, to one of the funny goofy guys along with Christian, posing for the benefit of those with flash photography. I became one of the most despised guys in the history of the WWE. As a matter of fact, I got thrown in the Long Island Sound. I had a live sex celebration. Thankfully with Lita and not Vicki Guerrero. And I would hope that through it all, I've earned the respect of everyone in that locker room. And I hope that I've earned all of your respect. Because no matter what, no matter what, I came out here and tried to give you guys as much as I had every single night. And in turn you guys gave it right

back to me ......"

Adam Copeland (EDGE) 12th April 2011 WWE Raw

There has been a lot written about how successful Owen Hart could have been, had it not been for his tragic accident at Over the Edge May 23rd 1999. Like I, many other wrestling fans believe he was ready for a major title run. Owen's skills in the ring were second to none, but it was his ability to interact with the crowd as a heel, such as getting the whole crowd to hate his character, chanting "nugget" or just plain hoping he loses, that was I feel his best attribute. His feud with his brother Brett was his break out moment, he would go on to win numerous tag team titles with wrestlers such as Yokozuna, Jeff Jarret and The British Bulldog. Owen also won The Intercontinental title twice and the European Title. As far as I remember he was the first wrester to come to the ring on a regular basis holding his "Slammy Awards". He was an excellent in-ring technical wrestler, and one of those wrestlers who had the ability to be able to have a great match with different type of wrestlers whether they were also technical (like his brother Brett), brawlers, high flyers or larger opponents.

Many of us fans have remembered where we were, and what we were doing on the day we found out about his accident descending from the ceiling during the Pay Per View 'Over the Edge' in 1999. Performing the high risk entrance from the ceiling, the stunt went terribly wrong and Owen fell, hitting the turnbuckle, and not being able to be revived. Doing my research for this book I have noticed numerous You Tube videos of the accident, but I have never, and will never watch any of them. There are just some things better left un-viewed. Owen you were a favourite of mine in the ring, I hear and read that you were a great father, husband and friend, and even 13 years on, the world is still a little duller since you have left.

It took me a while to fall under the Eddie Guerrero charm, but when I did I was hooked on the "Latino Heat" superstar. I was unfortunate to miss his run in his WCW days, but enjoyed his many feuds, matches, promos and skits while he was in the WWF/E. On November 13, 2005 Eddie Guerrero was found by his good friend, and nephew Chavo unconscious in a Hotel room. Attempts to revive him failed, heart failure being the cause of his death. I have read that he was due to regain the WWE title from Batista in the upcoming Pay Per View, so to lose a great and charismatic wrestler in his prime is always going to be a great tragedy. I will remember his title win from Brock Lesner at No Way Out in 2004, and had the privilege of watching him wrestle a great match live against Kurt Angle in Sydney. From his low rider entrance, his tag team skits with Chavo, to his signature frog splash, he is stilled missed greatly today.

One wrestler that has divided the wrestling community on how, or even if we should remember him, is Chris Beniot, and the murder and suicide that surrounded his death. Unlike stars such as Owen Hart and Eddie Guerrero, the circumstances surrounding Chris's death make it very hard to hold and remember him in high regard.

Prior to this terrible tragedy I was a Chris Beniot fan, I had enjoyed watching his rise through the WWF/E ranks to be one of the main event stars of the company. Rarely did he have a poor match, and when in the ring with the likes of Chris Jericho, Kurt Angle or Shawn Michaels you knew you had a classic match in the making. He was a shoe in to be one day in the Wrestling hall of fame, Royal Rumble winner, WWE World Heavyweight Champion, tag team champion and I am confident he had many more title reigns before he retired.

Many fans, just like I are torn in how and or whether we should remember Chris Beniot, while others are pretty clear cut in their beliefs. Many choose to only remember Chris's career and life before those infamous 3 days June 2007. Many have chosen to turn their backs on anything that Chris has done in the ring due to his actions on those infamous 3 days in June 2007. What makes it hard for people like me and other wrestling fans is that we all have a Chris Beniot wrestling moment that made us enjoy wrestling. For me it was Wrestlemania 20 with Chris winning the World Heavy Weight title for the first time, and celebrating in the ring with his good mate Eddie Guerrero. His matches against Kurt Angle, Booker T (in the best of 7 series) and the great ladder match against Chris Jericho at the Royal Rumble in 2001 are some of the great memories of his wrestling career I have with me. However being a father, I cannot understand what would make another father kill their own child. I know results have shown there was brain damage possibly caused by his wrestling career, and people theorise on steroid use and abuse. However when it is all said and done he murdered his wife and child, and that is something that many people cannot comprehend, and that is what we unfortunately remember most about him.

I currently work as a teacher at a correctional Centre (jail if you are in the USA), and often hear many different excuses about why inmates are in there. Very rarely is it 'their fault'. My personal opinion is there is a lot of people who do not take responsibility for their own actions, and instead tend to blame other people, society, government, the grog (alcohol), illnesses, their wives or husbands and so on. I have heard excuses such as I am in here because the cops were following me…not because they was selling drugs, or "I stabbed him because he got me angry", forgetting the fact that the 'act' of stabbing someone is wrong, or people who fight speeding fines, even though they were speeding and therefore breaking the law. People have made excuses for Chris's actions, and even looked at the wrestling industry as a scapegoat, and many that have known Chris have come out and said that his action on those days were completely out of character, but it doesn't change the fact that he acted on his own accord. I will not go into the incidents of the deaths of Chris and his family as I feel I am in no position to do so, however, I will send my thoughts and prayers to all of their family and friends who still grieve their loss.

The WWE acted quickly and removed all mention of Chris Beniot from their shows and merchandise and I commend them for that. As hard as it must have been for all those close to Chris, the WWE could not be seen promoting or endorsing the actions and career of a murderer in front of kids and families. When discussing wrestling with my kids, my favourite wrestlers and matches, I too choose not to mention Chris Beniot, but focus on other wrestling stars they should watch.

I could go into more depth about the Chris Beniot tragedy or other deaths in the world of professional wrestling however there are other books out there dedicated entirely to this topic which I would suggest reading. These include:

- *Benoit: Wrestling with the Horror That Destroyed a Family and Crippled a Sport (by Steven Johnson)*
  The life and alarming death of acclaimed professional wrestler Chris Benoit are explored in this timely and exhaustive biography. In June 2007 Benoit committed suicide after killing his wife and son, and the media coverage surrounding this event—as well as the facts of the case and its effects on professional wrestling—are all extensively addressed. Benoit's life prior to and during his pro wrestling career is examined, as is his significant impact on the wrestling world and widespread popularity. This close-up look at one of pro wrestling's greatest and most lamented figures also presents the place of his tragedy in the darker side of wrestling's history

- *Chris & Nancy: The True Story of the Benoit Murder-Suicide and Pro Wrestling's Cocktail of Death (by Irvin Muchnick)*

  Exploring the steroid-fuelled world of professional wrestling, this riveting chronicle lays bare the devastating events that led to the 2007 murder-suicide of Chris Benoit, his wife Nancy, and their seven-year-old son, Daniel. Benoit's performance-enhancing drug addiction—massive amounts of doctor-prescribed human growth hormone were found in Benoit's home—and subsequent suicide proved to be the tipping point for the professional wrestling world, resulting in unprecedented scrutiny of the sport's subpar health and safety standards. Using public records, dozens of interviews with those inside and outside of wrestling, and investigative results, this authoritative analysis provides an uncompromising look at the price athletes pay in this rough-and-tumble world.

- *Tributes II: Remembering More of the World's Greatest Wrestlers (Wrestling Observer) (By Dave Meltzer)*

This detailed chronicle looks at the lives, times, and deaths of the biggest names that the sport of professional wrestling has produced. Picking up where Tributes: Remembering Some of the World's Greatest Professional Wrestlers left off, author Dave Meltzer focuses on sports entertainment's most recent and high-profile losses, including Road Warrior Hawk, Curt Henning, Elizabeth, Stu Hart, Tim Woods, Davey Boy Smith, Gorilla Monsoon, Terry Gordy, Wahoo McDaniel, Johnny Valentine, The Sheik, Freddie Blassie, and Lou Thesz. Tributes II: Remembering More of the World's Greatest Wrestler also offers expanded versions of some of the most popular profiles from Tributes, including Owen Hart, and Andre the Giant. Offering candid and detailed accounts of bona fide wrestling legends and a foreword by Bret Hart, Tributes II takes its place among the most important books ever written on the world of pro wrestling

- *Broken Harts: The Life and Death of Owen Hart (by Martha Hart)*

Owen's wife Martha, tells the story of their life together from the days as high school sweethearts, through Owen's rise to fame in the WWF.

- *Gone Too Soon: Deaths That Changed Wrestling (byIan Hamilton)*

In the world of professional wrestling, we all have our heroes. But what happens when our heroes are taken away from us? "Gone Too Soon" chronicles the stories of three of wrestling's names who passed away too soon - Owen Hart, Eddie Guerrero and Chris Benoit - and the lasting effect they left on the industry.

Below is a list of the other wrestlers I have enjoyed watching since I started watching wrestling in the mid 1980's who have sadly passed on before the age of 50. As I am now in my very early 40's I think this list is a great reminder for me and others of similar ages to start having our (as my wife says) 'old man checks', keep fit and healthy and maybe slow down on the alcohol and bad fatty, sugary and salty foods.

Some of the below wrestlers were still in their primes with a lot still to offer the wrestling industry, while others were legends of the industry who didn't get to enjoy their retirements. This is not an extensive list of every wrestler that has sadly passes away, just a list of the wrestlers who were at some stage were regular viewing for me, and therefore 'my friends'. I send my wishes and thoughts to all their family and friends.

Lance Cade - 29

Crash Holly - 32

Test - 33

Owen Hart - 34

Yokozuna - 34

Brian Pillman - 35

Umaga - 36

Eddie Guerrero - 38

Davey Boy Smith - 39

Chris Benoit - 40

Rick Rude - 41

Miss Elizabeth - 42

Big Boss Man - 42

Earthquake - 42

Mike Awesome - 42

Brian Adams (Crush) - 43

Dino Bravo - 44

Curt Hennig - 44

El Gigante/Giant Gonzalez - 44

Bam Bam Bigelow - 45

Jerry Blackwell - 45

Junkyard Dog - 45

Hercules - 45

Toni Adams - 45

Andre the Giant - 46

Big John Studd - 46

Hawk - 46

Sherri Martel - 49

Steve Williams – 49

Chapter 10   When wrestling lets you down

Since watching 'The Empire Strikes Back" in 1980, I became a Star Wars fan for life. But even as good as the Star Wars movies were, there are moments in the franchise that you wish George Lucas should never have done. The Jar Jar Binks character in 'The Phantom Menace' is for nearly every Star Wars fan over 10 is a prime example of where George Lucas missed the mark, had a shocker or was drinking that day he came up with the character idea. The TV show Happy Days episode where 'The Fonz' jumps a shark while water skiing in his leather jacket coined the phrase "jump the shark" where a TV showed lost the plot and lost viewers. And even sporting teams sometimes miss the mark where CEO's, coaches and management loose fans by releasing players or signing players they shouldn't (in Australia any club signing Willie Mason is a prime example!). In the wrestling world, there is many times when the writers, wrestlers, company owners and even us fans have "jump the Shark", have had a shocker or just plain f*#k up!

As much as I personally enjoy watching my wrestling, there have been many matches and moments that have made me cringe, shake my head and just think "that was wrong". I am not talking about when one of my favourites loses a title or match or Christian losing the World Heavyweight title after only 2 days... or if there is a big face turn, or even someone winning a title who shouldn't (…Santino Marello holding the US title, or hornswoggle winning the Cruiserweight title, or Gillberg winning The light Heavyweight title!!). I am talking about moments where the idea, concept or gimmick should have stayed in the discussion room. Gimmicks such as The Gobbledygooker or Perry Saturn and his 'Moppy', or ideas that are of poor taste such as Big Boss Man driving a car and dragging Big Shows Father's coffin, or Big Boss Man getting Al Snows to eat his own dog, the Big Boss Man's Dog House in a Cell match against Al Snow, or the Big Boss Man being 'hung' after the Hell in a Cell Match against The Undertaker……..in fact really anything that involved the Big Boss Man in the 90's and beyond..(I offer no disrespect to Ray Taylor as in the late 80's and early 90's I enjoyed watching him perform, and he was one of my favourites during that time, it is just a lot of the story lines he had towards the end of his career in the WWE should not have occurred.)

Being a long-time wrestling fan I have seen many times where a wrestlers gimmick has been just plan awful, or inappropriate, or un-amusing, or just wrong. It could be a gimmick that is based on a current trend, that just did not work when transfer to the wrestling ring, or a gimmick that was before or past its time. For those NWF, when we are talking about wrestling gimmicks we mean:

> "A wrestler's personality and/or other distinguishing traits while wrestling. It can also be an implement used to cheat.[2] Some gimmicks, like CM Punk's being straight edge, are based on real life" Wikipedia 2012

The following list is those wrestlers whose gimmicks I did not enjoy, or did not understand or did not care about. These were wrestling gimmicks that missed their mark, and in some cases were dead set awful and I even felt embarrassed for the wrestler involved. Some of these wrestlers have been lucky enough to eventually find a gimmick that works for them others not so lucky:

- Fake (or the replacement) Razor Ramon and Diesel-1996 – When your 2 biggest draw cards jump ship to a rival wrestling company, what do you do?? Well since you own their gimmicks, how about replace the wrestlers but keep their gimmicks. Here we get a Razor Ramon who is not Scott Hall, and a Diesel who is not Kevin Nash. No surprise that it didn't go down well with us fans and was quickly discarded.

  A quick side note that the fake Diesel was none other than Glenn Jacobs. Glen would also have other failed gimmicks such as Issac Yankem DD (Jerry Lawler's personal Dentist in the WWF/E) and The Christmas Creature (USWA). However Glen would later get a gimmick he could use and make his own, that of WWE legend Kane!

- Giant Gonzalez 1993 – The idea, a giant near 8 foot man hired by Manager Harvey Wippleman, who burst onto the scene in the WWF/E and went on to attack and feud with the Undertaker. However for me and many wrestling fans it was his outfit that would not allow us to take him seriously (and the fact he was worse and slower in the ring that The Great Khali), no matter how hard the Undertaker tried to put him over. Gonzalez wore a full body suit that featured airbrushed muscles with bushy hair attached. After his feud with the Undertaker ended so did Gonzalez WWE and wrestling career.

- Zeus 1989 – Here is an idea….have the number 1 face of your company, Hulk Hogan star in a major movie No Holds Barred, so far so good even if the movie was not an academy award winner. Then to help promote the movie have that said top guy, Hulk Hogan feud with the actor who plays the villain in the movie Tom Lister Jr……..no wait, I have a better idea have your number 1 guy Hulk Hogan feud with the **fictional** villain character from the movie Zeus. So here we have now have a movie villain character wrestling the actor who starred as his nemesis in said movie…confused, not believable even for wrestling standards…...yep. No surprise that Zeus didn't hang around too long.

- Max Moon 1992 - was a cyborg soldier from The Future, we should just stop there, however it gets worse, like Giant Gonzalez, the costume he had to wear was just plain awful (and I have read it cost something like $1300…nearly as much as a Rick Flair robe!).

- Mantuar 1994 – I really like my Greek and Roman mythology and the many mythical creatures, and really like the history and story of the beast known as the Minotaur. However I do not enjoy my wrestlers coming to the ring wearing a great big bulls head and running around in circles like he has a bad case of mad cow decease. Enough said!

And just to show that bad wrestling gimmicks are not just a WWF/E thing, here are some of the best of the worst wrestling gimmicks in I have found in wrestling history.

- The Shockmaster 1993 – The blue glittered covered Storm Trooper helmet, wasn't the only thing that The

Shockmaster had against him. It is known as one of the most (unintentional) funniest things to happen in wrestling still today…

"He was set to debut in an 8-man tag match with partners Davey Boy Smith, Dusty Rhodes, and <u>Sting</u>. However their opponents wanted to know the identity of the mystery man, so they called them out on "A Flair for the Gold". Sting exclaimed, "All I can say is, he is going to "shock" the world, because he is none other than... The Shockmaster!!" (How could this go wrong, right?) There was an explosion, you could feel the suspense building. A large figure with a glitter helmet burst through the wall and....fell flat on his face. Fred Shockmaster scrambled to get his helmet back on (for fear of angering Darth Vadar). The host, Ric Flair, yelled out "Oh, God!" Davey Boy (God rest his soul) used some foul language. On a side note: He did not fall "on his arse", he fell on his

face...GET IT RIGHT SMITH! His voice over,

Ole Anderson, couldn't contain his laughter. It

turns out Ottman had been sabotaged. Not by

communists, but by David Crockett, Crockett

has nailed a piece of lumber to the wall, without

telling The Shockmaster, causing him to trip."

Nick Bolyard (Contributor) on March 7, 2011

The Bleacher Report.

Unfortunately for Wrestler Fred Ottman he also had to put up with other terrible gimmicks such as Tugboat, Typhoon and even The Super Shockmaster! Needless to say poor Fred didn't have a too successful career.

- Glacier (WCW) 1996 – a blatant rip off, of the Subzero character from the Mortal Kombat franchise, where his costume and ring entrance cost more than my entire yearly wage!!! I likes Subzero, this wrestler just looked like something from a very bad b grade movie.

- Arachnaman, (WCW) in 1991. – Another blatant rip off, this time of our real favourite arachnid, Spiderman. How this even got passed through a planning meeting is beyond me, but is was no surprise marvel comics also found it offensive!

While these bad gimmicks ended many careers, there have been many wrestlers who have returned strongly after receiving a bad gimmick. As mentioned previously Glen Jacobs would eventually have to go through 3 poor gimmicks before finding 'Kane". William Regal had the awful gimmick of 'The real Man's Man" which had him coming to the ring dressed from a lumber Jack to Construction worker. Chavo Guerro had to put up with his gimmick of "Kerwin White", a stereotypical, middle-class, white, conservative, Anglo-American man. Even The Rocks first alter ego of his Rocky Mavia sucked, before he turned it into The Rock. While there is sure to be further embarrassments for wrestling company's we can only hope that they have learnt from their pasts when deciding gimmicks for wrestlers......surely the Funkasaurus Brodus Clay isn't that bad......

Besides poor wrestling gimmicks, wrestling companies have also given us some absolutely terrible story lines. While I do not expect realism in all my stories (I am quite happy to believe The Undertaker has mythical powers), there are sometimes where stories have crossed boundaries and are of poor taste or do not make any sense or follow any logical at all, or the writers seem to run out of ideas and drop the story altogether hoping us fans will forget all about it. A great story can elevate matches between two wrestlers, while a poor story can do the complete opposite, and like a poor gimmick, can lead to the end of a wrestlers careers with a company.

Some of the poor wrestling stories that I remember, or made me feel either very uncomfortable or worse, made me tune our rather than tune into the show include:

- Mae Young and Mark "Sexual Chocolate' Henry's hand baby'. Yes you read that correctly in story which was bad enough to start off with, Mark Henry in his 'Sexual Chocolate' days started dating 76 year old Mae Young. If images of seeing these two sharing a bed, making out and talking dirty to each other wasn't enough to put you off, then having a 76 year become pregnant just about put this story in the ridiculous stakes. But then let's add in a 76 year old pregnant women getting power bombed through a table, causing an early labour. Then to top it all off, instead of having a baby, let's have the 76 year old lady give birth to a 'hand'! There are many other moments that I would rather forget that include Mae Young and a lack of clothes, so we will just leave it there. (On a quick side note, I did have a laugh when on Raw's 1000 episode Mae young was shown walking next to a giant hand!). Then there were those many wrestling swim suit contest, where we had to shy away from the TV when Mae Young decided she also wanted to "show her puppies" ....(throw up gargle)

- Many wrestling fans like myself will not only shudder at the thought of Mae Young naked, but also the name **Katie Vick**. This story and feud with Kane and Triple H, is still one of my low points as a wrestling fan. Without going into too much detail (there are plenty of references to be found on the internet), topics such as Necrophilia, drunk driving causing death, and autopsies are topics not for the wrestling ring (one of the good things about being the pg era is that stories like this will not happen again). To quote a very famous line (in Australia) from Derryn Hinch "Shame WWE Shame"!

- I would like to know what the WWF writers were thinking when they came up with this idea for the The Brian Pillman/Stone Cold Steve Austin feud. The idea was to have Pillman pull a gun and threaten to shoot Austin who had broken into his house. While breaking into other wrestlers houses has been done quite often, thankfully promoting gun violence has not.

- Every now and then we like to see the underdog win the big title. Shawn Michaels in his Iron Man match at Wrestlemania 12 being a prime example, Rey Mysterio beating Kurt Angle and Randy Orton for the Word Heavy Weight Championship at Wrestlemania and of course Christian beating Alberto del Rio in a ladder match to claim his first Word Heavyweight title to name a few.

But what annoys most of us fans is when people who shouldn't win or hold the main title of a company does. This story has unfortunately has a habit of re-occurring and includes those 'winners':

- Actor David Arquette winning the WCW
- Vince Russo holding the WCW title
- Sgt Slaughter winning the WWE title in 1989
- Mr Vince McMahon WWE and ECW titles

If you would like more reading on some of the "crap" that wrestling can sometime give us then get these books into your wrestling collection:

- *WrestleCrap: The Very Worst of Pro Wrestling (by R. D. Reynolds)*

Outrageous costumes, cartoonish characters, and scripted storylines are featured in this retrospective look at the no-holds-barred stunts pro wrestling promoters have used to attract viewers. Covering such entertainment catastrophes as an evil one-eyed midget, George Ringo the Wrestling Beatle, and Goobledy Gooker, the wrestler who emerged in the arena from an egg, this merciless evaluation of such organizations as World Championship Wrestling and the World Wrestling Federation will leave wrestling fans and critics alike in stitches. The choices of promoters and producers are reviewed in an effort to understand the motivations and imaginations behind the often incomprehensible and laughable stunts that have baffled even die-hard fans.

• *The WrestleCrap Book of Lists! (By R. D. Reynolds)* Ever wanted to know the worst career choices pro wrestlers made upon retirement? Or which kung fu chop-socky wrestlers would make Bruce Lee do a backflip in his grave? *The WrestleCrap Book of Lists!* Has all that — and much more. The gloves are off as best-selling author RD Reynolds and his co-author Blade Braxton pull no punches in looking at some of wrestling's biggest mistakes, most comical mishaps and most egotistical performers.

I have given wrestling companies and the writers a hard time over poor decisions made in gimmicks and stories, but we also should look at the wrestlers themselves, who can chose a path or make a decision they possibly shouldn't that has ended up hurting their careers and respect from us fans. Whether it has been the use of drugs (recreational, prescription or enhancing), infidelity, drink driving etc, wrestlers behaviour on the outside of the ring, especially now in the internet days, can affect how we fans perceive them in the ring. This is not just isolated to wrestling but I feel to all sports as here in Australia, League, AFL and Union sports stars a very quickly turned upon by fans for behaviour that is judged to be unacceptable. This has resulted in some players getting transferred from the current club, or sacked or even having to play a different code or play in a different country because of their actions. Just ask ex Canberra raider player Joel Monaghan, what a simple drunken photo with a friends dog can do for you career.

In fact usually when a wrestler does make a mistake, it is very quickly reported on, via news broadcasts or through wrestling websites. There have been many current and former wrestlers over the years that have ended up in these new reports, or even worse ended up behind bars due to something done away from the ring. Jeff hardy being a high profile example, due to his recreation drug use was nearly sent to gaol (jail) due his issues with drugs. It cost him WWF/E and TNA titles and contracts for periods of time, as well showed many parents that maybe he is not an ideal role model for their kids. Other well-known wrestlers to end up with their own personal mug shot include

- Billy Gunn / Kip James 1990 disorderly conduct
- Big Show Paul Wright allegedly exposing himself 1998
- Chris Jericho & Gregory Helms Public intoxication in 2010
- Jim Neidhardt drug possession 2010
- The Sandman resisting arrest 2008
- Razor Ramon / Scott Hall resisting arrest 2011
- Ric Flair road rage incident 2005
- Stone Cold Steve Austin striking in 2003

And just to show that it is not just the boys misbehaving out of the ring

- Sunny domestic violence issues 2012
- Lita / Amy Dumas driving offenses 2011
- Kaitland driving offences 2012
- Awesome Kong Driving offenses 2010

I enjoyed watching Matt Hardy wrestle. I enjoyed watching his career with the WWE/F through his tag team with his brother Jeff, and then onto his single career. I remember some great matches he was involved in, whether they were tag team (such as the TLC matches) or his matches with Edge, MVP or against his brother Jeff. I was also one of many fans who hoped he would eventually have a WWE major title run (besides his ECW world Championship). However in 2010 Matt Hardy went off the rails with some bazaar behaviour and internet blogs and videos. Many like me believe his behaviour was a result of pent up frustration about being overlooked by the WWE, however his rants, weird blogs only isolated himself from those same fans who supported him, rather than rallying us. Matt would end up with a brief stint in TNA, but again poor behaviour decisions including a drink driving charge led to his termination. Matt I have read has decided to get help, and I do wish him the best, and a return to wrestling someday.

If there was one wrestler whose behaviour and attitude destroyed what could have been a long and successful career was that of The Ultimate Warrior. At the height of his popularity, after being promoted to the face of the WWF/E, the Warrior would "self-destruct" and never be the same again. I recommend for those interested watching "The self-destruction of The Ultimate Warrior" for a full recount of exactly caused is downfall, and why many of us fans today believe that maybe he is a few shrimps short of the Barbie, or a few sandwiches short of a picnic, or a few beers short of a six-pack! Greed, thinking your bigger than the company itself, having to high of opinion of yourself while are good characteristics to have in the ring as a character, behind those curtains, those behaviours will not get you far.

What makes a good wrestling fan, is that we can acknowledge that our favourite form of entertainment is not perfect all the time, and for every bad gimmick, feud or story there are usually plenty of great gimmicks and stories to focus on. For every 'Shockmaster', there is an Undertaker, or a Kane, a Mankind or a Shawn Michaels to focus on, for every Katie Vick story/feud there is Stone Cold vs. Vince McMahon feud, or a Cm Punk and Chris Jericho Best in the World story. While disappointed with the actions outside of the ring of some wrestlers, I liked to think I will turn my attention to those who performance and attitude outside the ring are worthy of our respect, such as CM Punk, Christian, Mick Foley or Edge.

Chapter 11   My top 10 Wrestlers

This is the start of my 'list' chapters, and there were a couple of ways I could go. I could of listed who I think are the best wrestlers (and later matches, tag teams etc.), of all time, but there are so many criteria to determine this, and there are so many of these lists to be found on the internet, I'd feel I was just re-hashing lists already out there, as well as there are way more qualified people writing those list! So I have decided to list **my** top 10. These are the wrestlers (and next chapters the matches and tag teams) that made me glad I am a wrestling fan. These are the wrestlers I cheered for whether they were baby faces or heels, who I got disappointed when they didn't win, or ecstatic when they did, especially if a title was involved. These are the wrestlers whose matches I wanted to see and enjoyed watching, or whose promos I enjoyed hearing.

While I will give a quick Bio on each wrestler, if you want to find full information on their careers, including wrestling companies they performed in, titles won, movies acted in, music or books etc., then I suggest 'Google', I am going to give a quick breakdown of why they are **my** favourites. Like mentioned at the start of my book, many of these wrestlers had fantastic careers and matches other than just in the WWF/E, however it was through this company where I got to watch and enjoy these wrestlers perform.

Number 10 **Hulk Hogan**

* Date of Birth

11 August 1953, Augusta, Georgia, USA

Birth Name

Terry Gene Bollea

Wrestling names

The Hulkster

Hulk

Hollywood Hogan

Hulkamania

Thunder Lips (From the Movie Rocky III)

Mr America

Height

6' 4½" (1.94 m)

The Hulk Hogan that makes my list in from his performances in the 80's to early 00's, not his work now for TNA. Growing up in the 80's and being a wrestling fan, Hulk Hogan was the man, he was the face not only of the WWF/E, but for most of us he was the face of wrestling. He was the first person that I and my friends would talk about when our conversations turned to wrestling, He was the person we wanted to watch and see on TV or in a PPV, not only to enjoy his matches, but also enjoy (and then repeat over and over again) those wonderful promos (and well known quotes) such as ......
'To all my little Hulkamaniacs, say your prayers, take your vitamins and you will never go wrong;
Watcha gonna do brutha! when the hulkster runs wild on YOU? ;
Well, ya know something Mean Gene...

.....these what was we expected in promos in the 80's, over the top, loud and boy did Hulk Hogan know how to get you pumped and ready for his fights. He took on and beat all comers including

Rowdy Roddy Piper, Andre the Giant, King Kong Bundy, Earthquake and The Macho Man to name a few, and when he did loose, it was only because his opponent had to cheat!

While Hogan will never be classed as the greatest technical wrestler he did know how to get a crowd on their feet whether live at the event, or back home in our lounge rooms. The fans, I and my mates would leap of their seats when we first heard his ring entrance (*Rick Derringer's "Real American*) or when he started his customary legendary comebacks or otherwise known as "*Hulking up*". These included taking hits and punches from his opponent, shaking them off, pointing at his opponent, followed by several punches, an irish wip to the ropes, a big boot to the face, then when the opponent was on the mat, his famous leg drop, pin and victory. Then of course after his victory you got those famous Hogan poses, which every wrestling fan has done in the mirror once or twice in their life (those who say they haven't are lying!!!).

Hulk Hogan was the Ultimate Good Guy for me growing up, he was this generations John Cena, except loved by most not just those under the age of 12, and while I missed most of his WCW and New World Order run, I hear and read that he was just as impressive in the heel role, and initially it was some of his best work. While I will try and forget about his movie career (with the exception of his cameo role in Rocky III), his TV series "Thunder in Paridise"or his current work on TNA, his importance to me (and many older) wrestling fans cannot be denied.

Wrestlemania III, Hulk Hogan vs. Andre The Giant was where I became a Hogan fan. Watching Hogan overcome the odds, and beat 'The Giant' was the ultimate hero victory, and turned me into (for a while at least) a HULKAMANIAC! Some of his other matches that I suggest you watch, to understand his affect he had on the fans (including me), and why he is number 10 on my list are:

vs.   The Rock – Wrestlemania 18

vs.   The Ultimate Warrior – Wrestlemania VI

vs.   The Macho Man – Wrestlemania V

vs.   Hogan vs. "Nature Boy" Ric Flair, Bash at the

Beach '94

Number 9   **Ultimate Warrior**

Date of Birth

16 June 1959, Queens, New York, USA

Birth Name

Brian James Hellwig

Wrestling Names

Ultimate Warrior

Height

6' 3" (1.91 m)

When I first started watching wrestling, Hulk Hogan was

the top baby face, and stayed that way for a long time. Then in

1987, it wasn't a breath of fresh air, but more like a tornado that

came tearing his way through the WWE! Here came this

colourful face painted wrestler who sprinted to and then ran

around the ring, before shaking the ropes like a mad man. His

matches were always very fast paced, however like Hulk Hogan, the Warrior will never be known for his in ring technical wrestling, but for his power and energy in the ring.

While there are many issues relating to the Warrior behind the curtains (I recommend watching *The Self Destruction of the Ultimate Warrior* for further information regarding his reasonably short career) in those late 80's early 90's his matches were a must see. His feuds with The Honky Tonk Man, Rick Rude and Macho Man all helped established the Ultimate Warrior as mine (and many others) new hero. He has tried a few comebacks, all of which have been classed as failures, however it is initial run in the WWF/E which I will remember him fondly.

Also like Hogan, his promos were over the top, even though most of the times you didn't understand a single thing he was saying, although that was the entertaining part! He also like Hogan he had his own version of 'Hulking up', this was done by his opponents hits having no effect on him as he shook the ropes, before gorilla pressing, and splashing his opponent for the win. Wrestlemania VI was a definitely must see for me, as the main event of that match was Hulk Hogan vs. The Ultimate Warrior.

Sometimes anticipated matches have a way of not living up to the hype, this one didn't!

His flame burnt out as quickly as it was lit, but he was a major part of why I continued to watch wrestling. Two of what I recommend are his best matches, also make my top 10 matches list, which goes to show why he is number 9 on my list.

vs.   Honky Tonk Man – Summer Slam 88

vs.   Macho Man Randy Savage, career v career match Wrestlemania VII

vs.   Hulk Hogan – Wrestlemania VI

vs.   Ravishing Rick Rude – Summer Slam 1990 & SummerSlam 1989

Number 8   **Junkyard Dog**

Date of Birth

13 December 1952, Charlotte, North Carolina, USA

Date of Death

2 June 1998, nr, Forest, Mississippi, USA (automobile accident)

Nickname

JYD

Stagger Lee

Big Daddy Ritter

Height

6' 3" (1.91 m)

When I began my wrestling addiction, the first wrestler I'd always hope to see on those Saturday mornings was JYD, better known as The Junk Yard Dog. Whether it was his dancing, the fact I could imitate his voice (well at least I thought I could), his headbutts while on all fours, or his long chain and dog collar JYD will in my mind be the reason I am a wrestling fan today.

I was unfortunately only able to see him towards the end of his career, never saw him win any titles; in fact I cannot remember watching to many feuds where he walks out the winner. But that never diminished him as one of my favourites, and I am lucky with the internet I can go back and watch him in his prime. During his early WWF (WWE) days, he was only 2nd to Hulk Hogan as one of my favourites, but unfortunately never seen by the powers at be worthy of any title runs, whether that was political reasons, that's for another possible book.

These days wrestlers who bring kids into the ring and dance with them are not taken seriously in the ring (such as Brodus Clay), however JYD was the exception to the rule as he was seen as tough as nails while wrestling in the ring, but could celebrate in the ring with kids from ringside.

JYD had some memorial feuds with Greg Valentine, Terry Funk and 'King' Harley Race, and is number 8 on my list due to his importance in my wrestling history.

vs.   Greg Valentine. (03/31/85, Wrestlemania I)

vs.   Randy Savage. (11/07/85, The Wrestling Classic Tournament)

Number 7   **King Kong Bundy**

Date of Birth

November 7, 1957 (age 54)-Atlantic City, New Jersey

Wrestling Names

Big Daddy Bundy

Boom Boom Bundy

Chris Cannon

Crippler Cannon

Chris Canyon

King Kong Bundy

Man Mountain Cannon, Jr

Height

6 ft 4 in (1.93 m)

Another of my 80's favourites, and my first acknowledgement that a 'heel' can still be someone's favourite wrestle. From squashing jobbers on Saturday morning, to destroying his opponents with splashes and slams, King Kong Bundy for me was the ultimate heel. He was huge, angry, and aggressive and was someone you just wouldn't like to mess with. With his trade mark bald head, black singlet tights, and 458 lb (208 kg) frame King Kong Bundy lived up to his namesake!

Wrestlemania II where he fought Hulk Hogan for the title, was the first time I was cheering for another wrestler to beat

Hulk Hogan, which is why he is higher on my list. King Kong Bundy was one of those wrestlers who would 'put over' his opponent ("Putting over" simply means to make somebody look better (or stronger) than they were before) and just like my number 8 favourite JYD, King Kong Bundy would leave the WWF/E without a well-deserved title (I mean surely if Mark Henry gets a title run, then surely Bundy deserved one!!).

One of my all-time favourite Bundy memories is from Wrestlemania III where in a 6 man tag team match against Hill Billy Jim, that also included each wrestle have 2 little people as part of their team. Bundy had Little Tokyo and Lord Littlebrook, while Hill Billy had Little Beaver and the Haiti Kid. All match little beaver was annoying Bundy, to a point where to the disbelief of everyone, Bundy picks up Little Beaver, slams him, then follows that up with a big elbow!!! In today's standards it's not much considering what WWE Hornswoggle goes through, but in the 80's it was one of those "Holey Shit' moments.

Feuds with Andre The Giant, Hulk Hogan, JYD and Hill Billy Jim were the main focus Bundy had while in the WWF/E, and led to the following memorable matches, and the reason he is my number 7 favourite wrestler

vs.   S.D. Jones – WrestleMania I

vs.   Hulk Hogan – Wrestlemania II

               With Big John Studd VS Hulk Hogan & Andre the Giant – Saturday night main event 85

vs.   Hill Billy Jim – Wrestlemania III (was a 3 man tag match which includes The famous 'little beaver' squash)

Number 6   **Stone Cold Steve Austin**

Date of Birth

18 December 1964, Austin, Texas, USA

Birth Name

Steven James Anderson

Nickname

The Texas Rattlesnake

Stone Cold

The Bionic Redneck

'Stunning' Steve Williams

Height

6' 2" (1.88 m)

"Austin 3:16 says I just whipped your ass"......with that famous line Steve Austin went from just another wrestler, to be on his way to be the biggest star in the WWF/E. I did not get to see Steve Austin in his WCW run (as Stunning Steve Williams), and did not take that much notice of him as "The Ringmaster", along with manager "Million Dollar Man" Ted Dibiase, but I did start to take notice of him after winning The King of The Ring and uttering those famous words.

Then at Wrestlemania 13, in a submission match against Brett 'The Hitman' Hart, Stone Cold proved not only to me, but to many fans (and of course WWE powers at be) that he was a main event superstar. The match (will I will discuss later in the book) ended with Austin in the role of an anti-hero, who went onto a fantastic worked feud with the 'boss' Vince McMahon, that elevated Stone Cold to the top superstar in the WWE, and one of the main reasons why eventually WWF/E ending winning the 'Monday night wars'.

After 'King of the Ring', Wrestlemania 13, and the Vince McMahon feud, Stone Cold went on to feud with many of the top WWE superstars including Mick Foley, Triple H, The Undertaker, Shawn Michaels, but his Feud with The Rock, and their Wrestlemania matches at Wrestlemania 15, 17, and 19 that are a big highlight for me.

His out of the ring promos and segments were also essential viewing, whether it was driving to the ring in a beer truck or Zamboni, filling Mr McMahon's car with concrete, or fighting with Booker T throughout a supermarket (I recommend watching all 3 on you tube). Just like Hulk Hogan, Stone Cold had plenty of well-loved catchphrases including:

Austin 3:16 says I just whipped your ass!
And that's the bottom line, cause Stone Cold said so!
...and that's all I gotta say about THAT!
What?

I'm goin' stomp a mudhole in ya and walk it dry!

Drinking beers after (and possibly before) his matches, using his famous 'stunner' finishing move on everyone (which to me is one of the best ever finishing moves due to its simplicity yet still looks like it could end a match and the fact it could come out of no-where), and anywhere in the arena, Steve Austin was what the WWE Attitude Era was all about. Whether it was winning titles, Royal Rumbles or just 'kicking someone's ass, whenever Stone Cold was on TV you knew you were in for some great humour, sarcasm and action.

So grab a few cold beers and sit back at watch Stone Cold Steve Austin at his best during the following matches:

vs.   Shawn Michaels Wrestlemania 14

vs.   The Rock Wrestlemania XVII (actually any of The Rock and Stone Cold's Wrestlemania matches could be listed here!)

vs.   Triple H 2/3 Falls Match (Singles, Street Fight, Cage Match), No Way Out 2001 vs.   Bret Hart No Disqualification Submission Match, Wrestlemania 13

vs.   Royal Rumble 1997 (watch for the moment Austin looks at his wrist waiting for the next opponent)

Number 5   **The Rock**

Date of Birth

2 May 1972, Hayward, California, USA

Birth Name

Dwayne Douglas Johnson

Nickname

The People's Champion

The Brahma Bull

The Great One

The Rock

Height

6' 5" (1.96 m)

When Rocky Mavia first debuted at 1996 survivor series, with a terrible haircut, goofy smile and streamers as part of his ring attire, no-one would have thought that this 3rd generation clown, would turn out to be one of the best entertainers of all time. Originally he was pushed down our throats, by the WWF/E, with this backfiring with the fans, as they hated him and started chanting the now famous "Die Rocky Die!" and "Rocky Sucks"chants. Then came WWF Raw is War 8/18/97, where The Rock cut his first major promo on why he turned heel and joined the Nation of Domination. By starting to refer to himself in 3rd person as 'The Rock' and calling himself "The Peoples Champ', he was on the fast train to becoming the WWF/E biggest star.

Known as one of the best wrestlers on the mic, The Rock has many famous and well known catchphrases, which managed to get everyone off their seats screaming them with him. These include:

Finally...The Rock...has come back to [insert whatever city he's in at the time]

You want to go one on one with the Great One!

Who in the blue hell are you?

Can you smell what The Rock is cooking!

The Rock will take you down Know Your Role Boulevard which

is on the corner of Jabroni Drive and check you directly into the

Smackdown Hotel!

It doesn't matter what you think

This isn't sing along with the Rock

The Rock will take that .....[insert a item], turn that son of bitch

sideways, and stick it up your candy ass!

I suggest typing in "The Rocks best Promos" on you tube, and sit back and just admire his work and interaction he has with the crowds. From his "sing-a-long with the Rock", his backstage segments with 'The Hurricane', to his Stone Cold Steve Austin eulogy, The Rock rarely missed when he was given a microphone. Along with Chris Jericho, The Rock would be one of the only two wrestlers I know of where fans could sit back and watch them sing in the ring instead of wrestle and not get jeered out of the ring!

While he left wrestling, to go to Hollywood and make movies, and is possibly the only really wrestler to have a great and successful movie career (many have tried), his popularity in the wrestling world never diminished, and his yearlong Wrestlemania feud with John Cena in 2011/2012 is a tribute to his everlasting popularity.

The Rock has some great and intense feuds with Triple H, Mankind, Brock Lesner, The Undertaker, Chris Jericho but it was his feuds with Stone Cold Steve Austin that shows what great wrestling feuds should all be about. All their Wrestlemania matches, promos, and TV spots are all great TV viewing, and I am waiting very intently for a Rock V Austin DVD.

As good as The Rock's intensity could be, his humour in and out of the Ring was just as entertaining. His work with Mankind (The Rock'n'Sock Connection) is priceless (try and get copy of the Mankind's 'This is your Life' tribute to The Rock on Raw). His put downs of commentators, his fellow wrestles, the fans and anyone else in between are why he will be always regarded as one of the best wrestling superstars of all time. I recommend purchasing his DVD, but watching any of the following matches to see just how good he was in the ring, as a story teller, and performer:

vs.   Stone Cold Steve Austin Wrestlemania XIX (as above any of The Rock and Stone Cold's Wrestlemania matches could be put here!)

vs.   Hulk Hogan at Wrestlemania 18 (icon vs icon)

vs.   Triple H, Intercontinental Title Ladder Match, SummerSlam 1998

vs.   Mankind, I Quit Match, Royal Rumble 1999

vs.   Triple H, Iron Man Match for the WWE Title, Judgment Day 2000

Number 4   **Edge**

Date of Birth

30 October 1973, Orangeville, Ontario, Canada

Birth Name

Adam Joseph Copeland

Nickname

Adam Impact

Sexton Hardcastle III

The Rated R Superstar

Damon Striker

Mr. Money In The Bank

The Ultimate Opportunist

The Master Manipulator

Height

6' 5" (1.96 m)

Making his way to the ring through the crowd, performing with Christian and their five second poses "for those with the benefit of flash photography", (attempted) in ring sex to celebrate his first WWE title win, right from the start, and all the way through his career, Edge was to do things differently to every other wrestler I had seen before, which is the reason I enjoyed watching him so much.

After initial success early on in his career winning the WWF/E Intercontinental title, Edge would later join the stables of 'The Brood', followed by 'The Ministry', before forming a tag team with his kayfabe brother Christian. It would be this tag formation that was the start of placing both these wrestlers on to my top 10 list. From their goofy and cheesy '5 second poses', to their comedic spots in the back (especially with Mick Foley) to their skills, and risk taking in the ring, Edge and Christian were a must see for me. In the attitude era, it was their feuds and matches with The Hardy Boys and The Dudley Boys that were essential viewing every time these teams step into the ring together.

After the ending of their tag team, Edge would go on to win several more Intercontinental titles before an injury sidelined him. It was his return and heel turn at the Taboo Tuesday PPV in October 2004 that turned Edge from a successful mid-card wrestler to a successful Main Event star. His feuds, battles and matches with John Cena, Batista, DX (with Randy Orton) and The Undertaker were for me must see viewing.

If I think back to some memorable moments I have witness in wrestling, many of them involve Edge. He was the 1st (and 3rd) to cash in the 'money in the bank' contract on an injured, worn out champion, spearing Jeff Hardy (who was swinging holding onto the tag team belts) from a ladder, spearing

Mick Foley through the ropes crashing into a flaming table, being chokeslam through a ring by The Undertaker, being given a John Cena Attitude Adjustment through two tables and while losing his WWE Championship in the first Elimination Chamber at No Way Out in 2009 he would then knock out Kofi Kingston and take his spot and win the World Heavy Weight Championship in the 2nd Elimination Chamber later that same night, the only man to compete in 2 Elimination Chambers on the Same night.

For the majority of his career, Edge wrestled with the WWF/E, and his lists of accomplishments are that of a Hall of fame representative (which he also received in 2012):

- United States Championship (1 time)
- World Heavyweight Championship (7 times)
- World Tag Team Championship (12 times) – with Christian (7), Chris Benoit (2), Hulk Hogan (1), Randy Orton (1) and Chris Jericho (1)
- WWE Championship (4 times)
- WWF/E Intercontinental Championship (5 times)

- o WWE Tag Team Championship (2 times) – with Rey Mysterio (1) and Chris Jericho (1)
- o Fourteenth Triple Crown Champion
- o King of the Ring (2001)
- o Money in the Bank (2005 – first ever, 2007) - although his 2007 win, was in a singles match against Mr Kennedy where the brief case containing the contract was up for the winner of the match
- o Royal Rumble (2010)
- o WWE Hall of Fame (Class of 2012)

Sadly Edge would have to retire due to injuries after Wrestlemania 27, and I wish him all the best in his retirement. I have read his book, watched his move to the movie making business, and of course enjoyed reminiscing over his favourite matches and moments on his WWE DVD's, 'Decade of Decadence' and 'The Story of Edge'. If you really want to appreciate Edge's in ring career then first watch the series of matches with Christian against The Hardys and The Dudley's.

You could also watch any of his many of his Elimination Chamber matches, his Royal Rumble win, triple threat matches, TLC matches or Money in the Bank matches. But for just some classic, matches against some of the greats in wrestling then try these classics:

vs.   Chris Benoit (last man standing Match Backlash 2005)

vs.   Undertaker (Hell in a Cell Summer Slam 2008) – (any of the series of matches between these two you could watch and enjoy)

vs.   Mick Foley in a Hardcore Match (Wrestlemania 22)

vs.   with Lita and Foley vs. Dreamer, Beulah and Funk (ECW one night stand 2006)

vs.   Matt Hardy (Summer Slam 2005)

Number 2 – tied   **Christian**

Date of Birth

30 November 1973, Kitchener, Ontario, Canada

Birth Name

William Jason Reso

Nickname

Jay

CLB: Creepy Little Bastard

Captain Charisma

The Showstealer

The New People's Champion

The Instant Classic

Height

6' 2" (1.88 m)

The success of Edge and Christian as a tag team was due to a mix of skill in the ring, chemistry between the two, and the humour they generated. Watching these two you could actually see two friends having the time of their life. While Edge was the more well known of the two wrestlers, I found myself drawn to

Christian as the preferred member of the tag team. Whether it was those ridiculous sunglasses he wore, or being caught out by Mick Foley pretending to throw up, or the way he 'sold' moves, I enjoyed his role in this tag team. As with most tag teams in the wrestling industry, they were due for a falling out, with the traditional one member turning on the other. It would be Christian turning on Edge as a result of jealously after Edge had won Intercontinental title and the King of The Ring. While the majority of people supported Edge, it was here my 'fondnesses for Christian as a single wrestler took off, and I became a 'Peep'. With his tantrums in the ring during his losing streak, his win against Jericho at Wrestlemania or just his ability to get the crowd riled up all made Christian essential viewing for me.

I was very disappointed when he left WWF/E and signed with TNA, only for the fact I didn't have at the time access to TNA on my TV. While I missed watching his TNA run, I kept regular checks vie the TNA website, and enjoyed reading he was doing so well.

As disappointed as I was on Christian leaving the WWE, I was ecstatic on his return. To see him win the ECW title was great, but to see Christian finally win the WWE World Heavy title at the Extreme rules PPV event in 2011 I think I was nearly as excited and emotional as he was! (And as pissed as he was when he lost it 5 days later!!!)

I have never seen a poor match that involved Christian, this has included his tag teamwork, single of group matched such as Money in The Bank. While I missed viewing most of his work at TNA, I have been able to watch these matches via you tube. Whether he wins the match or loses, you know after watching the match that you have been thoroughly entertained. I have come to term with the fact he is used now as a top WWE superstar to put others superstars over, and help lift them from mid card to upper level. However I would like to see him with one good WWE or World Heavy Weight title run.

To appreciate the skills Christian has in the ring the firstly I recommend any of the tag team matches between Edge

& Christian vs. The Hardys vs. The Dudleys. As for his single career then I recommend these:

WWE career

vs.   Chris Jericho Wrestlemania XX

vs.   Shelton Benjamin   TLC 2009

vs.   Alberto Del Rio Extreme Rules 2011

Intercontinental battle royal   Judgement day 2003

vs.   Randy Orton any match from their 2011 feud

TNA career

vs.   Jeff Jarret Against all Odds 2006

vs.   Samoan Joe Destination X / Bound for Glory 2007

vs.   Kaz Ladder match Genesis 2007

Number 2 – tied   **The Undertaker**

Date of Birth

24 March 1962, Houston, Texas, USA

Birth Name

Mark William Calaway

Nickname

The Lord of Darkness

The Man From the Dark Side

The Phenom

The American Bad Ass

Big Evil

The Deadman

The O.D. - Original Deadman

The Punisher/Punisher Dice Morgan

Mean Mark Callous

Texas Red

'Taker

The Undertaker

The Last Outlaw

The Demon of Death Valley

Height

6' 10½" (2.10 m)

I could not split The Undertaker and Christian when it comes to my 2nd all-time favourite wrestlers. While Christian has battled to eventually rise to the top, The Undertaker has dominated since arriving at the Survivor Series PPV in 1990. For the past 20 or so years I have enjoyed watching The Undertaker change, adapt, morph, and return his character to suit the era of wrestling. The Undertaker has managed to stay a top level drawcard even though battles for the WWF/E and World Heavy Weight Titles have been limited compared to other main event wrestlers.

The Undertaker has been involved and responsible for developing some of the most unique matches in the history of wrestling. The Inferno matches against Kane, buried alive matches against Stone Cold, Mankind and Vince McMahon, Casket matches against Mark Henry, Yokozuna ad Kamahla and of course (including the very first) Hell in the Cell matches against Shawn Michaels, Brock Lesner, triple H and of the course Mankind. The Undertaker has feuded with the who's who of the WWF/E Universe including Hulk Hogan, The Rock, Kurt Angle, Edge, Batista, Rick Flair, Randy Orton, Triple H, Shawn Michaels, Brett Hart, Kane, Deisel (Kevin Nash) and Mick Foley.

His last 6 Wrestlemania matches between Batista, Edge and of course his classics matches against Shawn Michaels (25, 26) and Triple H (27, 28) have stolen the show on each night, and his Wrestlemania 'Streak' is now becoming a bigger match than any title and is the match I look forward to the most. I have just purchased The Undertakers Streak 20-0 DVD, and am currently enjoying revisiting some of his earlier Wrestlemania matches against Snuka, Bundy and Jake the Snake Roberts.

From his classic feuds and battles with Mankind and then his brother Kane, to feuds for titles against Batista, Stone Cold, Edge and Kurt Angle, The Undertaker was able to have fantastic matches with a variety of different wrestlers. Even feuds and matches against some weak (in skill level and ability) wrestling giants such as The Giant Gonzalas and Kahali have failed to derail The Undertakers legend status.

While The Undertaker only wrestles a couple of matches a year, and if they are as good as his last 4 Wrestlemania's then I hope he sticks around a few more years. One great Undertaker match a year, is a lot better than 10 Santino Marella matches. For those who want to experience why he is such a legend in the world of wrestling, then watch every one of his Wrestlemania matches. Other matches that showcase just how good The Undertaker is in the ring:

Hell in the Cell matches against Brock Lesner, Edge or the very first ever Hell in the Cell match against Shawn Michaels would be a great place to start after the Wrestlemania matches.

2007 Royal Rumble

Undertaker Debut   Survivor Series 1990

vs.   Mankind Hell in a Cell, King of the ring 1998

(Nearly any match between these two were classics, buried alive, boiler room brawls etc)

vs.   Undertaker vs. Kane Unforgiven 1998 (first ever inferno match)

vs.   Undertaker vs. Edge, One Night Stand (2008)

vs.   Undertaker vs. Kurt Angle, No Way out 2006

vs.   Kurt Angle vs. the Rock, Vengeance (2002)

vs.   Hulk Hogan, Survivor Series (1991)

Number 1

Mick Foley / Mankind / Cactus Jack / Dude Love

Date of Birth

7 June 1965, Long Island, New York, USA

Birth Name

Michael Francis Foley

Nickname

The King of Hardcore

The Boiler Room Dwellar

The Deranged One

Mankind

Dude Love

Cactus Jack

The Hardcore Legend

Height

6' 2" (1.88 m)

With stars like Shawn Michaels, Kurt Angle, Rick Flair, Brett Hart, John Cena, Randy Orton and Triple H or strong candidates for number 1 on a lot of fans favourite list, then how did Mick Foley make mine? Quite simply I enjoyed watching him perform in the ring, in a Cell, in a boiler room, or all over the arena. He has been one of the few wrestlers to have succeeded in all of the main wrestling companies WWF/E, ECW, WCW and TNA, as well as succeeded outside the ring (and my inspiration) in the literacy world with many successful books.

For me, here was a wrestler that looked like (minus the missing ear) a normal everyday person, not chiselled out of stone, 7 foot tall or had 24 inch 'pythons'. It showed me (and I assume many other fans) that you didn't need to look like a body builder or elite athlete (sorry Mick), to be successful in the world of wrestling.

While he has been called a glorified stunt man, by fans and even some of his wrestling peers, it is those risks and bumps he took, that made him a fan of mine. Whether it was those memorable falls from the top (and through) the Hell in The Cell, being slammed on hundreds of thumbtacks, being hit with a barbed wire baseball bat, being speared through flaming tables, or even just sitting in the ring pulling out his own hair, Mick's commitment to his style of wrestling in his career has made him, I feel, the success he is today. He was never going to win awards for technical ability, but the ability to take punishment, and make other wrestlers look good he excelled at. Aaron Hubbard said it best in 'The Contentious Ten 08.30.10: Mick Foley Matches'.

'.....*Mick knew that he could lose to anyone and stay over, so he made it his goal to get other people over. He was a star-maker that was so good at what he did that he became a star himself...*'

Mick Foley possibly has the worst win/loss record of any top draw wrestling legend, with the possible exception of King Kong Bundy. Wrestlers such as Randy Orton, Edge, Triple H, The Rock and of course The Undertaker had their status as wrestling legends increase after their battles with Mankind/Mick Foley. It was Mick's battles with the Undertaker that made everyone not just me stand up and really take notice just how good Mick Foley is.

The promos he did in his early WWF/E as Mankind were always very eerie, while towards the later of his career, he showed you can be humorous, and take the mickey out of yourself, however still be a big threat in the ring (Santina Marella study Mick's career!). His work with Edge and Christian as The Commissioner, and then with The Rock during the Rock'n'Sock during their run showed added another avenue for us fans to enjoy Mick Foley besides his hardcore Wrestling. From introducing us to 'Mr Socko', The Rock's This is your life, Dude Love's dancing, Mick could very quickly change gears from humour to derange as his intense feuds with Randy Orton, Rick Flair and Edge showed.

Away from the ring, Mick has become a very successful author (and as mentioned my inspiration for this literacy masterpiece), great work with charities and has his own comedy tour (which I hope he brings to Australia). He is a great family man, great entertainer and my all-time favourite wrestler after 30 years of watching. To show why he is number 1 on my list watch these matches:

vs.   Triple H Street fight Royal Rumble 2000

             And Hell in a Cell No way out 2000

vs.   Edge Hardcore Match Wrestlemania 22

vs.   Undertaker Hell in a Cell 1998 king of the Ring

vs.   The Rock I quite match

             WWE Championship No Disqualification Match:
             Raw is War 1.4.99

Mick Foley & Edge (w/ Lita) vs. Terry Funk & Tommy Dreamer

(w/ Beulah McGillicutty) ECW One Night Stand - 11/06/06

Vs.   Terry Funk King of the Deathmatch: 1995

vs.   Austin vs Triple H SummerSlam 1999

vs.   Randy Orton Backlash 2004

vs.   Sting for the World Title Lockdown 2009

Chapter 12   My top 10 Tag Teams

Now this list was actually very hard to come up with, as I wanted the list to not include those tag teams that were formed by two established stars. Teams such as 'The Rock 'n' Sock connection (The Rock and Mankind), 'The Brothers of Destruction' (The Undertaker and Kane), DX (Triple H and Shawn Michaels), Mega Powers (Hulk Hogan and Rand Savage), The Colossal Connection (Andre The Giant and Haku), and of course current tag team champions 'Hell No' (Kane and Daniel Bryan) etc. While all fantastic teams, they were always going to be successful due to their high profiles as individual wrestling stars. In fact there have been many wrestlers that have had many different but successful tag team partners. Wrestlers such as:

- Kane - has held tag team titles with The Undertaker; Mankind; X-Pac; The Hurricane; Rob Van Dam; The Big Show and now with Daniel Bryan.
- The Big Show – has held tag team titles with Kane; The Undertaker; The Miz and Chris Jericho

- Edge – has held tag team titles with Christian; Hulk Hogan; Randy Orton; Chris Jericho; Chris Beniot and Rey Mysterio

- Kofi Kingston – has held tag team titles with CM Punk; Evan Bourne and R-Truth

I have decided that my top 10 tag teams are those teams that either started out as tag teams, or were at the very least mid-card wrestlers that formed a tag team early on in their careers. As with my previous list, this is not a list of what I feel are the BEST tag team ever, just those teams who I barracked for and enjoyed watching. There is no surprise to see a lot of these teams I have selected as my favourites were around during the Rock'n'wrestle and attitude eras of wrestling.

Honourable mentions to those who just missed out on my list but could quite easily be on many other top lists include Legion of Doom; Paul London and Brian Kendrick; Los Guerreros; MNM; and The Nasty Boys.

10.   **Powers of Pain**

The Warlord and The Barbarian made up the physically intimidating duo of 'The Powers of Pain'. This team instantly became one of my favourites due to their "Conan the Barbarian" look, size and power (as I was a big fan of the Arnold Swarzenegger Conan movie). In a time when the tag team of Demolition was dominating the tag team scene, these two monsters gave us someone who could match not only them physically, but also not be intimidated by Demolition. Even in an era where big gimmicks ruled, the WWF/E, these two stood out as a team to watch. While there are many wrestling fans who believed these two were a basic Road Warriors rip off, with similar face paint, costumes and attitude, for us fans who only had the WWF/E to watch we were unaware of this, although I doubt it would have changed my opinion.

A great tag team finish move of the opponent being held in the Electric chair position by The Warlord, and getting a diving clothesline by The Barbarian, was the common way this team won their matches, mixed with strong power moves, slams and good team chemistry, this team from their debut against jobbers 'Iron Mike Sharp and Tony Ulysses were a force to be reckoned with. Although unfortunately for The Powers of Pain, this team would leave the WWF/E without holding the Tag team Titles. However prior to their WWF/E run, they did have some success while in Jim Crockett's Promotions.

The Powers of Pain had a fantastic feud with Demolition which included a fantastic double face/heel turn at the 1988 Survivor Series, where the then manager of Demolition Mr Fuji, would turn on his team and align himself with The Powers of Pain. They would continue this feud until Wrestlemania in 1989. Other feuds followed with The Bushwackers and The Rockers, before they split to try and find success as single competitors. Unfortunately success in single competition did not come, with the only notable record either achieving was The Warlords 20 year record of lasting only 2 second in the 1989 Royal Rumble.

Full Championships and accomplishments

- National Wrestling Alliance

- o NWA World Six-Man Tag Team Championship (1 time) - with Ivan Koloff
- Pro Wrestling Illustrated
  - o PWI ranked them #97 of the 100 best tag teams during the "PWI Years" in 2003
- Wrestling Observer Newsletter awards
  - o Worst Tag Team (1989)
- Other Championships and Accomplishments
  - o WWWA Tag Team Championship

9. **British Bulldogs**

My first viewing of the British Bulldogs – Davey Boy Smith and The Dynamite kid (Tom Billington), was at Wrestlemania III, and a long with Tito Santana were in a match against The Hart Foundation and Danny Davis. While they ended up losing that match, they became an instant favourite of mine. The combination of Davey Boy's strength and power, and the Dynamite kid's technical ability, made this team a formidable opponent for other teams. With their trade mark Union Jack ring attire, English entrance music, and Gorilla slam and diving head-butt combination finish, this team were always a joy to watch in the ring.

They had only one success at holding the WWF/E tag team titles, by defeating the "Dream Team" of Greg Valentine & Brutus Beefcake at Wrestlemania II, and would have to feud with that team all year to achieve that ultimate goal. They followed with feuds against The Hart Foundation, Demolition, The Fabulous Rougeaus and The Islanders and introduced us to 'Matilda', a British Bulldog as their mascot before matches. It would be a backstage falling out with The Rougeaus brothers that would lead to The British Bulldogs leaving the WWF/E.

Injuries and a falling out with Davey Boy Smith would hamper Tom Bilington's career, while Davey Boy Smith would go onto to have a great single career, with some great battles against his brother-in-law Brett Hart, which included what many believe is the best Summer Slam match ever, at Summer Slam 1992 held in Wembley Stadium in England for the Intercontinental title. Davey Boy Smith would unfortunately pass away in May 18th 2002.

Full Championships and accomplishments

- Pro Wrestling Illustrated
  - Ranked #5 in the top 100 tag teams of the "PWI Years" in 2003
- Stampede Wrestling
  - Stampede International Tag Team Championship (2 times)
- World Wrestling Federation
  - WWF World Tag Team Championship (1 time)
- Wrestling Observer Newsletter awards
  - Best Wrestling Manoeuvre (1984) Power clean dropkick
  - Tag Team of the Year (1985)

8. **The Hart Foundation (original)**

While many people would laugh at a tag team wearing bright pink outfits, this team had the muscle in Jim 'The Anvil' Neidhart, and the in ring technical skills of Brett Hart to back up their ring attire choice. I would always love watching the promos of this team which would have the serious Brett Hart, followed by that unique Jim Neidhart laugh. Just like the British Bulldogs, I first saw this team in that Wrestlemania III match, and while initially as they were heels, not liking this team, by the time of the face turn in late 1988, I was hooked on "The Pink and Black Attack".

They would go on to win the WWF/E titles twice, defeating the British Bulldogs in Feb 1987, and at SummerSlam 90, and then the Hart Foundation would defeated Demolition in a two out of three falls match for the tag titles in a classic match which showcases just how good tag team wrestling can be. The Hart Foundation would feud with all the top teams during their WWF/E run, including Demolition, The Fabulous Rougeaus, The Rockers, British Bulldogs, The Nasty Boys and Strikeforce.

A nice finish move called the 'Hart Attack" where Jim Neidart would lift an opponent in a bear hug like grip so the opponents head was above his, while Brett would bounce off the ropes and deliver a clothes line, was a great way for this team to win many matches. Early on in their career outside interference by their then manager Jimmy "the mouth of the South" Hart, would assist in many of their wins, however once their turn to fan favourites it was their skill, power and team work which would set up most of their wins.

While Brett Hart would go on to have a fantastic 'hall of fame' singles career, winning major Heavyweight championships in WWF/E and WCW, Jim would find some success back in the Tag team division with 'The New foundation' which included Brett's brother Owen. Both unfortunately would go on to have their fair share of controversy, with Brett's 'Montreal Screwjob' incident, and Jim being arrested on drug related charges.

Full Championships and accomplishments

- Pro Wrestling Illustrated
  - PWI ranked #37 of "The 100 Best Tag Teams" of the PWI Years in 2003
- World Wrestling Federation
  - WWF Tag Team Championship (2 times)

7.   **The Dudley Boys (Team 3D)**

Many have this team written down as the best Tag team in Wrestling History, due to their success in all of the major US wrestling companies. Bubba Ray Dudley, and D-von Dudley have dominated the tag team divisions not only at the WWF/E but also ECW, TNA, and even around the world in places such as Japan and the independent scene (as you will see in their list of championships and accomplishments).

My fond memories of this team, in their run with the WWF/E, was their great feuds and battles with Edge and Christian, and The Hardy Boyz, through cage matches, table matches and of course culminating in those infamous TLC (Table Ladder and Chair) matches. Like most fans I would scream with Devon for "Bubba Get the tables" and watch them put someone through a table, usually via their 'Dudley Deathdrop' finisher, or a Bubba power bomb. Usually it didn't matter who went through the table as long as someone did, whether it was the opponents, managers, or 80 year old Mea Young. We fans would also scream "what's up" or more like

"Whaaaaats uuuuuuuuuup!!!!" as D-von dove from the top rope into the groin area of his opponent Bubba Ray was holding. You knew every time that these two step into the ring, they were going to give you some great entertainment.

They would go on to hold the WWF/E title 9 times, dominating the Tag team division from 2000 to 2003, and feuding with other teams such as the New age Outlaws, The Brothers of Destruction and La Resistance. They could swap between face's and heels very easily, but not matter whether they were on the side of good or evil, they were a team you were hoping to see when watching the TV.

While both Bubba and D-von have tried a couple of times for single career success, it has only been in 2012 with TNA that they would have what you would call success. While Bubba did hold the WWF Hardcore Title 11 times, and D-Von did introduce us to Batista, neither had major single success in the WWF/E.

Full Championship and accomplishments

- All Japan Pro Wrestling

- o AJPW World's Strongest Tag Team League (2005)
- Cauliflower Alley Club
  - o Other honourees (1997)
- Extreme Championship Wrestling
  - o ECW World Tag Team Championship (8 times)
- Hustle
  - o Hustle Super Tag Team Championship (1 time)
- New Japan Pro Wrestling
  - o IWGP Tag Team Championship (2 times)
- Pro Wrestling Illustrated
  - o PWI Match of the Year (2000) vs. Edge and Christian and the Hardy Boyz in a Triangle Ladder match at Wrestlemania 2000
  - o PWI Match of the Year (2001) vs. Edge and Christian and the Hardy Boyz in a Tables, Ladders, and Chairs match at Wrestlemania X-Seven
  - o PWI Tag Team of the Year (2001, 2009)
  - o PWI Tag Team of the Decade (2000–2009)

- Total Nonstop Action Wrestling
  - NWA World Tag Team Championship (1 time)
  - TNA World Tag Team Championship (2 times)
  - TNA Tag Team of the Year (2005)
- World Wrestling Federation / World Wrestling Entertainment
  - WCW World Tag Team Championship (1 time)[1]
  - WWE Tag Team Championship (1 time[1]
  - WWF/E World Tag Team Championship (8 times)

6.   **The Hardy Boyz**

Team two of three that gave us those famous TLC matches, Matt and Jeff Hardy were the high flying, risk taking brothers that would always leave us wondering (especially with Jeff) what they would come up with next.

After being jobbers for early on in the careers, by 1998 they would start their ascent to the top of the tag team division. They stood out with their unique ring attire, gen Y attitude and of course their high flying moves in the ring. Not only could they fly, but also take a fair amount of punishment as the battles with Edge & Christian and The Dudley Boyz showed. It was their initial feud in the Terri Rennels invitational (for her services as a valet/manager) with Edge and Christian that made many, including me sit up and take notice of these two brothers.

Initially being managed by Michael Hayes, they would dump him and later add another high flyer to their team in WWE diva Lita. The three of them would all manage to attempt some type of move/s from the top rope on someone during their matches. Their first Tag team titles came against APA (or as they were known then The Acolytes -Farooq and Bradshaw), and would go on to hold tag team titles in the WWF/E 7 times.

One of the few tag teams that have managed to split and has both members have some success as individual wrestlers, with multiple single titles between them including Jeff with the WWE title and Matt holding the ECW title respectively. They would also go on to what I feel have one of the feuds of the year in late 2009 early 2010 when a jealous Matt would attack Jeff over not getting the opportunities that Jeff had received. Some great matches with their Wrestlemania 25 extreme rules match being a highlight for me (as I always preferred Matt over Jeff!).

Full Championship and accomplishments

- Elite Generation Wrestling
    - EGW World Tag Team Championship (3 times)
- Gas Chamber Wrestling
    - GCW World Tag Team Championship (1 time)
- New Dimension Wrestling
    - NDW Tag Team Championship (1 time)
- Organization of Modern Extreme Grappling Arts
    - OMEGA Tag Team Championship (1 time)
- Pro Wrestling Illustrated
    - PWI Match of the Year (2000) vs. The Dudley Boyz and Edge and Christian in a Triangle Ladder match at Wrestlemania 2000
    - PWI Match of the Year (2001) vs. The Dudley Boyz and Edge and Christian in a Tables, Ladders, and Chairs match at Wrestlemania X-Seven

- o PWI Tag Team of the Year (2000)
- World Wrestling Federation / World Wrestling Entertainment
  - o WCW Tag Team Championship (1 time)
  - o WWF/E World Tag Team Championship (6 times)
  - o Terri Invitational Tournament

5. **Demolition**

Many wrestling fans of WCW in the 80's claimed that Demolition were a rip off tag team of the Road Warriors at the time. Some others argue that the Powers of Pain were more of a rip off than Demolition, but for fans like myself who were kids at the time and didn't understand backstage politics of wrestling companies, the team of Ax and Smash -Demolition were just the toughest tag team I had ever seen.

With their KISS-like makeup, black studded leather outfits including those leather-covered hockey masks (although if someone said a tag team was wearing black studded leather today, I would have a different impression of that tag team!), physical size, and their *Demolition Decapitation* (Backbreaker hold/Diving elbow drop combination) finisher, this team would dominate the WWE from 1987 to 1991, and would hold the WWF/E tag teams titles 3 times including the period from March 27, 1988 - July 18, 1989 (478 days).

They had some tremendous feuds with the likes of the Hart Foundation, Strikeforce, The British Bulldogs, The Colossal Connection, The Brain Busters and of course The Powers of Pain, which included that famous double face turn at Survivor Series.

In 1990 Demolition added a third member to their team, Crush. While we now know this was due to food poisoning and injuries to Ax, who as the year went on, tended to compete less and less in the ring. In the 1990 Summer Slam demolition and The Hart Foundation would give us fans a classic 2 out of 3 falls for the WWF/E tag team titles. With interference from the Road Warriors, packaged for the WWF/E as The Legion of Doom, Demolition would lose this match, it was the last time they would hold the tag team titles. Ax eventually left the WWE, leaving Smash and Crush to be the only two Demolition members remaining.

Smash and Crush would both have very limited and some would say unsuccessful singes careers, but this doesn't dampen the image of Demolition being one of the great tag teams of all time.

Full Championship and accomplishments:

- Great Lakes Championship Wrestling
    - GLCW Tag Team Championship (1 time, current)
- Keystone State Wrestling Alliance
    - KSWA Tag Team Championship (1 time, current)
- Legends Pro Wrestling
    - XWF/LPW Hall of Fame Inductees- Class 2008 (2/22/08)
- Pro Wrestling Illustrated
    - Ranked #59 of the 100 best tag teams during the "PWI Years" in 2003
- Pro Wrestling Report

- o PWR Lifetime Achievement Award (2010)
- United States Xtreme Wrestling
  - o USXW Tag Team Championship (1 time, current)
- World Wrestling Federation
  - o WWF Tag Team Championship (3 times)

4. **The Rockers**

In an era of large men dominating the WWF/E, in both singles and tag team divisions, the Rockers 'flew' into many fans hearts due to their aerial and tag team combination moves. Shawn Michaels and Marty Jannetty while dominated in size, they would use their quickness to their advantage, quick double team moves, and of course fly from the top rope (which included my favourite move of theirs the double missile dropkicks from adjacent corners) to gain victories over their more physical opponents.

After a brief WWF/E appearance as the Midnight Rockers in 1987, they would return as the shorten The Rockers in 1988 and started feuding with The Brain Busters. Research tells me these teams had some tremendous non-televised matches with their match on January 23, 198 rated as one of the 50 greatest matches in the PWI 10th year anniversary issue. They would feud with many other teams over the next couple of years including The Fabulous Rougeau Brothers, The Bolsheviks, Twin Towers, Akeem and the Big Boss and The Powers of Pain.

In 1991 The Rockers went through series of miss-understandings in the ring would eventually break up on the infamous Brutus the Barber Beefcake 'Barbershop' interview segment on January 11, 1992, where Shawn Michaels would superkick Marty Jannetty and throw him through a window. Shawn would go on to have a fantastic Hall of Fame singles career, while Marty would leave the WWF/E and have a less successful career. This would lead to many Tag teams fearing 'The Marty Jannetty factor' of one member becoming successful, while the other having a failed wrestling career.

The history books show that The Rockers would never win the WWF/E tag team titles however this is not entirely true:

On this date in WWF history: The Rockers win the tag team titles -- but don't get to keep them

On October 30, 1990, "The Rockers" (Shawn Michaels and Marty Jannetty) won the WWF tag team championship by defeating "The Hart Foundation" (Bret Hart and Jim Neidhart) in a two-out-of-three falls match at a television taping in Fort Wayne, Indiana. They went on to defend their newly-won titles, successfully, just a few days later against the tag team of "Power & Glory" (Hercules Hernandez and Paul Roma). Neither of those bouts would ever make a televised broadcast.

That's because the WWF stripped The Rockers of the tag team titles and gave them back to The Hart Foundation.

But why?

"HBK" said in his book that "The Hitman" pulled a Hulkster and politicked his way back into the title. Other reports claim that Neidhart was being fired, which necessitated the change, but then took the titles back when the promotion reached an amicable agreement with "The Anvil."

Or maybe the match was just so bad, thanks to a broken ring rope, that no amount of editing could splice together something that didn't flat-out embarrass the product.

Whatever the reason, The Rockers wore the gold for a few days, even though the WWE still refuses to acknowledge it.

Indiana screwjob

(By Jesse Holland on Oct

http://www.cagesideseats.com)

Full Championship and accomplishments:

- American Wrestling Association
    - AWA World Tag Team Championship (2 times)

- Central States Wrestling
  - NWA Central States Tag Team Championship (1 time)
- Continental Wrestling Association
  - AWA Southern Tag Team Championship (2 times)
- Pro Wrestling Illustrated
  - PWI ranked them #33 of the 100 best tag teams during the "PWI Years" in 2003
- Wrestling Observer Newsletter awards
  - Tag Team of the Year (1989)

3.   **The New Age Outlaws**

Oh you didn't know............ your ass better call somebody!!!

It's me it's me it's that D.O.double g rollin with that a double crooked letter damn right... I'd like to welcome everybody to the Dogg House!! Ladies & gentleman boys & girls children of all ages.........

D-Generation X proudly brings too you.... Its/ soon to

be/WWF (The World Wrestling Federation) TAG

TEAM CHAMPIONS OF THE WOOOOOORLD

the Road Dogg Jesse James the Bad Ass Billy

Gunn......THE NEW AGE OUTLAWS!!!!

..........and if you're not down with that we got two

words for you SUCK IT!!!!!!!!

If like me, that entrance has you yelling and singing

along, then The New Age Outlaws of Road Dogg Jesse James,

and Bad Ass Billy Gunn were must see viewing during the

WWF/E attitude era. While along with Triple H, X-Pac and

Chyna they made up the New Degeneration X when Shawn

Michaels left due to his back problems, as a tag team, these two

would be on top for a long period of the attitude era.

While having fun in and out of the ring, these two could

switch to a vicious streak very easily as Mankind and Terry Funk

found out by being placed in a dumpster bin and rolled of the

stage, then beaten up further for good measure! While under

handed tactics usually aided their victories, it was this vicious streak and humour combo which appealed to me (and many other fans). Mick Foley would have a long ongoing battle with The New Age Outlaws, moving from tag team partners Chainsaw Charlie (Terry Funk), to Kane and even The Rock. The New Age Outlaws along with the rest of DX would battle the likes of The Corporation and The Nation of Domination.

When the team went their separate ways, both Road Dogg, and Billy Gunn had reasonable successful mid-card careers with both gaining championships such as Intercontinental and Hardcore titles.

Full Championship and accomplishments:

- Maryland Championship Wrestling
  - o MCW Tag Team Championship (1 time)
- Pro Wrestling Illustrated
  - o PWI ranked them #43 of the 100 best tag teams of the PWI Years in 2003
  - o PWI Tag Team of the Year (1998)
- TWA Powerhouse
  - o TWA Tag Team Championship (1 time)

- World Wrestling Federation
  - WWF Tag Team Championship (5 times)

2. **Bushwackers**

The Bushwackers Luke and Butch were destined to be one of my all-time favourites from the moment they made their debut in the WWF/E in 1989. Growing up in Australia, there weren't many 'local' wrestlers to support in the WWF/E. So when the Bushwackers came along, and I heard they were from New Zealand, I thought that is close enough to Australia to call them from my home town. It is something I later found out as I got older, that we Australians seem to do a lot (Actor Russel Crowe, Race Horse Pharlap, Music bands such as Split Enz & Crowded house).

Secondly, for reasons to this day I am still unaware of, when I was young my dad used to use the nickname Butch for me. So as there were no Craig's wrestling that I knew of, a tag team with a member named Butch was always going to grab my attention.

Thirdly, they managed to demonstrate a great combination of being portrayed as goofballs, (or hillbillies, or being few shrimp short of a Barbie), yet still being seen as a threat to opposition teams. It is something the likes of Santino or Zack Ryder should look closely at. Whether it was their signature arm movements, or their army pants and black singlet outfit, or their missing teeth or licking each other's, as well as opponents' and fans', heads, their comedy style appealed to me, to go along with their toughness in the ring. Their Sardine breath skits with Mean Gene always got a laugh out of me.

They would have some great battles and feuds with the likes of The Fabulous Rougeaus, Rhythm and Blues (Honky Tonk and Greg Valentine), The Nasty Boys, The Beverly Brothers, The Heavenly Bodies, The Natural Disasters, and The Headshrinkers. Leaving without ever holding the WWF/E tag team titles in 1996, The Bushwackers even 20 years on have left a memorable impression on me.

Just like many Tag teams of the rock'n'wrestle era, The Bushwackers had champion success in other wrestling companies in the 1970's and1980's, wrestling under the name of The Sheepherders. Under this name, Luke and Butch were less comical, and had a more violent and aggressive attitude in the ring.

As with The Warlord from the Powers of Pain, Luke would have his own Royal Rumble moment in 1991. Luke entered the ring at number 27 using the trademark Bushwhacker walk, but was grabbed, and thrown over the ropes by Earthquake, he didn't break walking form from the walk down, in the ring and then left the arena still swinging his arms up and down. It was the quickest elimination at the time of 4 seconds, and is still for me one of the funniest Rumble moments in history

Full Championships and accomplishments:

- Championship Wrestling From Florida
    - NWA Florida Tag Team Champion (1 time)
    - NWA Florida United States Tag Team Champion (1 time)
- Continental Wrestling Association
    - CWA International Tag Team Champion (1 time)

- Mid-Atlantic Championship Wrestling
  - NWA Mid-Atlantic Tag Team Champion (1 time)
- Pacific Northwest Wrestling
  - NWA Pacific Northwest Tag Team Champion (3 time)
- Stampede Wrestling
  - Stampede International Tag Team Champions (2 time)
- World Wrestling Council
  - WWC Tag Team Champion (2 time)

1.   **Edge and Christian**

Considering both wrestlers have ended up in my top 5 favourite wrestlers of all time, it is no wonder that they would top my tag team list. With a mixture of great humour in and out of the ring, great in-ring skill at either technical, hardcore or if need be high flying skills, this team I feel had it all.

While Edge had been around the WWF/E a little while, it was joining forces with his good friend Christian in 'The Brood' that he and Christian would start their successful tag team run.

Starting with a great series of matches with the Hardy Boyz for the Terri Invitational Tournament, and then of course moving to those TLC matches with The Hardys and The Dudleys, Edge and Christian delivered every time they were in the ring.

The backstage segments with Mick Foley, their "five-second pose" where, "for the benefit of those with flash photography", their con-chair-to (both Edge and Christian hitting an opponent in the head with a chair at the same time from different sides) and their goofy outfits, this team 'reeked of Awesomeness' and as far as I was concerned must see viewing every week on Raw. As a team they would hold the Tag team titles 7 times, and each would go on to hold the tag team titles with other partners after their split in 2001.

Their split as a result of Christian's jealousness towards Edge's success, would lead to a series of great matches between the good friends, and send them both on to successful singles careers, with major WWE / Heavyweight Championships between them. With Edge's career ending injury, a last Edge and

Christian tag team run will not occur which would of been great to see!

Full Championships and accomplishments:

- Insane Championship Wrestling
  - ICW Streetfight Tag Team Championship (1 time)
- New Tokyo Pro Wrestling
  - NTPW Pro Tag Team Championship (1 time)
- Pro Wrestling Illustrated
  - PWI Match of the Year (2000) vs. The Dudley Boyz and The Hardy Boyz in a Triangle Ladder match at WrestleMania 2000
  - PWI Match of the Year (2001) vs. The Dudley Boyz and The Hardy Boyz in a Tables, Ladders, and Chairs match at Wrestlemania X-Seven
- Southern States Wrestling
  - SSW Tag Team Championship (1 time)
- World Wrestling Federation/WWE
  - WWF Tag Team Championship (7 times)

- o WWE Hall of Fame (Class of 2012) - Edge
- Wrestling Observer Newsletter
  - o Tag Team of the Year (2000)

I should also point out that there were some great tag teams from other companies such as WCW, TNA who possibly would have been on my list had a watched these companies more. Teams from WCW such as:

- Midnight Express
- The Road Warriors
- Arn Anderson and Tully Blanchard (the Brain Busters in WWF/E)
- The Fabulous Freebirds
- The Steiner Brothers
- Harlem Heat

Over at TNA, while only a newish company, has already produced some great tag teams, such as:

- Beer Money Inc.
- The Motor City Machine Guns
- The British Invasion

13   My top 10 matches

This list is not what I think are the best 10 matches of all time as determining what makes a great match, whether it's wrestling, football, cricket or tennis, has many personal inputs to take into account. For example here in Australia one of the greatest Rugby League Grand Finals played was the 1989 Balmain Tigers vs. Canberra Raiders. Now due to the result, my team of the tigers losing, it all of a sudden becomes for me the worst Grand Final ever, one in which I will NEVER….EVER…. watch ever again. Super Bowl XLII between the Patriots and Giants is rated by many as one of the best Super Bowls ever, however I doubt many Patriot fans rate it so high. Wrestlemania 21 had what many believe to be an absolutely classic match between Shawn Michaels and Kurt Angle. However for me the highlights for that night was Edge winning the first ever Money in the Bank match, Undertaker beating Randy Orton and Batista beating Triple H, so The Michaels /Angle match was quickly forgotten by me.

These are the 10 matches that pulled at MY emotions, made me say "what just happened!" matches that I have watched numerous times, or were memorable because of the time, place, built up story or people I was with. Matches that made me laugh, matches that made me (nearly) cry and matches that left me feeling drained at the end. Some of these matches are not the best technical matches ever, and some many people might query why a match would make anyone's top 10, so possibly a better name for this chapter would be *"My top 10 most memorable matches"*. These are the matches that make me glad that I am a wrestling fan and continue to be a wrestling fan.

Some of these matches were at the end of a very well thought out stories and feuds, some were unexpected gems, some were huge surprises and some just were fantastic matches to watch due to the skill, commitment, and showmanship of the wrestlers involved. Some of these matches are not what you would class as traditional matches as they involve chairs, ladders, cages and tables, however, there are still a couple of traditional style that made my list. I would have loved to make this list a top 20, but we will have to settle for the top 10 for now.

Number 10

Funaki vs. Jamie Noble – March 3rd 2006 Sydney
Smackdown's Road to Wrestlemania Tour

I know a lot of wrestling fans would be asking how can this match, between these two wrestlers be in anyone's top 10 lists. At best, these two wrestling superstars managed cruiser weight titles, but wouldn't even be called mid card wrestlers' in fact these two were more jobbers than wrestlers.

Even on this night, these two with no current TV 'storey' behind them, came out as a filler between matches, but however in my opinion this match stole the show (and considering the main event was a fatal four way between Kurt Angle, Undertaker, Randy Orton and Mark Henry, it's even more impressive!), and its why it is my number 10 match of all time. Both wrestlers came out to what you call a polite reception, with most of the fans in attendance (including me), expecting a quick

5 minute match. After all we were there to see The Undertaker, Randy Orton, Booker T, not a couple of lowly mid card jobbers. After the 5 minute mark, with a mixture of nice cruiserweight moves, the first cover (as hoped), occurred, and followed by a kick out. Over the next 5-10 minutes we were witness to reversals, near falls and some great wrestling, with Funaki and Noble managing to bring the previous quiet audience into the match. The atmosphere went from being "I hope this ends quickly" to the "Ooohs and Ahhs and cheers when another kick out occurred.

I would love to give a play by play recount of the match, but unfortunately being a house show, way back in 2006, in Sydney there are no *You tube, DVD or even VHS* copies of the match (if you happened to be in Sydney that night and illegally taped the show, call me!).

While Funaki walked away with the win, the fact that these two went from polite acknowledgment by the fans in attendance, to a standing ovation, is why we wrestling fans, enjoy the 'sport' and not just the headlining names. This match showed me on that night that any match on any show, should be treated with respect, as you just do not know when a gem of a match will occur. I know a lot of people use these matches for toilet breaks, but in doing that you may just miss a little gem like this.

Number 9

Ultimate Warrior vs. Honkey Tonk Man IC title,

SummerSlam 1988

A match that last less than 1 minute, makes my list because of the way both wrestlers played their parts, the shock value of how the match came about and unexpectedness of what happened, (something that is becoming rarer and rarer today due to internet blogs, spoilers etc.).

Here we have (possibly) the greatest Intercontinental Champion of all, time and the longest reigning IC champion of all time in the The Honky Tonk man, currently in the middle of a feud with Brutus The Barber Beefcake. Due to injury Brutus is unable to wrestle, the IC title match at the first ever Summer

Slam in 1988. A replacement is found, but no-one one knows who. Honky Tonk is out in the ring waiting (evens grabs the mike and says "send anyone out, I don't care"). The crowd is restless, when all of a sudden, we hear the Ultimate Warriors music play. Out he comes at a million miles an hour, the fans in attendance started going absolutely wild. The Warrior jumps in the ring, bounces off the ropes clothes lines Honky Tonk, bounces of the ring again, pumps his arms to the crowd as the bell rings. A couple of more quick clothes lines and a big splash, a pin...and in less than a minute we have a new Intercontinental Champ!

If you decide to look at or revisit the match, watch carefully how well both The Honky Tonk Man, and Jimmy Hart react and 'sell' the shock of who it is and the mayhem that The Ultimate Warrior brings to this 1 minute match!

Number 8

Mankind vs. The Rock empty arena match Jan 1999

This match was in the middle of The Rock and Mankind's feud, and was something that I had never seen before, or since and held during half time of the 1999 super Bowl. For me it was either this match or the "I quit" match between these two at the 1999 Royal Rumble as my number 8 match. I ended up choosing this one, as like I mentioned I had never seen anything like this before, and to be able to pull off a great match with no energy from a crowd to feed off, makes their performance even more impressive (I still recommend watching their 'I Quit" match anyway). These two (who would later go on to entertain us some more as the 'Rock'n'Sock Connection) delivered a serious of matches that helped put over The Rock as a genuine Champion, and Mankind as a genuine main event superstar.

Here you had both The Rock and Mankind excelling at what they both best were known for. Mankind for his ability to take punishment such as being kicked and rolling down the arena stairs, to being thrown into chairs, fridges and a buffet table, And The Rock for his entertainment through his trash talking all the way through the match. It is not the best hardcore match ever, not the best falls count anywhere match, why it makes it on my list is because of the uniqueness of the match and how well both wrestlers played their roles. It was also had a brief return of somewhat, of Vince McMahon to the commentary role, and his bias towards the Rock and terrible lines like "if you can't take the heat..." while they were wrestling in the kitchen just plain corny but entertaining.

Other highlights for me during the match include Mankind attacking The Rock with a large bag of popcorn, The Rock trying to chat up an office worker during the match, Mankind taking and delivering a beating, yet still asking a forklift driver to "get out please", and the final image of Mankind holding the belt and saying "yo Adrien - I did it again!"

This match would of been higher on my list had the ending been shot or edited better, I enjoyed the idea of the ending, it just wasn't executed well, and took a lot of the gloss off the match.

Number 7

Triple H vs. Shawn Michaels vs. Chris Beniot Wrestlemania 20 (World Heavy Weight Title)

As mentioned in Chapter 8, when it comes to Chris Beniot people are very torn on whether he should be mentioned or not. I thought long and hard about including this match on my list. Why I shouldn't include it has already been discussed (Chapter 8), however, why I should include it eventually outweighed the negatives and why I put it on my list. This match also adds to Shawn Michaels 'Mr Wrestlemania' legacy, and why Triple H was the face of the WWF/E for so long (and not just because he married the boss's daughter!).

The build up to Wrestlemania 20 helped set the match, through the acknowledgment of Chris's 18 year history in wrestling, and never making to the top, Chris winning the Royal

Rumble to earn his shot, and the bad blood at the time between Triple H and Shawn Michaels. Triple H and Shawn were in the middle of a great feud that had already produced two classic matches, and Shawn Michael's had interfered at the Triple H/Beniot contract signing, by signing his own name on the contract, and hence adding extra friction between him and Beniot into the match.

The match itself was one of the best triple threat matches I have seen, with each wrestler getting their opportunity to shine, as well as great use of ring steps, ring posts and of course the poor old Spanish announce table. Each wrestler at different stages look like they were going to win, and both Triple H and Shawn Michaels ended the match with blood streaming down their faces.

I like many other people sitting at home, and the thousands in attendance at Madison Square Garden, leapt off our seats when Chris finally won a major WWF/E title. I will also admit to a little tear forming as Chris and Eddie Gurrero hugged in the middle of the ring, confetti falling from the ceiling, both as major WWF/E champions. It is one of those everlasting images of wrestling that makes it a great entertainment past time.

Number 6

Hulk Hogan vs. Andre the Giant at Wrestlemania III

When you have over 93 000 screaming fans on their feet, the biggest name in wrestling up against the biggest man in wrestling, you are set for not only a wrestling match but a wrestling event. If you are hoping for a fast pace, countering, technical match, then look elsewhere. Here you have a slow match dominator by Andre The Giant, until the Hulk Hogan's traditional 'Hulking up', followed by THAT body slam.

From the face-off at the start of the match, where Andre is just looking at Hulk, while Hulk Hogan is mouthing off, Hogan failing a body slam and nearly getting pinned in the first 30 seconds, and the electric atmosphere at the Pontiac Silverdome in Michigan, the match grabbed a hold of you and didn't let go until the end. This was good vs. Evil at its core, with 'The Giant' seeming unbeatable, and our 'hero' doing everything he can just to stay in the match. The commentary by both Gorilla Monsoon and Jesse 'The Body' Ventura helped sell the story of Hogan's back being damaged and how dominate Andre is during the match. This match shows just how good a wrestling can be with large athletes, and you don't always need the high flying moves to get crowds out of their seats.

If there was a roof on the Pontiac Silverdome it would have been blow off when Hogan finally slams Andre, and then performs his customary leg drop at the end of the match, and to many including myself, still to this day the best Wrestlemania ever!

Number 5

Mankind vs. Undertaker King of the Ring -- June 28, 1998

I know, after reading Mick Foley's 'Countdown to Lockdown' he has a great love/hate relationship with this match. While this match has helped cement his place in not just WWF/E history, but in wrestling history, he mentioned in his book he would rather not talk about this match again, due to it being nearly the first match talked about when people meet him. But after watching the match you can see why. Whether it is the image of Mick Foley being thrown off the top of the cell, 15 feet down through the announce table, The image of Mankind (Mick Foley) falling through the cell to the ring below, or the image of Mick Foley smiling while a piece of his tooth is in his nose.

Before this match, The Undertaker and Mick Foley as Mankind had already battled in many unique and dangerous matches that include:

- Boiler Room Brawl

    SummerSlam 1996

- First ever Buried Alive match   In

    Your House 1996

- Paul Bearer hanging in a cage match

    Survivor series 1996

The Undertaker vs. Shawn Michaels at Bad Blood in 1997 was the first WWF/E Hell in a Cell, however The Undertaker vs. Mankind match at King of the Ring in 1998 match showed us fans just how dangerous the Hell in The Cell can be. Many watching thought the match was over after Mankind firstly was thrown off the top, then after he was choke slammed through the Cell roof. Mankind managed to eventually get up after both falls, and even inflict The Undertaker with pain. The introduction of thumbtacks only added to the drama of this battle.

The drama that was added to the match included Terry Funk coming down to check on Mankind (Mick), even though they were currently in a feud of their own, and even Terry taking a cheap shot from The Undertaker to give Mankind some precious few minutes. While being stretched from his first fall from the cell, the image of Mankind, hoping off the stretcher and climbing straight back up the cell showed me his insanity and toughness all rolled into one.

While both The Undertaker and Mick Foley would be part of many more Hell in The Cell matches against a variety of opponents, this is the match I first think of when someone mentions Hell in the Cell, or Undertaker vs. Mankind.

Number 4

Undertaker vs. Shawn Michaels Wrestlemania 25

Before deciding on this match, I basically got a coin out of my pocket and flipped it. Heads was the Undertaker vs. Shawn Michaels Wrestlemania 25; Tails was The Undertaker vs. Shawn Michaels at Wrestlemania 26 (I recommend that you should watch both anyway). The Undertaker's undefeated Wrestlemania streak really started after his match against Rick Flair in Wrestlemania 18. After defeating Flair, The Undertaker then raised up 10 fingers singling that he is 10 – 0 at Wrestlemania. The Undertaker's next 6 Wrestlemania matches the Streak continued, and started to become a goal of many wrestlers to try and end and a match equal to that of a championship.

By Wrestlemania 25 many believed that The Streak will never be broken, especially after the last couple of 'Streak' matches at Wrestlemania (and no disrespect to any of the Wrestlers involved) against Mark Henry, Batista and Edge, while they were all enjoyable matches, the streak did not seem to be in any great threat. By mid-way through his match against Shawn

Michaels at W25, many fans including myself thought that the streak was going to be ended by 'Mr Wrestlemania'.

The match had just about everything you wanted in a classic match between two of the best ever in the WWF/E. The match had numerous near falls, many were after finishing moves were performed, high flying action by both Michaels and The Undertaker, and the build-up of atmosphere generated by the match had everyone at the edge of their seats (either at home, or at the event).

While the streak would continue, this match would set up a return match at Wrestlemania 26, and then matches between Triple H and The Undertaker at Wrestlemania 27 and 28. All three of those matches could have easily made my list!

Number 3

Shane McMahan vs. Kurt Angle Street Fight King of The Ring 2001

This match will shock many traditionalists and wrestling fans, considering Shane McMahon is not a wrestler. But he has many highlight matches included matches against his dad Vince, and ambulance match against Kane, and a falls count anywhere match against The big Show, which included him Jumping of the Titantron (Backlash 2001).

In this match Kurt Angle made Shane look good, (in fact Kurt Angle can make anyone look good in the ring) and delivered some of the most devastating moves I have seen. Throwing Shane through 2 glass plain windows would seem bad enough, however each took 2 to 3 attempts before breaking, and each failed attempt Shane landed awkwardly on his neck. Trash cans, and other around the ring equipment used, and the match only ended after an Angle slam from the top rope. At the height of the attitude era, this was the type of match that fans came to expect, mainly due to my number 2 favourite match…...

Number 2

Edge & Christian vs. The Hardy Boys vs. The Dudley Boys

Tables ladders and Chairs (TLC) SummerSlam 2000

This was firstly a matter of which match between these three to choose from. They were involved in 3 TLC matches, although their 3rd TLC match had the team of Chris Jericho and Chris Beniot as a fourth team, so should not be included. Then there was their straight ladder match at Wrestlemania 2000, and there TLC rematch at Wrestlemania X-7 which many believe was better than the one I selected, the first TLC match at Summer Slam 2000. I chose this one, as the Wrestlemania X-7 match had outside interference from Lita (although she did quickly interfere at the end of the match), Rhyna and Spike Dudley, while the Summerslam match was purely between these 3 teams and the first time I had seen anything like it.

Highlights of this match were many, and what these six put their bodies through was just amazing. But the major talking points after the match were:

- Bubby Ray's Bubba Bomb on Christian from the ladders
- Jeff Hardy falling on a ladder, and see sawing it into his brother Matt's face
- Jeff Hardy's Swanton off a 20ft Ladder through a table
- Bubba Ray being pushed Off the 20 foot ladder out over the ring crashing through 4 tables!
- Matt's Twist of Fate on Christian from high on top of the ladder
- Matt Hardy Being pushed of the 20 foot Ladder through tables
- Jeff and Devon hanging from the championship belts high above the ring

I have read that all six participates received a standing ovation by their fellow wrestlers once they went behind the curtains, which says a lot of what even other wrestlers thought of their performance that night. A match I have enjoyed revisiting while writing this book, and I am sure I will revisit again sometime soon!

Number 1

Ricky The Dragon Steamboat v Macho Man Randy Savage

Wrestlemania III

Besides my list, this match has also ended up being number 1 on many other peoples list as either their favourite, or one of the best matches of all time. The fact that it happened over 25 years ago, and still number 1 on peoples list, just goes to show the quality and the performance of Rickie 'The Dragon' Steamboat and Randy 'Macho Man' Savage delivered on that night, and why this match stole the show at Wrestlemania III.

So what made this match so great? It was a combination of great story writing, Steamboat returning from an injury suffered at the hands of Savage, as well as, Steamboats last chance at Savage's Intercontinental Title. Add in the ringside history between George 'The Animal' Steele and Miss Elizabeth, 93 000 screaming fans, and even before the ringing of the bell you have great tension and electricity in the air.

Then we get a great one on one wrestling match, that was fast pace, multiple pin attempts and off course multiple kick outs. Neither Savage nor Steamboat dominated the match for long periods, and each had great opportunities to win. The commentary from Gorilla Monsoon and Jessie Ventura was first class, and why they still are my favourite commentary pairing of all time. The ending, which was set up to mirror how Savage injured Steamboat a year ago, as well as having an ending that came from nowhere all added to the drama that happened in the ring during that match. It shows that even though chairs, tables, ladders, cages, cells, chambers, barbwire and blood are all great in a wrestling match, but when done properly a classic one –on-one match between two great wrestlers can be even better.

Honourable Mention:

Tyson Gibbs vs. Jack Bonza IWA Tournament final, IWA Wild West Tour Dubbo 23rd June 2012

There are many criteria that can make a match great, memorable, unforgettable and a totally enjoyable experience to watch and be a part of. Whether it's the wrestling chemistry between the wrestlers in the ring, the story that is told during the match, the emotion of the story/feud leading to the match or if the match has a memorable spot in it. Another criteria that can be added to what makes a great match is the atmosphere generated by the fans at ringside.

The match on this night was the final of a tournament for the IWA trans-tasman Championship (an independent wrestling company in Australia), held in front of around 200 people, of which (including my 4) 60 kids at our local RSL club in Dubbo. The final of the tournament was between the 'Our local boy' from Dubbo Tyson Gibb vs. the main heel of the night (played beautifully all night) Jack Bonza. As any dad would do to stir up his kids, I went for the heel on the night, with my 4 kids supporting Tyson. The match itself was of high standard, with some nice spots, and two wrestlers who even though had wrestled two matches already that night giving it all for us fans in attendance. From 'our hero' being locked in a submission hold, to our villain tormenting the kids at ringside, and a nice 'super' move to finish, these two local Australian wrestlers put on a well-designed match. The images I will take away from the match, and why I am giving it a very high honourable mention on my favourite match list, is due to the fun I had not only watching the match, but also watching my kids reactions and excitement they had throughout the match. Images that made me smile throughout the match include my 9 year daughter Ruby, leaving her seat and making her way to the front, so she could get a better look (she is my regular wrestling companion) at one of her new wrestling heroes and my other daughter (10 year old Zara) continually covering my mouth every time I yelled support for Jack Bonza. My oldest son Connor (10), chewing nervously on his jacket as the match progresses, and finally the image my youngest boy Max (7) screaming out at Tyson not to tap while being held in the STFU. Their cheers and relief on their smiling faces when Tyson won is a wrestling image and memory I will take with me forever.

Just missed out

There are many other matches that could have quite easily made my list. As mentioned any of The Undertaker's Wrestlemania matches from Wrestlemania 26-28, as well as these classics which just missed out:

Macho man vs. Ultimate Warrior Wrestlemania 7 Career ending match

Shawn Michaels vs. Kurt Angle Wrestlemania XXI, 2005

John Cena vs. CM Punk Money in The Bank 2011

Undertaker vs. Triple H III Wrestlemania 28

Bret Hart vs. British Bulldog (intercontinental match London), SummerSlam, 1992

Steve Austin vs. Triple H (3 stages of hell) No Way Out, 2001

Mick Foley vs. Triple H Street Fight Royal Rumble 2000

Mick Foley vs. Triple H Hell in a Cell No way out 2000

Honourable Mention (2):

The Royal Rumble

While this is type of match, rather than a particular match, I wanted to give this a special mention. Besides Wrestlemania, this is the Pay Per View and event I look forward to the most every year, and have ever since I saw my first Royal Rumble in 1990 which incidentally was won by Hulk Hogan. By this time there had already been two, with wrestling Legends Hacksaw Jim Duggan, and Big John Studd winning respectively.

In 1992 Ric Flair won the Royal Rumble, and with it the WWF/E championship which was up for grabs for the winner that night. From the next Rumble in 1993 and still today, the winner of the Royal Rumble gets to have a major title match at Wrestlemania which has added to the excitement and drama to the Royal Rumble match. Now while the Pay Per View itself also includes other matches, some of which have been stand-outs (Mick Foley vs. Tripe H street fight Royal Rumble 2000), I am specifically talking about the actual Royal Rumble match.

What makes this match so enjoyable is you have the battle royal style match, which is a multi-wrestler match where to be eliminated from the match you must be thrown over the top rope and have both feet hit the floor, mixed with the excitement of not knowing who is coming through the curtain next. You could end up with one on one in the ring, 3, 4, or even 10+ wrestlers in the ring at one time. The crowd will countdown the last 10 seconds of the time interval, and all heads would turn to the curtain to cheer, jeer or be shocked at who was coming down the ramp next. Over the years we fans have been shocked many times by surprised entrants, including female wrestlers Chyna, Karma and Beth Phoenix, a 'celebrity' Drew Carey, retired legends such as Rowdy Piper, wrestlers returning from injuries, and even the announce team of Michael Cole, Jerry Lawler and Booker T all participating! While there is usually 30 participants, by the time the Rumble comes around there are usually 4 to 5 wrestlers who due to current story lines can win the Rumble. These are usually one of the main event Superstars, as they will be heading to Wrestlemania later in the year. Now just to throw us fans for a loop, I would love to see just once a WWE superstar come from nowhere to win. A Superstar which is classed as mid-card or even upper mid card who we as fans know isn't going to win, but just give a great performance, last a long time or dominate for sections of the Rumble. I would love to see a WWE Superstar such as Christian (obviously), Drew Mcintyre, Damien Sandow, Cody Rhodes, Kane or even Mark Henry shock us one year and win!

While the entering the rumble last (usually the number 30 entrant), would usually give you some advantage, the same amount of winners (2) have won from entering last, as well as entering first! There have been rumbles where someone has dominated (Kane eliminating 11 men in the Rumble 2001), people that have won more than one Rumble (Stone Cold Steve Austin, Shawn Michaels and Hulk Hogan), a drawn rumble (Brett Hart and Lex Luger in 1994), and even Wrestlers that are returning from injury managing to win (Triple H, John Cena and Edge). The Rumble has been a match that has started many feuds, or given us a taste of a match we want to see (Hulk Hogan and Ultimate Warrior stare down (at the 1990 Royal Rumble).

While there have been 25 Rumbles so far (1988-2012), there have been those Rumbles that have stood out more than others. Whether it was who the Rumble winner was, magical moments from the match, records broken during the rumble or even those surprise entrants, there are Rumbles I preferred to over others.

The following are the highlights and reason why these are my top 10 most memorable Royal Rumbles:

- Royal Rumble 1990 – Hulk Hogan winning, my first Rumble. The Rumble that has started my love affair with this match and Pay Per View. This Rumble also had the first coming together of Hulk Hogan and the Ultimate Warrior, which would eventually happen a couple of months later at Wrestlemania VI. While only brief before being interrupted by the number 27th Entrant The barbarian, this meeting between Hogan and the Warrior gave us all a taste of something we really wanted and needed to see. Other highlights of my first Rumble, were Hogan winning, Andre The Giant catching his tag team partner and stopping him from being eliminated, and seeing The Bushwhackers win on the undercard (this didn't happen to often!!).

- Royal Rumble 2010 - Edge returning and winning. After being away from the ring for around 6 months due to injury, Edge returned at the 2010 Rumble entering at position 29. After spearing all remaining entrants upon entering the ring, Edge would eliminate Chris Jericho, fight with Shawn Michaels on the outside of the ropes, before quickly eliminating John Cena for the win. This Rumble is also remembered for the start, when a then NEXUS stable leader CM Punk, entered the match at 3, eliminated the first 2 wrestlers and started talking how he was going to win the Rumble. He would continue eliminating and talking up his chances for the next 4 participants, until Triple H came in to shut him up!

- Royal Rumble 1997 - Stone cold wins after being eliminated. Stone Cold Steve Austin enters the 1997

Rumble at number at number 5. He dominates early, to even be at a couple of stages in the ring by himself, doing push-ups, or looking at (a pretend) watch on his arm waiting for the next opponent. Late in the match, Undertaker and Mankind start brawling outside the ring, which takes all the ring referees to try and brake up. During this time, Brett Hart eliminates Stone Cold. As all the referees were distracted, Stone Cold quickly slides back into the Ring and eliminates al the remaining contestants, winning his first of 3 Rumbles.

- Royal Rumble 2004 - Chris Beniot wins after entering at number 1. While Shawn Michaels had won from the number 1 position before, it was done on a shorten Rumble, so not many people expected it to happen again, especially considering some of the big names that were entered in this year's Rumble. Starting with Randy Orton who entered at number 2, Chris Beniot would battle, for over an hour to be left in the ring with the Big Show at the end. When The Big Show went to chokeslam Beniot over the ropes, Chris hung on and dragged Big Show over the rope and then eliminating him from the Rumble. Chris Beniot would eliminate 5 wrestlers, and be speared, chokeslamed, power bombed and generally smashed by the other 29 superstars for the 1 hour 1 minute he was in the ring. Beniot would eventually use this win to main event Wrestlemania and win his first World Heavy Weight Championship.

- Royal Rumble 2006 -Rey Mysterio's dedication to Eddie Guerrero. With the death of his friend Eddie Guerrero still fresh on his mind, Rey Mysterio dedicated the 2006 Rumble to his friend. The dedication didn't start to well, when Rey became the second entrant and to win the rumble would have to go through all 29 other contestants. Over an hour later (he holds the current record for longest time in a Rumble) Rey would eliminate Triple H and Randy Orton to win the Rumble. He became only the 4th man to win the Rumble from either entrant 1 or 2, and would eliminate 6 wrestlers on his way to victory. A rumble that for me was a great tribute to a great wrestler Eddie Guerrero.

- Royal Rumble 2004 - Kane's 11 eliminations in 1 night. While Stone Cold Steve Austin was the eventual winner of the 2001 Royal Rumble, this Rumble is better known for one of the most dominate performance from one man in the history of the Rumble. Kane would enter the Rumble at the number 6 position, and would go on to eliminate 11 competitors in one night. This included every competitor from positions of 7 to 12 in succession. The list of people Kane eliminated that night included: Raven; Al Snow; Perry Saturn; Steve Blackman; Grand Master Sexay; The Honky Tonk Man; The Rock; Tazz; Albert; Crash Holly; and Scotty Too Hotty. While it doesn't count Drew Carey eliminated himself rather than face Kane, so Kane should at least get the assist. Kane would be eventually eliminated last by Stone Cold, but leave a lasting impression on his dominance on this night. Add in the use of chairs, garbage cans and other around the ring equipment, and this Rumble is quite easily one you can watch over and over again!

- Royal Rumble 2002 -Maven eliminates The Undertaker. Entering the Rumble as the number 8 entrant, The Undertaker dominated eliminating 7 wrestling superstars. The last 2 people he eliminated were the Hardy Boys Matt and Jeff. Matt and Jeff did not leave quietly, distracting The Undertaker. Entrant 11 was tough enough winner Maven, who while The Undertaker was yelling at the Hardy's would drop kick the back of The Undertaker, eliminating from the match. Like the Hardy's The Undertaker did not go quietly returning and eliminating and destroying Maven throughout the arena, including smashing him through a pop corn machine! As for the rest of the Rumble, it was won by a returning from injuryTriple H, who eliminated Kurt Angle for the win.

- The next is not a particular rumble but two great athletic spots taking advantage of a Royal Rumble loop hole. One of the few rules to a royal rumble is that to be eliminated BOTH feet must touch the FLOOR. We have seen Shawn Michaels take advantage of this to win The Rumble in 1995, and we have also seen some other wrestlers use this stipulation to great effect. John Morrison "Spiderman" 2011 and Kofi Kingston handstand in the following Rumble in 2012, showed the great athleticism of these two, and that you can steal the Rumble highlights and not win. John Morrison would end up on the outside of the ring and shoved. Instead of falling to the floor, he lept over to the security wall and hung on. Climbing up, then walking along the wall, he then jumped to the ring steps, kicked an eliminated William Regal in the head, and proceeded to re-enter the Rumble! The following year, Kofi was forced over the top rope, and ended up with his feet on the ring apron and hands on the floor. The Miz pushed Kofi's leg to hopefully eliminate him, only to have Kofi walk on his hands over to the ring steps, and re-enter the rumble!

- Royal Rumble 1998 -The 3 faces of Foley. Starting at the number 1 entrant, Cactus Jack would enter the Rumble. After being eliminated reasonable early I was a little disappointed my favourite for the night was gone so early. The countdown to entrant 16 occurs and my hopes of a Mick Foley win are again high as Mankind would enter the Rumble. But he too would be eliminated, and again lose my favourite pick to win. Then as the countdown for entrant 28 finishes, out through the curtain...Dude Love! Here I thought is it, surely Foley can win it now! Sadly he was eliminated by eventual winner Stone Cold Steve Austin, wrecking my dream of seeing Foley win a Rumble.

My number one all-time favourite Royal Rumble match is.......

- 2007 Royal rumble – Undertaker Wins. The Undertaker had entered the Rumble7 times since 1991, and 2007 would be his eighth attempt to win. While he has dominated sections of his previous rumbles he had never gone on to win any. We had to wait until he arrived as the last entrant at number 30. He quickly disposed of Khali who had himself dominated and eliminated 7 men, then eliminated MVP, leaving himself, Shawn Michaels, Randy Orton and Edge as the final 4. After Michaels eliminated both Edge and Orton it came down to Shawn and The Undertaker for the win. We next witness a series of near eliminations, chokslams, superkicks between these two (which possible planted seeds for their Wrestlemania Match the following year). In the end The Undertaker dodged a superkick, and eliminated Shawn, becoming the first man to win the rumble coming in as the last entrant.

This Rumble also had some great ECW moments where Sandman entered the Rumble bringing in his Singapore cane, and Kane choke slamming Sabu out of the ring and through a table. It was the year that big men dominated the rumble with Kane and Khali dominating for long periods and of course The Undertaker winning.

Chapter 14   My Ultimate Wrestlemania

The Grand Final (or super bowl depending which country you come from) of wrestling is known as WWE's Wrestlemania. Starting back on March 31 1985, it is now the show piece event on not just the WWE calendar, but on most wrestling fans calendars. It was the brain child of Vince McMahon, and many believe was the start of turning wrestling from a local product into the world-wide phenomenon it is today. Vince risked his company and fortune on Wrestlemania, which was not only successful but also transformed wrestling itself.

Over the past 29 years I have seen some of the most memorable matches in wrestling history including; Undertaker vs. Shawn Michaels 1 & 2; Macho Man vs. Rickie The Dragon Steamboat; Shawn Michaels vs. Brett Hart Iron man match, as well as many memorable moments such as Hulk Hogan slamming Andre the Giant; Edge spearing Mick Foley onto a burning table; the sight of Eddie Guerrero and Chris Beniot celebrating at the end of Wrestlemania 20; Shawn Michaels saying "I'm Sorry, I love you" before beating Rick Flair; or Mr McMahon and Stone Cold joining forces in Wrestlemania 17 after years of feuding together.. From the very first money in the bank match, first ever ladder match, Hardcore matches, cage mages, Hell in a Cell, battle royals, to classic one on one wrestling matches, in my opinion Wrestlemania has very rarely fail to produce. Along with the Royal Rumble, it is the Pay Per View I budget for and order every year, and as with the Royal Rumble, one of my Bucket list items to attend live before I die.

With the build up to Wrestlemania starting now at The Royal Rumble, we get 3 months of building feuds, matches and stipulations that have most fans like myself bursting come March/April. I do feel these days that the Elimination Chamber pay per view is wasted as the last PPV before Wrestlemania. In the last few years it has become either too predictable in who is going to win, or actually breaks any momentum two superstars were having since the Rumble. If there must be a pay per view, then swap the Chamber to the PPV before Summer Slam, with the winners of each Chamber facing the Champions at Summer

Slam, and move a genetic PPV before Wrestlemania where feuds can be enhanced and developed further. This is just one fans opinion, and since it is my book, I thought I would share it with you.

While there have been 28 Wrestlemania's, for me Wrestlemania III will always be my favourite. It was my very first Wrestlemania I watched, my very first wrestling pay per view I watched, and was, as mentioned earlier in the book, the wrestling event that return my love of wrestling after a break of a couple of years. Besides the fact there were 12 fantastic matches to watch and enjoy there were many magical moments such as "Hogan's Body slam of Andre the Giant", or " King Kong Bundy's Squash of Little Beaver", Alice Cooper with Jake 'the Snake 'Roberts, and even the little wrestling ring vehicles they rode to the ring. I have spoken numerous throughout the book of the quality and importance of some of the matches on the Wrestlemania III card, and reminiscing while writing this book there are not too many matches I didn't enjoy watching. For those interested here is a quick match list for Wrestlemania III:

1. The Can-Am Connection (Rick Martel and Tom Zenk) vs.
Bob Orton and The Magnificent Muraco (with Mr. Fuji)

2. Billy Jack Haynes vs. Hercules (with Bobby Heenan) - battle
of the full nelsons

3. Hillbilly Jim, The Haiti Kid and Little Beaver vs. King Kong
Bundy, Little Tokyo and Lord Littlebrook

4. Harley Race (with Bobby Heenan and The Fabulous Moolah)
vs. The Junkyard Dog – loser must kneel down to the victor

5. The Dream Team (Greg Valentine and Brutus Beefcake) (with
Johnny Valiant and Dino Bravo) vs. The Rougeau Brothers
(Jacques and Raymond)

6. Roddy Piper vs. Adrian Adonis (with Jimmy Hart), hair vs
hair match

7. The Hart Foundation (Bret Hart and Jim Neidhart) and Danny
Davis (with Jimmy Hart) vs. The British Bulldogs (Davey Boy
Smith and The Dynamite Kid) and Tito Santana

8. Butch Reed (with Slick) vs. Koko B. Ware

9. Ricky Steamboat (with George Steele) vs. Randy Savage (c)

(with Miss Elizabeth)

10. The Honky Tonk Man (with Jimmy Hart) vs. Jake Roberts
(with Alice Cooper)

11. The Iron Sheik and Nikolai Volkoff (with Slick) vs.The
Killer Bees (B. Brian Blair and Jim Brunzell)

12. Hulk Hogan (c) vs. André the Giant (with Bobby Heenan)

Going through all 28 Wrestlemania PPVs I wondered
what would be my dream or my ultimate Wrestlemania. That is a
Wrestlemania made up of the best matches from the past 28
Wrestlemania's. This would need to be a 12 match card (I chose
12 matches to honour my favourite Wrestlemania) and have on it
some of (what I feel) are my most memorable matches (and
moments) that have occurred in Wrestlemania History. This is a
list for a single Wrestlemania card, let's call it The Ultimate
Wrestlemania. If I was to produce a list of the best Wrestlemania
matches, then this list would look completely different.

My criteria for selecting matches was to only give each
wrestle 1 match otherwise The Undertaker and Shawn Michaels
would be wrestling 5 to 6 matches!(in fact you could just have

either a Undertaker Wrestlemania or a Shawn Michaels Wrestlemania and it would be a great show / DVD). However Hulk Hogan, Edge and Brett Hart have managed to sneak into 2 matches (and unfortunately for Edge he will end up being a very sore man at the end of my Ultimate Wrestlemania!). I also wanted to only have 1 WWE title match, 1 tag team title match, 1 World Heavy weight title match, and only 1 Intercontinental match. I will not give a play by play recount of the matches, just why they made my 'Ultimate Wrestlemania, I would rather you go and watch each match to experience why they are on my list.

I would like to have some honourable mentions to WWE starts such as Triple H, John Cena, The Big Show, Eddie Guerrero, Ultimate Warrior and tag teams such as Demolition, Hart Foundation, The British Bulldogs who have given me many great matches and moments during Wrestlemania, but unfortunately have missed out on my list here. Triple H's vs. Undertaker 2 (with Shawn Michaels) in Hell in a Cell and both career ending matches of Rick Flair vs. Shawn Michaels, and

Randy Savage vs. Ultimate Warrior were matches I wanted to include but could not fit in under my criteria I set.

Other matches that I thought long and hard about including that I feel deserve at least a mention include:

- Kurt Angle vs. Chris Jericho vs. Chris Beniot (European & Intercontinental title match Wrestlemania 24)

- Hulk Hogan vs. Ultimate Warrior (Wrestlemania VI)

- Hulk Hogan vs. King Kong Bundy (WWF Champion ship Wrestlemania 2)

- Shawn Michaels vs. Kurt Angle (Wrestlemania 21)

- The Rock vs. Stone Cold Steve Austin (Wrestlemania 19) - actually any of the three Rock vs. Stone Cold matches could have made my list.

- The British Bulldogs vs. Greg Valentine and Brutes Beefcake (Wrestlemania 2)

So here is my Ultimate Wrestlemania, like I said go on YouTube, your dvd library etc. and watch, agree or disagree, but enjoy these 12 great Wrestlemania Matches:

Match 1

Edge & Christian vs. The Dudley Boys vs. The Hardy Boys in TLC II for the World Tag team titles. – (Wrestlemania 17)

There was the initial ladder match between these three teams at Wrestlemania 16, The Table, Ladders and Chairs (TLC) one at Summer Slam 2000 (which I have already spoken about), table's matches and cage matches between these 3 teams over a 2 year period. I have chosen this match between the 3 teams as nobody (including myself) thought they could outdo the first TLC….. But they did, and Edge flying through the air and spearing Jeff hardy while he is swinging from the belts still has me hitting the rewind button every time I watch it. What these 3 teams put themselves through for us fans show 6 wrestling superstars who not only love their job, but want to go out and give 100% for us fans, which they did.

Match 2

Owen Hart vs. Brett Hart (Wrestlemania 10)

There has been a lot written about Owen Hart's death, and how he could have been an all-time great had he been still alive today, which I agree 100% with. And those who haven't seen just how good he could have been, then this is the match I suggest you watch. A great back and forth match between 2 brothers that show just how good a classic wrestling match can be. This match showed many people like, myself that Owen could make the leap from mid-card level wrestler to main eventing PPV's.

Match 3

The Rock vs. Hulk Hogan (Wrestlemania 18)

Standing face to face in the middle of the ring, looking at each other, then to the fans, these two different generation icons sent goose bumps down my back even before the first punch was thrown. There are many 'dream' matches we would all love to see pitching 2 wrestlers from different eras or companies together in their respective primes (see my next chapter for some great match-ups I would have loved to see).

Wrestlemania 18 we got to see a match many people had on their dream match list. What made this match even more remarkable was Hogan was meant to the 'Heel" of the match and The Rock "the babyface', however the fans in attendance did not see it that way. By The end of the match the fans were cheering for Hogan, and booing The Rock, although personally I did want The Rock to 'Lay the Smackdown' on Hogan!!

Match 4

Kurt Angle vs. Rey Mysterio vs. Randy Orton – World Heavyweight Championship – (Wrestlemania 22)

While personally I feel the triple threat match between Shawn Michaels, Triple H and Chris Beniot World Heavyweight Championship was a better triple threat match, I have decided to go with Kurt, Rey and Randy's match due to Shawn will be involved in my main event match later on.

Rey had dedicated his Royal Rumble win, and this match to the memory of the late Eddie Guerrero, Randy Orton was on the rise back from his first run as Champion, and Kurt Angle, well Kurt Angle is arguably one of the best wrestlers of all time. A typically great see sawing match in which any of the three would have been deserved winners, and each had their moments through the match where you thought they were going to win. However an ending that just pulled at your heart strings as a wrestling fan was the correct decision.

Match 5

Trish Stratus vs. Mickie James – WWE Womens Championship – (Wrestlemania 22)

You cannot have a Wrestlemania without showcasing the WWE Divas. Unfortunately most of the diva / women's matches at Wrestlemania are not great and are placed and used as a 'break' for the fans, or placed just before the main event, are used as toilet breaks for us serious wrestling fans and usually involve some gimmick (lingerie, pillow fight, guest celebrity as a wrestler etc.). However this match at Wrestlemania 22, showcased what these female athletes can do when given an excellent couple of months lead in story line, and given a decent time limit to tell a story during a match. On top of that you have 2 of the better Diva wrestlers performing. Combining all those ingredients you get this fantastic match.

Match 6

Money in the Bank – CM Punk vs. Shelton Benjamin vs. Chris Jericho vs. Carlito v MVP vs. Mr Kennedy vs. John Morrison (Wrestlemania 24)

Before it had its own PPV, The money in the Bank was a Wrestlemania initiative, and has produced some fantastic moments (or spots) in each of the Wrestlemania's it has been a part of. It has also been responsible for lifting the winning wrestlers from the 'mid-card' level to main event stars of the company, such as Edge, Rob Van Dam, Daniel Bryan and CM Punk.

I chose this Money in the Bank, as it showcases some wrestlers who used this type of match to shine. Wrestles such as Shelton Benjamin and John Morrison excelled in this environment. There were also many unbelievable 'spots') including Morrison climbing a turnbuckle and performed a moonsault onto other competitors outside the ring while holding a ladder against his chest, or Benjamin climbed another ladder placed adjacent to the first one and performed a sunset flip powerbomb on Kennedy, who in turn superplexed Morrison from the top of the ladder!

Match 7

Macho Man Randy Savage vs. Rickie the Dragon Steamboat for the Intercontinental Title – (Wrestlemania 3)

See my previous chapter on my favourite all time matches, and there is no way this match wasn't going to be on my Ultimate Wrestlemania!! Not only one of the best Intercontinental matches at Wrestlemania, but one of the best Intercontinental matches ever.

Match 8

Edge (with Lita) vs. Mick Foley Hardcore Match –

(Wrestlemania 22)

Classed by many (including myself), as the best every hardcore match seen at a Wrestlemania. It also involved 2 of my all-time favourite wrestlers, and gave us fans many great images and moments to talk about at the end of the match. This match had everything I enjoy about quality hardcore matches, brutality from the 2 combatants, barb wire, thumb tacks, tables, and blood and of course the added fiery table at the end of the match. While many who witness ECW at its best, or wrestling in Japan might feel this match tame in comparison, for us without that wrestling background this match delivered.

The images of both Edge and Foley bleeding, battered and burnt left me in no doubt about why I enjoy watching these two in the ring, and why although it's sad they both no longer wrestle, am happy to see that they both can walk around and enjoy their retirement, even after a match like this.

Match 9

Brett Hart vs. Stone Cold Steve Austin Submission match –

(Wrestlemania 13)

A match that included a double face/heel turn, the famous image of Stone Cold screaming in pain, face full of blood, but refusing to tap out, and a man who was the WWF/E wrestling hero when all the big names left in the early 1990's, turning on his fans. This was one of the only matches I know where even I changed who I support at the end.

While historically this match has great importance to the way the WWF/E went forward, the actually match itself was of high quality, stole the night at Wrestlemania 13, and showed the great wrestling and storytelling of both Superstars in the ring.

Match 10

Hulk Hogan vs. Andre The Giant for the WWE title –

(Wrestlemania 3)

As with the Steamboat vs. Savage match before, this match is also on my top 10 list of my favourite all time matches, so needed to be placed on my Ultimate Wrestlemania card. Now while the WWF/E title usually main events and ends Wrestlemania, I felt that sometimes Wrestlemania gives us a better more deserving match to main event or end Wrestlemania.

Match 11

Hillbilly Jim, The Haiti Kid and Little Beaver vs. King Kong Bundy, Little Tokyo and Lord Littlebrook – (Wrestlemania 3)

Many matches take their toll on us fans as well as the competitors. Our emotional rollercoaster of highs and lows do leave as feeling drained and needing to take a breath. Often Wrestlemania will give us a match that gives us a chance to get our breath back while still enjoying some excellent wrestling action. What better way to get our breath back, then watching this classic match (and moment). It also gave me a chance to include King Kong Bundy in my Ultimate Wrestlemania.

Plenty of humour, some great midget wrestling, 2 wrestling legends and of course a great ending, especially if you love to see Giants squashing people!!

Match 12

Undertaker vs. Shawn Michaels - Career vs. streak match –

(Wrestlemania 26)

After recently purchasing The Undertaker's Streak DVD, I have had a chance to watch both Undertaker vs. Shawn Michael's matches, and The Undertaker vs. Triple H (Wrestlemania 27 and 28). Deciding which match to end my Ultimate Wrestlemania was not an easy decision. The Undertaker and Shawn Michaels match at Wrestlemania 25 was a better match, and The Undertaker and Triple H match at Wrestlemania 27 and 28 more violent, and told a great story through the match, I chose this match for a couple of reasons.

The first, most people believe The Undertaker will never lose a match at Wrestlemania, however this match there were no spoilers or rumours that Shawn was set to retire, so, I like many people thought there was a great possibility that Shawn could actually win this match and end The Undertakers streak. Now while end of career matches do not always mean end of career

(Savage, Foley, Flair are just some names of people who lost career matches only to return to the ring), with Shawn's age and career injury history, a return to the ring if retired didn't seem likely.

Second, Like me, many people didn't believe that 'Mr Wrestlemania' Shawn Michaels would lose 2 Wrestlemania's in a row, and thought that The Undertaker would return the favour and lose to Michaels this time. What we got, was a match that for the first time since The Undertakers streak was talked about, a strong belief that the streak could end. In the end we had a roller coaster of a match that could have gone either way, but in the end we got an ending fit for a retiring legend.

Chapter 15   My Top 10 Fantasy match ups

I always feel it is very hard to compare 2 (or more) athletes from different eras when it comes to sport. Many people always wonder for example, is Tiger Woods better than Jack Nicholas? I feel we cannot compare these two due to golf clubs and ball technology being so much more advanced today; golf courses are made longer due to golf balls going further due to these technologies. I would love to see Tiger Woods, play a round of golf with clubs similar to what we all had back 20 years ago. Imagine Tiger Woods using his drivers and wood that was actually made from wood, and were not the size of Andre The Giants closed fist. Golf clubs not made out of graphite, titanium or whatever space age metal they are made from now. Only after Tiger has played a round or two with those clubs, then we can think about comparing.

Would Rafer Nadel be as good as Bjorn Borg on clay courts playing with an old style wooden racquet?, With all we know about training and conditioning athletes now, is Usain Bolt better / faster athlete than Carl Lewis?, what if Usain had the same training and conditioning that Carl had back in the 1980's, would he be as fast today? It is fun to think about which generation star is better, but until we all have computer programs like the one on the"Rocky Balboa' (Rocky VI) movie we just will never know.

What I like a lot about the WWE games (such as Raw vs. Smackdown, WWE 12 etc) is that we as fans can make some of our fantasy wrestling matches from wrestlers from different era's. We can have Hulk Hogan vs. John Cena, or DX vs. Demolition or even Rick Flair vs Christian. It is through games playing such as this, that we really start to think what are our absolute fantasy wrestling matches? I have compared in previous chapters different wrestling eras, and different wrestling companies, but what if everyone from different eras and companies had a chance to fight each other, what matches would I love to see? We as wrestling fans have been lucky to witness 2 of these 'fantasy' match ups and for me both matches didn't disappoint. The Rock vs. Hogan at Wrestlemania 18, and The

Rock vs. John Cena at Wrestlemania 28. I have already spoken about the Rock / Hogan match and how much I enjoyed it, and last year's Rock / Cena match while for me not as anticipated, but with the year build up, the generation vs. generation match up I thoroughly enjoyed the match, and thought it a good way to end Wrestlemania. There are always talk and rumours running around the internet about possible fantasy match ups happening such as Stone Cold vs. CM Punk, or even The Undertaker vs. Sting, as well as many lists like the one I am going to do. With all fantasy match ups, the participates competing would be in the prime of their careers, I would also like to see these as traditional wrestling matches rather than any type of gimmick match, which may or may not spill to the outside of the Ring. Some of my fantasy matches that almost made their way onto my list were:

Kurt Angle   vs.   CM Punk

Abyss   vs.   Jake the Snake Roberts

Brett Hart   vs.   Daniel Bryan

Samoan Joe   vs.   Triple H

Aj Styles   vs.   Shawn Michaels.

5 great matches, would possible make a lot of fans fantasy lists, but unfortunately did not make the cut for my top 10. My 10 fantasy matches I would love to see are:

Number 10

Randy 'Macho Man' Savage vs. Christian

There are many wrestlers I would love to watch in a match against Savage, which just goes to show what a talent he was in the ring (let's all forget about his music career). In fact you could possible list most of the WWF/E attitude era superstars, or current WWE or TNA stars against Savage and it would be instant classic match. I would have loved to see Savage against wrestling superstars such as Edge, The Rock, CM Punk, Daniel Bryan, Randy Orton, Chris Jericho, Dolph Ziggler, John Cena or even Kurt Angle. In fact you could possibly just have a list dedicated to people you would have loved to see wrestler Randy Savage.

In the end I chose Christian vs. Savage as my first Fantasy match for a few reasons. Firstly both are similar styles of wrestlers, good technical wrestlers, as well as both enjoy utilising moves from the top rope. Second both wrestlers are good at countering other wrestler's moves, using underhand tactics when need be, can take a good bump, as well as both have a great repertoire of moves lists they can draw upon. I cannot think of a poor match had by either wrestler. Thirdly, as I spoke about in an earlier chapter, Christian is one of my all-time favourite wrestlers, I have yet to see a disappointing match wrestled by him, and I think a match against savage would really show his skills and talent. Finally both wrestlers are good on the microphone, so the lead up promos would great to watch, and having one of Christian's 'Peep Show' Segment between the two, well we all know how that would end. If you add in the Intercontinental title up for grabs I think you would have a match that would steal the show. This being a fantasy match and considering both at one stage had female support coming to the ring, we may as well have Miss Elizabeth in Savage's Corner, and Trish Stratus in Christian's.

Number 9

Hulk Hogan vs. John Cena

The face of the WWF/E in the 1980's vs. The face of the WWE in the 2000's. There would be coloured shirts everywhere. Hogan's fans will be wearing his red and yellow, whilst Cena's fans would be wearing their Fruity Pebbles coloured variety of shirts of red, green orange or purple (I will admit I do own the orange shirt). We would have the Hulkamaniacs vs. the Cenanation; the taking your vitamins vs. Hustle loyalty and respect; the "Whatya going to do brotha" vs. "The champ is here!" and finally we would have the 'Hulking up' vs. 'Super Cena'. You would have nearly everyone under the age of 14 supporting Cena, while Hogan would get those fans over the age of 30. Those in-between (15-29) would possibly go to the bathroom during this match.

I would see this match very similar to the Hogan / Warrior match from Wrestlemania VI. I would see both wrestlers would dominate patches of the match, each using their strength as the choice of weapons, and both wrestlers would need to have their 'classical' comebacks at some time through the match. You wouldn't see a great amount of technical wrestling, but then again we never watch Hogan or Cena for their technical wrestling skills. I would see Hogan kicking out of Cena's AA(Attitude Adjustment), while Cena would kick out of Hogan's Leg Drop. A match that would end with a handshake, hug and of course pose off.

And just to add spice to the match, have The Rock as the special guest referee, in which case the match would end with a series of 'Rock Bottoms'!!

Number 8

The Rockers vs. The Hardy Boys

Here we have a classic match where the challengers (the Hardy Boys Matt and Jeff Hardy) would be facing their inspirations to their wrestling careers The Rockers (Shawn Michaels and Marty Jannetty).

A tag team match which would be full of some high flying moves, great team moves and fast quick action would be a joy to watch. Shawn and Jeff flying off the top ropes, Marty and Matt flying through the ropes to the outside, Jeff flying off the crowd barriers, I feel this match would spend more time in the air than on the ground.   The high flying action would be matched by the quick double teams, quick reversals and of course ladders would have to come out and be used at some stage.

At the very end of the match, Marty and Matt can have a talk on having to live in the other partners shadow after their respective tag teams have broken up. In fact they could start their own support group for all tag team members who have fallen by the way side, or watched on as their former tag team partners have gone on to great things, such as major wrestling titles and careers. 'The Marty Jannetty Factor" support group would include such members as:

Marty Janetty	The Rockers
Matt Hardy	The Hardy Boys
John Morrison	The Miz and Morrison
Jim 'The anvil' Niedhart	The Hart Foundation

Stevie Ray   The Harlem Heat

Brian Pillman   The Hollywood Blondes

Number 7

Chris Jericho vs. Ricky "The Dragon' Steamboat

Just like Randy Savage there are many people who I would love to of seen wrestle Ricky The Dragon Steamboat. While I missed most of the classic Steamboat matches, what I saw of his abilities in his Wrestlemania III against Savage, and my looking back through you tube during this writing process, is what has put him in my fantasy list. Wrestlers such as Kurt Angle, Edge, Punk or The Rock are just some of the big names that I would have enjoyed in a match against Steamboat. While (as mentioned) I have only seen glimpses of the Steamboat in his prime, his matches against Rick Flair are legendary, and I would see this match as no different.

Chris Jericho has been a star for me ever since I saw him on his debut in the WWF/E on Raw on August 9, 1999. He has been in some great matches with people such as Shawn

Michaels, Kurt Angle, The Rock and Chris Beniot, and I can see a match against Steamboat being as good as any of those.

Although we did see this match at Backlash 2009, and briefly at Wrestlemania 25, theses matches were only teasers of what could have been. Ricky Steamboat put on a great show at age of 56, and in fact I believe Steamboat got his match at Backlash due to his performance against Jericho at Wrestlemania 25. Just imagine how good the match at Backlash could have been had Steamboat been twenty years younger.

The wrestling skill of both wrestlers would make for a match full of great wrestling moves, great counters and reversals and many near falls and near submissions.

Number 6

The Rock vs. The Ultimate Warrior

The Rock has been one of the few wrestlers that have transcended Era's by having classic matches with Hulk Hogan, Ric Flair and John Cena. And on each occasion these matches either headlined or stole the show they were on. In fact if there was a wrestler who could promote a fantasy match you would want it to be the Rock.

The Ultimate Warrior while burning out quickly in the world of wrestling, did burn very bright during the late 80's early 90's. The energy he brought to the ring, often made up for his limited wrestling repertoire, and through his matches with Hogan, Savage and Rick Flair showed he could match it in the Ring with main event stars. I feel that a match between The Rock and The Ultimate Warrior would top that of the Warrior and Hogan's match at Wrestlemania XI.

While The Rock would have to do a lot of the pre match promo work, mainly due to no-one being able to understand what the Warrior would be talking about. The image of these two staring off at each other in the middle of the ring is giving me Goosebumps as I am writing. The most electrifying man in sports entertainment vs. the man with the most energy in sports entertainment would result in a very explosive match.

The Ultimate Warrior would have the advantage in strength and energy, The Rock in wrestling skill and strike power; however they would both cancel each other out with intensity. While it wouldn't be a classically long match, with The Ultimate Warrior wrestling at 100 miles, he didn't have too many long matches, it would still make for essential viewing.

Number 5

DX (Triple H/Shawn Michaels) vs. nWo (Scott Hall / Kevin Nash)

Special guest referee Sean "X-Pac" Waltman

Two of the biggest stables during the "Monday night wars" started with members of The Kliq. The Kliq in the world of wrestling is known as a close the group of friends (Triple H, Shawn Michaels, Sean Waltman, Kevin Nash and Scott Hall) that in the early 1990's were believed to have very strong influence in the booking of shows. Many believed they held and refuse to put over other talent in the WWF/E at the time. The group is also known for breaking the wrestling code, and performing the now known "curtain call" on May 19, 1996 at Madison Square Garden. At the time Triple H (heel) was battling

Scott Hall (face) and Shawn Michaels (face) was battling Kevin Nash (heel). Hash and Hall had just signed a contract with WCW, and on this night, it was the last night they would wrestle for WWF/E. After the final match, all 4 members, broke kayfabe and hugged in the ring. Hall and Nash went onto form the nWo, while Triple H and Shawn Michaels went on to form DX, both wrestling stables were very anti authority against wrestling management. So essentially the Kliq ran the wrestling world from 2 companies during The Monday Night wars!

A match against nWo and DX would include some great lead up action, Shawn and Triple H dressing as the nWo, Hall and Nash attacking DX back stage. You could just image the fun these 4 would have with the pre match feuding.

We have seen how good Scott Hall and Shawn Michaels were in the ring together through their great ladder matches, and Nash and Triple H would add the power (and the sledge hammers) to the match. I see all four participates while friends, walking away from this match very sore, bleeding and leaving us fans wanting m

Number 4

Brett Hart vs. Kurt Angle

The age old saying of "you do not know what you have till it's gone" sums up my opinion of Kurt Angle. There isn't a poor match I can think of I saw involving Kurt, but it was only once he left the WWF/E I realised how much I enjoyed his matches. I have only seen glimpses of his work on TNA, however have read how great his matches have been against the likes of Samoan Joe, AJ Styles and Jeff Jarret.

While many believe DX, Stone Cold and the Rock saved the WWF/E, I always thought that it was Brett Hart who held the WWF/E together once Hogan, Savage, Hall and Nash moved to WCW. It was the quality of matches he produced against people like Stone Cold, his brother Owen, and Shawn Michaels that kept WWF/E fans loyal to the company.

Two of the best technical wrestlers I have had the privilege of watching in the ring, would make an absolute dream match to watch. Whether it was a submission match, iron man match, or just a straight one on one contest, this match would have people selling the grandmothers to get tickets to see.

Submission moves, counters, reversals, and even some moves off the top ropes, this match would include just about everything you would want out of a wrestling match. I have watched Kurt Angle wrestler similar style wrestlers in Chris Beniot and Chris Jericho, and each one of those matches were instant classics. Brett has also had some fantastic matches with legends such as Mr Perfect, his brother Owen as well as Chris Beniot. So a match between Angle and Hart would have been an ultimate dream match to watch.

Number 3

The Undertaker vs. Andre The Giant.

Just the other day a saw a fantasy match voting choice that had Andre The Giant vs. The Big Show. From my many years of watching wrestling, I have never really enjoyed too many big man vs. big man wrestling matches. Big Show and Mark Henry did surprise me last year, and I remember King

Kong Bundy vs Big John Studd matches from the early 80's, and The Undertaker vs. Desiel (Kevin Nash) at Wrestlemania 12 was another exception to the rule. But for me, the only person I would love to see wrestle Andre would be The Undertaker.

Wrestling fans know how big the Hogan / Andre match was at Wrestlemania III. We wrestling fans know how big the last 4 Undertaker streak matches against Michaels and Triple H have been. So by placing Andre vs. The Undertaker in Wrestlemania streak match would blow the roof of any stadium.

There have not been too many large wrestlers we fans have taken as serious threat to the Undertaker. Khali, Hiendenriech, Gonzalas are just some of these wrestlers brought in to feud with the Undertaker, but turned out to be very poor wrestlers. Here we have Andre, arguably the one of the best large wrestlers there have been who himself had a pretty impressive streak, up against The Undertaker, one of the best I have ever seen. Andre size would nullify Undertakers moves such as 'Last ride' and even the Tombstone, so he would have to rely on his more agile move repertoire. Andre would dominate in strength, and slow the match down, add in a Bobby 'The Brain' Heenan in Andre's corner and The Undertaker's streak would be in real danger.

Number 2

Stone Cold Steve Austin vs. Goldberg

2 of the biggest names and drawcards for their respective companies, Stone Cold Steve Austin and Goldberg was a match most of us fans wanted to see during the Monday Night Wars, as well as soon as the wars were over, and especially when we heard Goldberg was coming to the WWE. But due to injuries this match never happened.

The Stunner vs. The Spear, Goldberg's strength vs Stone colds tenacity, this match would not include too many technical wrestling moves, just a straight out slugfest, power moves and 1 finger salutes. With both the Stunner and Spear being moves that can come out of nowhere, this match could end quickly, or be a drawn brawl that would spill to the outside of the ring, into the crowd and of course destroy the poor Spanish announce table.

Number 1

Traditional Survivor series match

Evolution   vs.   The Hart Foundation

(Triple H, Ric Flair,   (Brett and Owen Hart,

                                        British Bulldog

Batista, Randy Orton)   Jim Neidhart)

In 1997, the formation of 'The Hart Foundation" stable dominated the WWF/E holding at one time all of the major WWF/E Championships. From WWF titles, Intercontinental and European titles to of course Tag team titles.

In 2003 Evolution was born, and also dominated the WWF/E with also at one stage holding on to all of the major championships on Raw. Every member of the Evolution stable did have, or went onto hold multiply world wrestling titles. If I wanted to end my fantasy match list, then this is the match I would like to see.

Each team had its power house; Batista vs. Jim Neidhart, each team had its experience and mentor role; Rick Flair vs.

Brett Hart, each team has its wrestler with huge potential; Randy Orton vs. Owen Hart, and finally each team had their dominate wrestler: Triple H vs. British Bulldog. While my fantasy match is a 4 on 4 tag match, each of those individual match-ups are fantasy match-ups on their own that I would enjoy watching.

A traditional elimination survivor series style match between these two stables would headline not only Survivor Series, but any PPV it would be on.

I have included below further matches that also just missed out on my list as I feel they would of all had to of been specialty / gimmick type matches. So these are my top 10 speciality matches I would love to see or my ultimate extreme rules PPV!

The Dudleys Boys vs. Demolition	tables match
Mankind vs. King Kong Bundy	Boiler room brawl match
Undertaker vs. Sting	Hell in a Cell
Kane vs. Abyss	Inferno Match

Kurt Angle vs. Daniel Bryan	Ironman Submission match
APA vs. The Nast Boys	Hardcore tag team match
Shane McMahon vs. Rob Van Dam	Falls count anywhere match
Batista vs. Goldberg	last man standing match
Stone Cold vs. Hulk Hogan	Steel cage match
Shelton Benjamin vs. Jeff Hardy	Ladder match

Money in the bank match:

Rey Mysterio vs. Christian vs. Shawn Michaels vs. Razor Ramon (Scott Hall) vs. Eddie Guerrero vs. Rob Van Dam vs. Shelton Benjamin vs. Kofi Kingston

Chapter 16   Some wrestling ideas/improvements

Now after having my say in chapter 5 about if internet wrestling fans didn't like the product they are watching then don't watch, then this chapter seems a little hypocritical on my behalf. However if you noticed in chapter 5, I did say if you have a concern there is a polite way you can go about suggesting ideas. If my ideas are not taken, then that doesn't mean I will stop watching. Some of the suggestions I have are currently in the process of happening, so who knows; by the time this gets finished or maybe even published these suggestions might be redundant, in that case you may want to skip this chapter. While the majority of these suggestions are aimed at the wrestling product I watch the most (The WWE), some I hope are to help the establish wrestling here in Australia some more, while other ideas are to improve other wrestling products and experiences for other fans

Make the WWE minor titles mean more – At the time of writing Cody Rhodes, Christian, The Miz and now Kofi Kingston have done an excellent job of re-establishing the WWE Intercontinental Title as a prestige title worth winning. When I look back at some of the battles and matches that used to occur for this title from the previously mention Steamboat / Savage match at Wrestlemania 3, to the battles between the Ultimate Warrior and Rick Rude, or the Shawn Michaels vs. Razor Ramon Ladder matches, this title used to mean something to the fans as well as the wresters. I have seen the current battle between Cody Rhodes and Christian, The Miz and Rey Mysterio, and now Kofi Kingston and Wade Barret lifting this Title back to those Heights. By keeping these feuds going with future and past world Champions, this title will always be a great stepping stone for the move to (and back) to the main event scene.

The US Title needs a similar injection of focus, at the stage of writing current US champion Santino Marella has a match at WWE's No Way Out against...ring announcer ***Ricardo Rodriguez***. Nothing against each person as entertainers but I wonder how former Champions such as Harley Race, Rick Flair, Brett Hart, Lex Luger and Booker T feel about the title they fought so hard for. To make it a meaningful title again, rather than a title to give someone who needs a little push or thank them for all their comedy routines (sorry Santino). I remember a great best of seven series in 2005 between Booker T and Chris Beniot for this title. The matches went over a couple of months between Raw shows and PPV's and even ended with Randy Orton subbing a match for Booker T. There was also another, best of seven series between for this title between Booker T and John Cena that included match 3 at the *WWE Return of The Dead Man Tour* in Sydney 2004 which I managed to be there to see. The match for us in Australia was a big deal as it actually meant something in relation to an ongoing story line on Raw. The last time I felt a feud was done correctly for the US title was in 2007/2008 between MVP and Matt Hardy, as it was the last time I really cared about the title.

While under the current 'pg. era' I cannot see it happening, I would love to see the Hardcore title brought back, especially under the 24/7 rule. For those who missed it, the

Hardcore title could be defended 24 hours a day, 7 days a week,

thanks to comments by Crash Holly. I have fond memories of

Crash Holly having to defend this title in his hotel room, laundry

matt and even the airport! The 'battle royals' for this title, and

the backstage impromptu matches added humour and some great

hardcore action to Raw shows or PPVs.

Decent Mid Card Feuds - There is often criticism that there is no

wrestler in the mid card level ready to step up, and that the WWE

can struggle if 2 or more main event superstars are injured or out

of action (due to suspensions). But what are needed for these

wrestlers to prove they can handle the spot light are meaningful

feuds lasting over a couple of months, that make their matches

worth watching and not a time to duck off and go to the toilet.

Currently in the WWE, the majority of the mid card talent are

being used to get over a current champion, the current champions

challenger, or to put over a new superstar. By placing these mid

card wrestlers in a decent meaningful feuds can show us fans if

they are capable of main eventing future WWE shows.

I remember watching during the rock'n'wrestle, and attitude eras some great midcard battles that had nothing to do with titles but were as intense and must see viewing as the battle for the championship was. Jake 'The Snake' Roberts vs. Rick Rude is a great example how 2 midcard based wrestlers can have a feud and series of matches that the audience at home and at the show just have to see. Other great midcard feuds I remember include

Eddie Guerrero vs., Rey Mysterio

Jerry 'The King' Lawler vs. Brett Hart

Shawn Michaels vs. Razor Ramon

Mankind vs. Triple H (1997 version)

Stone Cold Steve Austin vs. Owen Hart

What makes for interesting reading of those midcard feuds is that nearly all went on to become main event stars.

What are some of the feuds that have worked before? The most common mid card feud usually involves a tag team splitting, when done correctly can lead to a great series of matches, and elevate at least 1 of the team. Shawn Michaels and Marty Janette – The Rockers is the best known example of how a tag team split can elevate 1 member into greatness. Most of us old timer wrestling fans still have the image of Shawn throwing Marty through a window on The Barber Shop in 1992 officially ending the Rockers as a tag team, and then the matches that followed. Other tag teams splits that lifted at least one wrestler to the top level include Edge and Christian, The Hardy Boys while in WCW Harlem Heat (Booket T), and currently in TNA you have Beer Money splitting with James Storm now being the longest running TNA champion of all time. Unfortunately for the WWE, this option is not really a viable option (see next suggestion on the tag team division).

Another option to lift some mid card wrestlers is to put them in a feud with an established main event star. The Undertaker, Brett Hart and even the Big Show are prime examples of big main event wrestlers who have the ability to lift mid carders to the next level. Brett Hart did it with Shawn

Michaels, Steve Austin, and his brother Owen just to name a few. The Undertaker is has done it with Jeff Hardy, The Great Khali (his only decent WWE run, which says a lot for what the Undertaker can do) and it was The Undertakers battles with Mankind which showed us that Mankind can handle being a main event superstar. The Big Show has even recently helped elevate Cody Rhodes to many now calling for a main event title run for him, as well his initial Battles with John Cena, help John on his way to greatness. Although this option is also limited due to the current amount of main event starts available.

Then there are feuds between 2 mid carders that when done well have lifted at least one if not both of the wrestlers to main or at least upper mid card level. The feud between Chris Jericho and Christian (That included Trish Stratuss) showed that two these could be eventually main event superstars. Early feuds between Edge and Kurt Angle (with the famous Hair vs. Hair match at Judgment Day 2002) helped these 2 superstars onto greatness. As mentioned above the great feud between Jake The Snake Roberts and Ravishing Rick Rude, in 1988 even went as far as Rude wearing a pair of tights with Jake's wife on them, established both these superstars as regular drawcards for their WWF/WWE runs. To me the last well run mid card feud was between Matt Hardy and MVP over the US Title. This ran over a couple of months, elevated both stars for a small time, and gave us some fantastic matches. There are plenty of story ideas, feuds ideas that could happen, if I could conquer Raw vs Smakedown 2009 general manager mode by repeating stories, surely WWE writers can re-use stories as well if they are struggling for ideas. Stealing girlfriends, any country vs. USA, disgruntle superstar if the story is told and played out well, it will make these matches more exciting for us fans. Look at the current WWE roster and just think about how much better matches such as Drew McIntyre and Tyson Kidd, Ted DiBiase and Wade Barrett or R-Truth and Jack Swagger could be if we as fans could involve ourselves emotionally into their battles.

Return the WWE tag team division to mean something – At the 1988 Survivor Series, there was a traditional Survivor Series match between 10 tag teams (The Powers of Pain {The Warlord and The Barbarian}, The Rockers {Shawn Michaels and Marty Jannetty}, The British Bulldogs {Davey Boy Smith and Dynamite Kid}, The Hart Foundation {Bret Hart and Jim Neidhart} and The Young Stallions {Jim Powers and Paul Roma} **vs.** Demolition {Ax and Smash}, The Brain Busters {Arn Anderson and Tully Blanchard}, The Bolsheviks {Nikolai Volkoff and Boris Zhukov}, The Fabulous Rougeaus {Raymond and Jacques} and The Conquistadors {Uno and Dos}). Today the WWE would struggle to make 1 side of a traditional Survivor Series match. In the early 2000's you had The Dudleys, Edge and Christian and The Hardy Boys dominating and stealing the shows at PPV's.

Sadly in today's WWE we have mid card wrestlers thrown together for a small feud between another pay of mid carders thrown together. In the past 2 years Kofi Kingston has won tag team titles with CM Punk, Evan Bourne and R-truth. Those tag teams not in the tag team title picture are usually the ones jobbing to the tag team champs or the tag team champs current opponents. Further proof that the tag team titles are not as important is the fact on the MITB PPV, the tag team champs were on a dark match before the show, while during the PPV, 2 other tag teams were shown. With Raw now moving to a 3 hour show, maybe this will give the tag team division a chance to shine. Like the mid card wrestlers, the tag team division excel when you have decent run feuds and stories that do not always have to be about the titles. I have enjoyed watching many tag team feuds including:

The Hart Foundation had many great feuds with tag teams such as The British Bulldogs, Demolition and The Rougeau Brothers. Demolition and The Powers of Pain had some great battles and even had the manager of Demolition trade sides to The Powers of Pain. Later on Demolition would have some great matches and feuds with the Brain Busters (Arn Anderson and Tully Blanchard), the Colossal Connection (André the Giant and Haku) and Legion of Doom (L.O.D.).

As mentioned many times throughout the book Edge and Christian, The Dudleys and The Hardy Boys feud in the early 2000's was essential viewing for all wrestling fans.

(As I near the end of this book, just recently with the Kane and Daniel Bryan story line, and the increase in tag teams such as 'The Prime Time Players', 'Epico and Primo', 'The Usos' and the emergency of Cody Rhodes and Sandow- 'The Rhode Scholars have me excited about tag team wrestling again for the first time in a couple of years!!!)

Less WWE Pay Per Views – I feel there are too many PPV's throughout the year at the moment. This for me leads to not enough build up time for feuds and match anticipation. I assume I am like, most people and cannot afford every PPV, so less of them throughout the year would mean I would possible order more, as all of a sudden they become a little more important. I would get rid of at least 2 PPV's and re-arrange some of them. Below is the current schedule of PPV's for the WWE in 2013:

- The 26th Annual Royal Rumble- January 27 from the U.S. Airways Center in Phoenix, AZ
- Elimination Chamber- February 17 from the New Orleans Arena in New Orleans, LA

- WrestleMania XXIX- April 7 from the MetLife Stadium in East Rutherford, NJ

- Extreme Rules- May 19 from the Scottrade Center in St. Louis, MO

- [to be named]- June 16 from [to be announced]

- Money-in-the-Bank- July 14 from the Dunkin' Donuts Center in Providence, RI

- The 26th Annual SummerSlam- August 18 from the Staples Center in Los Angeles, CA

- Night of Champions- September 15 from [to be announced]

- Over The Limit- October 6 from the Quicken Loans Arena in Cleveland, OH

- Hell in a Cell- October 27 from the Consol Energy Center in Pittsburgh, PA

- The 27th Annual Survivor Series- November 24 from [to be announced]

- WWE TLC: Tables, Ladders & Chairs- December 15 from [to be announced]

If I was to plan the schedule there would be no PPV's between the' Royal Rumble' and 'Wrestlemania'. This makes the Rumble more important to win (one chance at headlining Wrestlemania), as well as more importance for the WWE writers to start feuds at the Rumble. Being eliminated at the Rumble by someone was always a great way to start a feud build up for Wrestlemania. You would then have nearly 2 months to build feuds, stories, match stipulations etc and add in the fact there is a 2 month gap between PPV's, buy up rates would increase for both.

I would then move 'Money in the bank' (MITB) from its current placement to the first PPV after Wrestlemania, so that the winner/s have 1 full year to cash in their briefcase, which makes for great story line writing for those champions as they have done with Dolph Ziggler in 2012. The will he / won't he cash in the brief case has had everyone guessing all year. To replace the MITB spot, I would move the 'Elimination Chamber', where the winner will headline Summer Slam. This way only 1 Chamber is needed, and you could have many lead up, matches on RAW and Smackdown to find the participants for the Chamber.

Lastly merge 'Over the Limit' and 'Hell in A Cell' as 2 PPV's in the one month is a waste of time and money, as most people if ordering will only order one anyway, so buy Rates would be split between the 2. There is no real time to build any new feuds, so most of the matches will be between the same participants as well.

Have the WWE help promote Australian Wrestling companies when touring Australia – Ever since I have been a wrestling fan, the local wrestling product in Australia, has been lacking in very low profiled. I am not knocking the performers who give just as much to their matches as the well established stars in WWE and TNA today. It is just the Australian TV companies do not promote it, and you cannot get excitement and atmosphere, when they are performing in front of 20 people at The Rooty Hill RSL club. As a wrestling fan, I would love to turn up to a WWE show in Sydney and see 1 match between an established WWE star, not in a current story line take on the champ from either AWF (Australasian Wrestling Federation) or the IWA (International Wrestling Australia). I can just image a match like The Miz vs.

IWA Champion **Tyson Gibbs** or maybe Kofi Kingston vs. **Jake Bonza,** Or even a battle royal between members of IWA, AWF or both with the winner to face a WWE superstar. There are many ideas how this could work, and if WWE and the Australian wrestling companies need a middle man, then I would love to volunteer my services (with a small fee of course ☺)

A match at a WWE house show by a wrestler/s from an Australian company would lift the profile of these wrestling companies here in Australia, and the WWE can have yet another feeder company to draw talent from. I see it as a win / win / win...a win for Australian wrestling giving these guys some great exposure and development by mixing with the WWE, a win for us Australian wrestling fans as it will give us another outlet to enjoy watching wrestling, and a very small win for the WWE.

Some WWE merchandise ideas – I am not going to be silly enough to list my ideas here, but if you're reading this book Mr McMahon I would love to discuss these ideas with you.

Bring Back General Manager mode on WWE games – I loved this element of the Raw vs. Smackdown games, and while this will not improve wrestling greatly, it will make me more likely to buy the next WWE game. And after this year's Wrestlemania you could have a general manger mode of Team Teddy vs. Team Johnny to finish the game off....I expect to see WWE 14' with this included!!

A WWE Films project – Like my General Manager Mode idea, this will not improve wrestling, however may attract newer fans to the WWE, through film success. I have already mentioned that I have enjoyed a few of the films that have been developed by WWE films, and thought what would be better than seeing one of my favourite wrestlers in a movie, seeing lots of my favourite wrestlers in a movie, such as Adam Sandler's remake of 'The Longest Yard'. Well my remake would be *'The Dirty Dozen',* which for those who were too young for the movie, or those who have forgotten this classic was:

A Major with an attitude problem and a
history of getting things done is told to

interview military prisoners with death

sentences or long terms for a dangerous

mission; to parachute behind enemy lines and

cause havoc for the German Generals at a

rest house on the eve of D-Day.

While three TV movie sequels were made, none were as impressive as the original. With that in mind, I come up with the table below which gives the character name, original cast member and the WWE Superstar I would have in that role:

NAME (Character)	Original Cast	Wrestling cast
MJ John Reisman	Lee Marvin	The Rock
Gen.Sam Worden	Ernest Borgnine	Triple H
Franko, V. R.	John Cassavetes	Drew McIntyre
Vladek, M.	Tom Busby	Heath Slater
Jefferson, R. T.	Jim Brown	Mark Henry
Pinkley, V. L.	Donald Sutherland	Christian
Gilpin, S.	Ben Carruthers	Primo
Posey, S.	Clint Walker	CM punk
Wladislaw, T.	Charles Bronson	Randy Orton
Sawyer, S. K.	Colin Maitland	Wade Barret
Lever, R.	Stuart Cooper	Justin Gabriel
Bravos, T. R.	Al Mancini	Santino
Jiminez, J. P.	Trini Lopez	Alberto Del Rio
Maggott, A. J.	Telly Savalas	Steve Austin

The last two ideas, are ideas not to improve the wrestling product, but improve wrestling experiences for us fans.

Wrestling camp –Well let's say I am very close to 40 years old, and quite content to have missed the boat on any type of in ring wrestling career, I would like however to have a week's wrestling training, just to get a taste of what these athletes go for. Ideally my training would occur in a type of wrestling camp. Inspired by The Simpson's episode 293 titled "How I spent my Strummer vacation" where Homer spends a week at a Rock camp hosted by Rock legends such as Mick Jagger , Tom Petty, Keith Richards, Elcis Costello, Lenny Kravitz and Brian Setzer, I feel a wrestling camp hosted by some former wrestling legends would by just the ticket. (I should wack a copy write © on that idea as well!). The camp open to all those fans like myself who have visions of grandeur, or those internet fans who bag wrestlers in ring performance to put their money where their mouth is, or just those who may have an interest in a possible wrestling career. The camp would be an intensive training camp, as well as looking at other elements that go into a wrestling show, such as setting up, costume design, how to do a promo, coming up with their own wrestling name, how to do promotion of wrestling shows etc. At the end of the week (or two), the 'campers' can put on a small show for their friends and family. In fact the more I think about the idea and with my experience running camps, Mr McMahon give me a call and I think we can get this off the ground!

Upon nearing completion of my book I did come across this which may interest at least one of kids (my wrestling buddy Ruby) in a few years. It is from the AWF (Australian Wrestling Federation), and it is for a 'dreamcamp' for interested wrestling fans aged 12 and above:

AWF looks forward to introducing a swag of new students to training, and hopefully producing some excellent future wrestling talent!

DREAMCAMP 2013 (AGES 12 & ABOVE)

MON 7 JANUARY - THURS 10 JANUARY, 2013 - $300

4 Day Fun Training Camp to be held at Penrith, NSW - Receive a DVD & Posed Picture on completion!

Email info@awfwrestling.com.au for an application and join now

And if I was perhaps 10 to 20 years younger I might be interested in this training course the AWF has to offer:

AWF SCHOOL OF PRO-WRESTLING DEC 2012 – JAN 2013 TRAINING SCHEDULE

Training to take place at 123 Coreen Ave, Penrith, NSW

NEXT BEGINNERS COURSE DATES WILL BE:

MON 17 DEC - FRI 21 DEC: 9AM - 3PM DAILY - $400

Suitable for Male & Female aspiring Wrestlers, Managers and Referees aged 16 and over

To be held in Penrith, NSW

Full payments and Applications to be in before 14 December no exceptions. Get organised!

Email info@awfwrestling.com.au for an application and join now!

Wrestlemania holiday tour- This one is for my fellow Australian wrestling fans. As the WWE already have Wrestlemania packages such as this Wrestlemania 29 package (care of WWE.com);

WWE Travel Packages include tickets to:

- Wrestlemania 29 at MetLife Stadium on Sunday, April 7, 2013

- WWE Hall of Fame Induction Ceremony at "The World's Most Famous Arena" Madison Square Garden on Saturday, April 6, 2013

- Wrestlemania Axxess at the IZOD Center, where you can meet your favourite WWE Superstars, from Thursday, April 4 – Sunday, April 7, 2013

- Monday Night Raw at the IZOD Center on Monday, April 8, 2013 (only with 4-night hotel accommodations)

- Hotel accommodations in New York City

For us out of Towner's, i.e. from Australia, New Zealand, England etc. then the above package would also need to include:

International airfare

Transfers to and from the hotel

Breakfasts every day

A package like this, with a limited number of places I feel would sell fast, and of course need a Australians chaperone (ie ME) to tag along free of charge to help out.

Chapter 17   My Wrestling Bucket list

Bucket list: a number of experiences or

achievements that a person hopes to have or

accomplish during their lifetime (Oxford

Dictionary)

As we grow old, we start to think up more and more

things that we would like to do before we die, i.e. what we can

add to our bucket lists (as well as we start to think why hair all of

a sudden starts growing in our ears, why our eyebrows now need

grooming, why we have to eat more fibre based cereals, and how

every year we now have to doctors checks on our cholesterol,

sugar, weight and our PSA count!). Some things we are quite

happy to cross off our bucket lists that we know we will never

end up doing, such as I am quite happy now to never bungie

Jump or Sky dive, while others items we miss out on are

disappointing such as becoming a wrestler (or at least a pesky

annoying wrestling manager). With this in mind my wrestling

bucket list is therefore:

All the things a person wishes to do, see and be part of that has to do with wrestling.

My Wrestling bucket list items are the things that will highlight my wrestling career as a fan, and things I have wanted to do or see for a very long time. I believe some of these items are reachable, while others may be a little out of reach, but that is the good thing about bucket lists, you can be as realistic, or as imaginable as you like. I have crossed off quite a few things off my wrestling bucket list already, these have included:

- Going to a live wrestling event;
- Seeing a WWF/E wrestling event;
- Seeing The Undertaker at a live wrestling event
- Taking my kids to a live wrestling event.

However there are still quite a few things I wish to see and do as a wrestling fan, so here are my wrestling bucket list items:

1. Write my wrestling book – Obviously if you are reading this, then I can tick this off my list! As I have mentioned at the start of this book, I have been thinking and wanting to write my story, autobiography on how wrestling has influenced my life. Now while unlike many other wrestling books, I did not follow the path of a wrestler, I feel my path as a wrestling fan has had many highs and lows which I would like to talk about and share with you readers. I hope it has given you Non Wrestling fans an appreciation of why we enjoy our 'sports entertainment' and I hope it given wrestling fans some discussion topics they can talk about and discuss.

2. Attend Wrestlemania – This would also include all of the lead up fan events and of course the WWE Hall of Fame ceremony. While I have seen quite a few Live wrestling events, seeing the main wrestling event of the year is a must not just for me but I feel for any wrestling fan. I am resigned

to the fact that by the time I possibly get to go to a Wrestlemania I will miss an Undertaker 'streak' match, and seeing him continue his streak, but I would settle seeing Christian win the WWE title instead .

3. Attend The Royal Rumble - The Royal Rumble is my favourite wrestling PPV, and therefore a PPV just like Wrestlemania I would love to experience live and in person. I would enjoy doing the countdown of wrestlers appearing just the other thousands in attendance, and of course seeing Christian win the Rumble would top it off!

4. Sitting Front row – We all watch the TV shows, PPV and attend the live house shows, and secretly curse and hated those fans who have gotten the front row seats. Just once I would like to be one of those people being cursed and hated by the fans not sitting in the front row. Ideally Front row at the Royal Rumble or Wrestlemania of course would kill two birds with the one stone.

5. Taking my daughter Abbey to a live wrestling event – I have had the privilege of taking 4 of my kids (Zara, Connor, Ruby and Max) to a couple of wrestling events, and enjoyed watching them enjoy the event as much as I do. I will also get the privilege of taking my sister and her family to their first live wrestling event, and look forward to seeing my 2 nephews Rhyse and Jak enjoy seeing their heroes live for the first time. Currently my little angel is only 15 months old, so in about 5 to 6 years' time, I would love to let her enjoy the fun of live wrestling.

6. Meet Mick Foley – not only meet Mick, but I would love to invite him and his family around for a BBQ. I saw the episode of celebrity wife swap he was in with his family, and I am sure his wife would get on with my wife, and all our kids should get along as well. Not only would I get him to personally sign all his books and DVD's I have got, but to have a chance to talk about his career,

favourite matches, favourite feuds etc. (I promise Mick not to mention that Hell in a Cell match with the Undertaker!). *This bucket list item is now somewhat on the way of happening as I have purchased meet and greet tickets to Mick Foley's Sydney's leg of his Australian Comedy tour. This has meant I better get my arse into gear and finish this book!!!*

7. Meet Vince McMahon – For just plan business advice, I would love to pick Vince's brain, as well as have the opportunity to thank him for over 30 years of entertaining me. I of course would love to also discuss my merchandise, and marketing ideas with him....for a small fee of course.

8. Be behind the scenes of a WWE show – whether it be a Raw, Smackdown or just a live show in Australia, it would be good to be able to see the show from behind that mysterious curtain the wresters walk through. To meet and talk to all those involve in the whole process from setting up

to packing up, watch the production crew in flight or even and of course mingle with the wrestlers back stage.

9. See a show in Mexico or Japan – I have only ever heard positive things about wrestling in these two countries. I hear that the fans in these two countries are nearly as big of fans of wrestling as I am. I would love to experience firstly a Lucha style wrestling show in Mexico. The high flying style, learning aboutthe history of their masks, and of course the atmosphere thousands of locals would bring to the show. Japan while being a different style and atmosphere would just be as exciting, especially if somewhere on the show there was a match similar to the "King of death Match' 1995 between Mick Foley and Terry Funk. (if you have never seen this match give it a look, makes current hardcore matches look very very soft)

And finally

10. My last Bucket list item would be a second wrestling book. I already have the title in mine "<u>A wrestling Fan's Bucket List</u>". Now if I could just find myself a backer for that project...... someone with a lot of money..... Someone who knows about the wrestling industry....... and someone who likes to help the little guy....... Give me a call Mr Trump!

I have missed my opportunity at a few wrestling experiences, so my bucket list will always remain that little unfulfilled. Things I have missed out on seeing include;

- Seeing Hulk Hogan, Stone Cold Steve Austin and of course Mick Foley wrestle live. I would have loved seeing at least one match of these three in their prime, Hearing Hulk's music blast through the arena, jumping out of my seat at the sound of Stone Colds breaking glass, and of course watching Mick Foley in a hardcore / extreme match all would of been (as the Miz would say) 'Awesome' to see.

- As mentioned briefly, missing out on seeing The Undertaker at Wrestlemania. After the last 4 mania's, the streak match has outshone the other main events, and the atmosphere that I have seen on the PPV during these matches would be an absolute dream to be a part of!

- Now while at 40ish year of age, I have missed my opportunity to become a wrestling star, I would of at least like to of tried some training, or tried out just to see how hard it is. And since this bucket list item is truly long gone, getting trained in the Hart Family dungeon would have been my ultimate wrestling training fantasy. Maybe in the next life!

Chapter 18   Wrestling Glossary

TERM	DEFINITION
Angle	A wrestling plot / story which may involve only one match or may continue over several matches for some time. The reason behind a feud or a turn.
Baby face	A good guy, the hero.
Blade	Cutting oneself or being cut with a part of a razor blade that was hidden by the wrestler in order to produce blood. Usually cut on the hairline or in the upper forehead.
Blind	A referee has his back turned while the other side is cheating.
Blow off	The big money match to settle a feud between two rivals. The tension builds until it needs to be blown off. Usually done at a

	Pay per view or large house show.
Blow up	To become very fatigued or exhausted, during the match.
Booker	The individual responsible for writing the angles, storylines, finishes of match. Also helps in the hiring and firing in a promotion.
Bump	A fall or hit to the mat which knocks the person down.
Card	The series of matches in one location at one time.
Cleans house	When a wrestler(s) eliminates every other man in the ring.
Curtain jerker	Wrestlers who usually opens the shows up. Basically the first match on the card.
Curtain Call or The MSG	the incident at Madison Square Garden in the spring of 1996, when WWE superstars Shawn Michaels, Diesel, Razor Ramon, and

Incident	Triple H (The Clique) broke kayfabe in front of a live sold out New York crowd, playing it out in a farewell to the crowd and a group hug
Dark match	A match performed before the live TV/PPV show. Seen by the live crowd but not by the TV audience.
Draw	To attract fans. The popularity of a wrestler, the ability to bring in fans.
Dud	A particularly bad and totally uninteresting match.
Fall	A referee's count of three with the loser's shoulders on the mat.
Feud	A series of matches between two wrestlers or multiple groups. Many times they will interview and bad mouth the other wrestler(s).

Finish	The event or sequence of events which leads to the ultimate outcome of a match.
Garbage	Matches or promotions that have no wrestling but pure violence. Use of nothing but weapons and violent gimmick matches.
Gorilla position	The area wrestlers wait their turn to come out for their match/run-in/interview. Most all the time it's the area right behind the curtains.
Green	Not good due to inexperience in the ring.
Heat	Enthusiasm, a positive/negative response from fans.
Heavy	The opposite of getting light. Basically being dead weight and not helping your opponent get you in any type of move.
Heel	A bad guy; rule-breaker.
House	The wrestling audience in the building

House show	A wrestling event that is not televised.
Job	A staged loss. A clean job is a staged loss by legal pin fall or submission without resort to illegalities.
Jobber	An un-pushed wrestler who does jobs for pushed wrestlers. Usually a wrestler who is on a long losing streak.
Juice	Blood. Also means steroids
Juicing	Means two things; A wrestler who is be bleeding. It also means a wrestler who is taking steroids.
Kayfabe	Of or related to inside information about the business. To break kayfabe is to break out of your character. It is also used by wrestlers to kayfabe each other, which means to keep quiet on certain things with other people and to not let them know.

Kill	To stop a gimmick or match that is not getting a good response from the crowd.
Mark	A member of the audience, presumed gullible. Basically a wrestling fan who attends all the shows, buys all the merchandise etc.
Mid-carder	A wrestler who wrestles on the under-card but is usually well known.
Over	When a wrestler's gimmick is well liked by the fans or he receives a great amount of heat whether it be cheers or boos. To be over is to get a big response from fans whenever a wrestler comes out.
Paper	Free complimentary tickets, given to fans and friends/family of wrestlers to make the arena look as if it sold out.
Pop	A loud sudden heat from a house as a

	response to a wrestler's entry or hot move.
Post	To run or be run into the ring post.
Push	When a wrestler starts to go on a winning streak or is shown to be really dominate by performing a lot of squash matches. Also gets more interview time and TV time and possible title shot.
Psychology	To tell a story by working over a certain body part, making a series of moves make sense in the ring. Working the crowd at the right moment, and to sell a lot.
Rest hold	When wrestlers need to take a rest during a match, or figure out the next series of moves, or they can't decide what to do next. They will apply some type of boring non-damaging hold. It only serves to stretch out the match and give the wrestlers time to breathe.

Run-in	Interference caused by a non-participant in a match.
Save	A run-in by another wrestler or wrestlers to protect a wrestler from being beat up after a match is over.
Screw-job	A match or ending which is not clean due to factors outside the rules of wrestling.
Sell	To act hurt and use facial expressions when a move has been applied or performed.
Shoot	The real thing. A match where the participants are really attempting to hurt another.
Smark	A smart mark. A guy who thinks he knows everything there is to know about wrestling. Doesn't care much for gimmicks or angles. Like good matches with psychology.
Spot	A sequence/series of moves which makes a

	particular match distinctive, the climax of a match.
Spot fest	High impact moves after high impact moves.
Squash	Where one wrestler completely dominates another.
Stable	Multiple wrestler's that have form a group.
Stretch	To stretch someone is to get a wrestler in a submission and stiff him by pulling back.
Tap out	To give up whilst in a submission manoeuvre by tapping your hand signalling your quit.
Turn	Change in orientation from heel to face or vice-versa.
Tweener	A wrestler who is part heel and part face. He isn't classified as a heel or face, he is more in the middle.
Work	Anything such as story or incident planned to

	happen, but seems real.
Worker	Another term for wrestler.

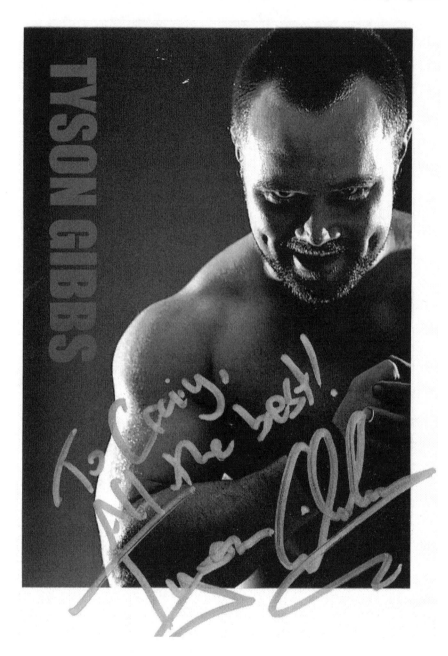

Tyson Gibbs IWA star and Son of a friend at my work currently in the US

Bop 'n' Wrestle, the original wrestling game!!! – We have come a long way in the gaming
industry

The two signs used at the WWE Global Warning tour 2002

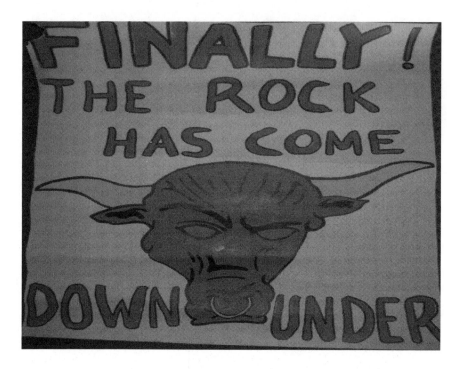

Some other creative signs that were used by my daughters at the WWE show in Sydney 2011

Afterthought

Now I can understand why not everyone writes books, writing a book is so hard. And considering this is not a master piece of award winning writing, I can dip my hat to all those writers out there with a new sense of respect. The writing, deleting, restarting, the mental blocks, the weird hours of inspiration and then to finish the book and not be 100% happy were things I did not expect at the start of my book writing journey. But after months of some self-editing, some final adjustments to some paragraphs and chapters, I think I can say I am up to 85% happy with what I have produced.

With new and exciting things happening on the WWE in the past 6 months, it has made me change some of things I have written, or at least acknowledge change was on the way. So this meant having to re-write some paragraphs, or add onto the end of a paragraph. And with the Royal Rumble 2013 not far away, then Wrestlemania 29, if I do not finish the book soon, it may never get done as there will be always something new to write about!

It was funny when inspiration hit, it was usually just when I rolled into bed, and an idea for a chapter, of a paragraph would just fill my mind up. Early on in the writing process I would make a mental note to write the idea in the morning, but 9 times out of 10 would forget. So towards the end of the book, I would get up at 11:00pm write myself a quick note, before jumping back into bed and trying to get some sleep before my brain ticked over again. While at work I would also be hit be inspiration, and again had to find a way to jot down these thoughts before they went away. Very rarely did inspiration hit, when I had a free afternoon, weekend or day off, I only hope other writers have had this problem!

The second frustrating part has been trying to find an agent and/or publisher to get this book published (and there's a whole other book on that process), which means as I type this I know this may never get published and if it does it might be as I have to self-publish. But my goal was to write a book, in which case I have at least technically completed that goal.

After my wife finished reading and editing this book the first question I asked was not did you like it but have you learnt more about wrestling in which she replied "yes". The same response occurred when I asked my brother after he read the book. Whether I have converted them or not is beside the point, as that was not my intention, my intention was to give wrestling fans a nice trip down memory lane, and the opportunity to discuss issues, matches and wrestlers with their friends, online or even with me, as well as just to give those non-wrestling fans a small insight into why we love our wrestling, and I feel I have accomplished that.

Thank you for reading, now go and switch on some wrestling

Made in the USA
Lexington, KY
06 April 2017